The Spanish Blue Division

To my father, Jaime Dolado, and to my Godfather Gregorio del Pozo
that, coming from the S.E.U. and the Youth Front Centuries,
served together as volunteers of the Division and the Blue Legion.

To my brother Jaime, who with his example maintained alive
the Service and the Spirit Sacrifice, inherited from our father.

Jesus Dolado Esteban

To all my "Carmenes," for being my sunshine each morning.

Eduardo Ramos Redondo

To our Youth, so the example of those who fought for one ideal will
help them become themselves in today's society.

Eduardo Esteban Robles

The Military Intervention Corps of the Spanish Blue Division in the German *Wehrmacht* 1941-1944

Organization • Uniforms • Insignia • Documents

Jesus Dolado Esteban
Eduardo Ramos Redondo
Eduardo Robles Esteban

Schiffer Military History
Atglen, PA

Notes from the Translator

In translating the Spanish edition of this book, I attempted to maintain the ideas, integrity, and concepts used by the authors. There are some expressions or names, that in translation into the English language, would not make sense or, would degrade the strength of the word, phrase or paragraph. In those occasions, I decided to use a less literal approach with another word, modifying phrase or paragraph.

There are also words, that although, found in the English language, have little modern use or a different meaning. In those cases, I used my judgment to maintain the idea of the original Spanish script.

I also included, with the permission of the authors, a brief explanation of the modern ***Intervention Corps*** in the Spanish Army, to help the reader better understand their function and grouping within the Spanish Armed Forces.

!Arriba España!

Mariano V. Fernandez Jimenez
Miami, May 2007

Book translation by Mariano V. Fernandez Jimenez
Book Design by Ian Robertson.

Library of Congress Control Number: 2008930914

Printed in China.
ISBN: 978-0-7643-3102-2

This book was originally published in Spanish under the title
Revista de Comisario El Cuerpo de Intervención Militar en la División Azul
by AF Editores

We are interested in hearing from authors with book ideas on related topics.

Published by Schiffer Publishing Ltd.
4880 Lower Valley Road
Atglen, PA 19310
Phone: (610) 593-1777
FAX: (610) 593-2002
E-mail: Info@schifferbooks.com.
Visit our web site at: www.schifferbooks.com
Please write for a free catalog.
This book may be purchased from the publisher.
Please include $5.00 postage.
Try your bookstore first.

In Europe, Schiffer books are distributed by:
Bushwood Books
6 Marksbury Avenue
Kew Gardens
Surrey TW9 4JF, England
Phone: 44 (0) 20 8392-8585
FAX: 44 (0) 20 8392-9876
E-mail: Info@bushwoodbooks.co.uk.
Visit our website at: www.bushwoodbooks.co.uk
Free postage in the UK. Europe: air mail at cost.
Try your bookstore first.

Contents

Preface

In the Spanish Armed Forces, there is a Corps with specific functions for matters of an economic and administrative nature, law, notary, and auditor responsibilities. This Corps has passed, as has modern Spanish history, through several and profound modifications.

From the original military carrier title (Commissary of War), to the civil character given to them by the Republic during the pre-Civil War times, to the new military title and function of the law of 1999, they overcame obstacles to maintain their level of responsibility and military character for which they fought and is deserved.

The armies needed those functions and technical expertise offered by the War Commissaries, or Interventors. From the simple daily report of active personnel available for combat, to the logistic and budgetary functions. In this matter, they earned a position within the modern Spanish Armed Forces.

One of the functions that is often overseen was their service as attorneys and prosecutors in cases of Court Martial, and those derived from the Notary services. These were of great value to our brave men and women in uniform when serving the interest of the State far away from their Mother land. The simple will or the necessary power of attorney needed when one is confronting the danger of death in combat, to guarantee the property rights of their families, is a well earned service, due to all our men and women in uniform.

In this book, there is special consideration given to those volunteers serving in the Blue Division, and later the Legion, that served with Intervention capacity. To the surprise of many, these interventors were combatants, as they were troop commanders in all the fronts. While the High Command still had all their needs covered with their reports and daily work, the interventors' efforts made possible the work performance of the Unit.

They served as procurement officers, attorneys, prosecutors, auditors, bankers, and payers securing the funds for the Unit, their salaries, and materials. Although there is a close correlation with the Intendance Group, their mission is as important and as varied, and well deserves a special mention in this book.

Although the English language definition of their mission would be "Auditor," it falls short of the real definition of their functions. As a result, the English translator decided to use the more parallel and literal translation "*Interventor*." The Spanish law of May 18, 1999, created the Corps, defining their new ranks and duties, and giving them again the Military status lost before the Spanish Civil War.

Law No. 17/1999, of May 18, published in the B.O.E. No. 119. Regulation of Personnel of the Armed Forces, Article 40:

The Military Intervention Corps:

1. The members of the Military Intervention Corps, grouped in a Superior Scale of Officers, had as assignments, in the scope of the Ministry of Defense and its independent Organisms, to carry out the internal control of the management and economic-financial functions.

They will exercise the functions as Interventors, with the specific functions of the financial control and audit, by delegation of the General Interventor of the Administration of the State, in the terms anticipated in the General Budgetary Law.

They will also serve as the Military Notary's office in the form and conditions established by the laws, and the advisory functions in all economic matters. They will be the public prosecutors, and will prepare and submit information and reports as required of them in the matter of their jurisdiction by the superior authorities of the Ministry of Defense.

In the performance of their assignments, they will be able to assume the command function in centers or organisms. Also, the logistic and administration function corresponding to them, and of support to the control, technical, and educational functions related to these assignments.

2. The ranks of the Intervention Military Corps will be those of Lieutenant to Major General, with the denominations of the corresponding rank followed by the term "**Interventor**."

Introduction

In 1941, Europe was submerged in a confrontation of ideologies of gigantic proportions. Under the conventional appearance of fighting between nations, what was really at stake was in fact a war between different visions of the world, a true "religious war."

Fascist totalitarian regimes and liberal-parliamentarian democracies fought, on the grounds of Europe, in support of their idea of the sense of life and history, their conception of the political and economic life of the nations, and their XX century vision of the individual and collective morale of man.

In 1941, the conflict had just started. The explosive news, breaking the air waves on that Sunday morning of 22 June, left everyone breathless. At three thirty that early morning, the Third Reich military machine began the invasion of the Soviet Union. The communist paradise was going to be crushed by more than three million men, unfolding north to the south, throughout a 1,600 km front, on an unprecedented scale in world war history. It opened the controversial "second front" of the German war, and with it a third ideology, Communism, entered the conflict.

This Second Front came to be the final answer to the ideological tension that had built up in Europe from 1919 to 1939, between Communism, fascism, and capitalist parliamentary liberalism.

The three natural adversaries procrastinated in having a three party confrontation, following the model described by the *Sorbonne* professor, J. B. Duroselle. It was obvious that two of them would join forces to defeat the third one.

However, in any war or battle, there can only be present two contenders. The decision of Germany to confront communist Russia after rolling over but not completing their victory of the liberal-capitalist nations of western Europe, gave a definitive form to the war. Germany would end up losing, perhaps due to these circumstances.

At the end of the war a new period of tension would arise, this time between the winners; the USSR and the western democracies that were allies, against their nature, in order to defeat Germany during the war.

This period has been called the Cold War, and concluded with the "fall of the wall" and the dismembering of the Soviet Union. In 1989, after those events, we would see if, in today's surviving world, liberalism would be capable of demonstrating its capacity of survival, and if it deserved the achieved success. In addition, the remaining social democracy would need to prove if it was capable of taking XXI century man from a nihilist dead end, in which reasoned pride had placed them, to radical liberal individualism and its motto of world secularization.

In Spain the news of the USSR's attack produced a big wave of enthusiasm, materialized in numerous adhesion demonstrations on the war against Russia and the participation of Spain in the fight. (Russia as a victim in fact, rather than the "Russia is guilty" of the political slogans, as *Jose Antonio Girón* wrote in his memoirs[1]).

This opportunity was not only celebrated to "return the visit of the international brigades to Spain," but also it was mainly thought to be part of the creation of the new European Order, which would arise after the doubtless victory in the arms of the Axis. A European order, "heroic and popular," in the words of *Dionisio Ridruejo*, was built, according to what was expected, on the ruins of Soviet Communism and the western capitalist plutocracies.

In order to understand well this yearning, it is necessary to know the European feelings between the wars. After the Great War of 1914, parliamentary liberalism was the object of enormous disrepute in all of Europe. The "crisis of the democracy" was a subject accepted by most of the narrators of the '20s and '30s.

The incapacity and passivity of this aged system worried more about parliamentary procedures and interests than about economic oligarchies. The attention of large sectors of the European population, being directed towards new authoritarian formulas, was less interested in facing the innumerable urgencies and social responsibilities of the modern mass society for the XX century. They were also more concerned about the details of political representation than in the hierarchic and effective political and economic organization of the nation, making the material aspirations of each town with a vision towards modernization and social level elevation more urgent. One is necessity, which had increased more and more since the Great Depression of 1929.

Fascism, mainly in the years before World War II, attracted the interest of ample sectors of middle-class Europeans that aspired to a modern lifestyle and a political system to guarantee it. Communism, on the other hand, exerted the same exact fascination, and for the same reasons prevailed in the mentality of the left wing and the radicalized proletariat. All—Tirius and Trojans—were convinced that Europe needed new political solutions, and that it was urgent to create a new order, and no one doubted that order would be a fascist or a communist totalitarian regime.

The already mentioned form of triangular ideological conflict consisted of the revolutionary rivalry established between fascism and communism. The objective of both sides was to destroy its two opponents, and also to supplant with historical advantage the discredited system of liberal-parliamentarian and inherited capitalism of the XIX century.

In Spain, the Phalange shared in this vision, and for that reason was inclined to take part in the war on the Axis side. The young phalangists were convinced that after conquering Moscow (Russia was still at that time the "question of a day"), Europe was going to have a great spiritual and regenerating revolution like the one Phalange was promulgating in Spain.

In that spirit, from the first day, and to their own risk, FET and of the JONS, by order of Jose Luis Arrese, his brand new Secretary General, opened in all their centers pennants of enlistment for the young people who wanted to serve as volunteers in the primitively named Phalange Division that was going to Russia. The name came from the people in charge of the Party that had conceived it as a phalangists' Corps of Volunteers.

While the relations between the forces that composed the new Spanish regime of 18 July were not absolutely idyllic, the Army, alarmed by what it considered an interference of the Party in their assignments and duties, took immediate action and demanded the control of the process. The Army wanted, without a doubt, to lead with professional criteria and personnel.

In this underground struggle, Varela, Minister of the Army, also demanded that the official denomination of the unit be the Spanish Division of Volunteers (DEV), and thus it was. But for everyone, in world history, and of course for the legend, the name by which the Spanish presence in Russia would be remembered was The Blue Division. For the Germans it was Division 250 of the XVI Army of Army Group North. The Russians called it, in their language, the *Galubaya Divisia*.

In July 1941, the Blue Division departed to meet the *Wehrmacht* units at the Eastern Front, after a short period of training in Grafenwör (Germany). Those first eighteen thousand men (of the approximately fifty thousand who passed through Russia in the different relief groups) left in the middle of an inexpressible enthusiasm, as can be verified in the cinematographic documents from that time.

It was a time of revolutionary ambitions and heroic utopia, reasons why it was not strange that they marched toward the war (as surely is our postmodern weak mentality), to the suffering and the danger, singing gladly, and with great enthusiasm. (The pains and the omens were carried inside for sure, as was the proper decorum).

They felt, without a doubt, they were going to construct the new Europe demanded by the times; thoughts felt since they were volunteers from Spain placed in the front lines. They also felt that history passed through their hands and nerves, and that they could direct it. History was for them to make. As Enrique Sotomayor (fallen in Possad) wrote, "a fight generation, that had to buy and pay with blood its place in the hierarchy of the new order."

It was a revolutionary time in which, indeed by being there, the youth had great difficulty in opening their passage as the new protagonists of history, as until then, it was just a phase of life that "would be cured with age," and since then, a factor for the change.

Those boys are today aging older men. Although it is easy to imagine them, thanks to the photos of the time, with their young faces, to the point of being almost infantile, wearing a soldier's uniform. Surely it will be that striking appearance that God has reserved for their memory until the end of time. Men of today, those boys of yesterday, whom we must admire with the greatest respect, not only due to their sacrifice, but mainly because they coherently accepted to risk their own lives to make a reality the dream of this utopia, that at the time seemed possible.

They also knew how to take the best Spanish spirit to Russia, that was left to cultivate the fields forever with their accomplishments and works. Since then that corner of the world, that extreme piece of Russia, has always had something from Spain in itself, just as Spain will always have a little part of Russia brought by those that returned, printed in their souls and memories, and also in their pain. As a memory of this, four thousand fallen volunteers were left there by the Division. In addition to the desperation of the Germans, they showed a Christian and simple brotherhood with the civil population, regardless of whether it was Russian, Polish, Jewish, or even enemy prisoners.

Scorn for death, tenacious heroism, and deep humanity were three identifying signs left before Russians and Germans, in the name of Spain, left by these ambassadors sent to hell's very doors. Soldiers weathered and feared in an extreme situation, and were able yet, with compassion, to compose a complete and finished human spirit model, with which surely God would be reasonably satisfied.

There are two images gathered by Dionisio Ridruejo in his campaign dailies[1] that we know are not isolated, but habitual episodes that reflect and summarize the spirit and the temperament of the division. The first one occurred during the extraordinarily long trip to get to the front, at the entrance to Poland in one of the trains:

"In the morning, in the first stations or stops, children assaulted us, poorly dressed but very sweet; they were 'Polish Catholics,' advised already by the passage of other convoys that we were the Spanish Catholics. You should have seen with what degree of tenderness those coarse soldiers attended and welcomed these children, distributing among them the few articles they had." And he added, "These poor kids, so happy, no longer have a mother country. With those two or three Spanish words that learned, without really comprehending them, perhaps in a near future would remind them of those moments as a seed to bring to life a hidden dream or thought about a wonderful Spain."

The second narrative corresponded to the Possad battle of December 1941: "We saw fall, one by one, the defenders of a near position. When there was only one left, to our surprise, angered he started to sing the 'Cara al Sol,' like a demon, black by the powder, shooting hand grenades. The position was yielded by the attackers to him. I have never seen a miracle of the power of personality like that one."

The behavior of the Blue Division men in itself is a monument to the human spirit. If we join it with the epic they wrote, and in which they took part, they exceed the reasons why their memory must never be lost nor forgotten. Their memory must serve as a reference for future generations. Not for ours today, so soft, so ...to the end of history, so weak of thought, so overwhelmed with interminable rights, egoism, so little of duties, so ready always to give the reason to any enemy from the West, so sentimentally kind; but perhaps for the children or grandsons of this one, who will manage again to reach a strong and ascetic sense of life, of the world, and its importance.

They will need then references and moral anthropological models, not of their ancestors, to whom the law of life made little case, but of new classics, which by all means will have to be the military, and the humanistic history, that composed the value, charity, and strength of the Blue Division.

It is time to see the necessity of reconstructing and maintaining that reality, in all its authenticity, without automatic complacencies and justifications, without coruscation, and with the desire to reveal the truth as only can be done by those who lived it. With this aim all books, testimonies, photographs, film, memories, and bulletins, and even the most modest paper become indispensable.

All these we expect are in the care of the existing Brotherhood and the Blue Division Foundation. But it is precisely for those future generations, to encourage the legend and the myth, to write and to conserve narrations that would embolden them, that will move them to grow vertically, and help them to reunite a man's life in a total and solid vision in a new "strong thought." In this the Blue Division memory will be an important element, not the only one of course, but essential for a "new mythology."

The authors of "The Military Intervention Corps in the Blue Division" contributed with their perspective, very well documented, and with a great photographic dossier, to the composition of the whole picture, that was never finished about the Division. The authors, as well as this humble writer, are still young men, who by all means did not experience first hand the context they study in this book. We are members of an intermediate generation, who in their childhood in the '60s and '70s had the rare opportunity of being educated through some of their family atmosphere, and others in the rows of the Spanish Youth Organization of those years (La O.J.E.), with the style—or way to understand life—with the spirit, and of the necessary generational adaptations of those heroes of our legends.

We considered ourselves forced continuers of that style and that spirit and, for that reason, and given the present circumstances, we assumed, along with many others, to be the loyal and jealous protector of the Legend of the Blue Division. We are the quiet copiers of the "narrations of Russia," the historians of the events; in short, an anonymous bridge that joins the shores of the past with the shores of the future and more vigorous generations, morally superior to the ones of our time, thanks to, among other things, the examples given by the men of the Blue Division.

Sergio Brandao Cardoso
"*Hermandad Doncel*" Association President
B.A. in History and Geography

Notes on the Blue Division

by: Carlos Caballero Jurado

This book does not try to be a written global history of the Blue Division, but rather to analyze a very narrow aspect of it: *the importance the Officers of Intervention had in the Division and the War*. The reader who wishes to know more about the history of the Division as a whole must know that there are, at his disposal, remarkable historic studies[2] and documentation. Nevertheless, we must, for the reader's benefit, make a brief introduction on what it was, as well as the origin of the Blue Division, so as not to force the reader to read this text along with other documents or books.

In the early hours of 22 June, the Spanish ambassador in Berlin, Espinosa of the Monteros, telephoned Ramon Serrano Suñer,[3] Foreign Minister of Spain and brother-in-law of General Franco, about the beginning of Operation Barbarossa, with which Hitler tried to devastate the Soviet Union with a lightning punch strength strategy (*blitzkrieg*).[4]

The biggest military conflict in world history had just started.

When the news was confirmed by the German ambassador in Madrid, Von Store, *Serrano Suñer* hurried towards the "*El Pardo*" (Official residence of General Franco, near Madrid) to meet with the Head of State.

Franco, connoisseur of the news, was awaiting the visitor. *Serrano Suñer*, perhaps the best known German sympathizer, tried to convince "*El Caudillo*" of the possibility of attacking Communism in its own den, as well as of the future advantages of Spanish participation in this offensive next to the Germans. As a remainder and context note, we must remember that the *Wehrmacht* Divisions were also present at the Pyrenees to pressure the Spanish government into taking sides.

The Hendaya meeting between Hitler and Franco (October 1940) did not answer any questions, nor offer a solution to the problem; the two opposing positions remained firm and distant. The reader must evaluate that at the time of the famous meeting Hitler and Stalin were very close allies. Germany and Russia had divided their Polish bounty. While Stalin saw how the Germans conquered and destroyed the Scandinavians, Holland, Belgium, and France with his supplies of oil and raw materials, Hitler observed without any action how Russia annexed the Baltic countries and destroyed Finland and Rumania.

Visceral animosity and anti-communist furor surged on April 1, 1939, towards Russia, and the communist party. It was not rare for the support of the German "*realpolitik*" to be mixed with the sympathized admiration expressed towards the III Reich and the eternal gratitude that existed for the heroic Legion Condor. It is important to point out that the authors, who were looking for any trace of proof joining Hitler and Franco together as conspirators, forgot the close alliance that existed between the III Reich and the USSR during the first phase of World War II.

With the beginning of the Barbarossa operations, the conflict took a complete turn of events. The attack by Germans on Russia caused great expectation in Europe. In countries like Finland or Rumania, where Russia had taken possession of territories without any criticism by other countries, the time for vengeance and justice had arrived. The other German allies that were not previously notified of the invasion made clear their willingness to join efforts in the campaign. Sweden was first among the countries joining the efforts to support the war against Communism.

The rest of Europe, under the *Wehrmacht* invasion, applauded the action even when they were under the German presence. Even exiled Russians and other soviet national circles expressed their enthusiasm. In Croatia, a Czarist general offered himself to start recruiting to create a Russian Legion Anti-Bolshevist. In Rumania, with Antonescu's blessing, the Ukrainian Legion was formed.[5] It was Germany's own fault and loss not to allow the participation of these exiled communities.

There is no doubt that the place where the Russian invasion caused the greatest popular euphoria was in Spain. The people,

A magazine cover from that time.

spontaneously, made popular demonstrations not even imitated in the Reich. The Spanish Civil war was for the victorious group, the Spanish Crusade against Communism, "*La Cruzada contra el Comunismo*," but until then, it was condemned to have no further continuation, since the German/Russian courtship in the beginning of the conflict.

Now, with the overwhelming power of the German military Forces in soviet territory, WWII was acquiring an understandable and assumable new meaning for the Spanish people. "The Spanish Crusade against Communism" would be revived as the "European Crusade."[6]

In Spain at that time, the young Spanish evolutionary political body was forming. Their Regimen, created after the 18 July military uprising known as "*El Alzamiento*," had not yet clearly marked the direction lines. There was a clear power struggle between the *Falange* and the Army. There were more important reasons for the struggle, as the direction of the country with a line as " National Catholicism" or "National Syndicalism" was dividing the right and the left.

The first one was based in deep monarchic conservatory roots, with clear nostalgia for the throne, and supported by the church with intellectual side allies like Balmes and Menendez y Pelayo.

Assault Section of the III Battalion, 262 Regiment headed by Alferez Nuñez. (Archives Ripoll)

The second option was not naming a restoration, but a regeneration, and claimed to be the estate of the ninety-eight philosophies defined by the *Ortega y Gasset* or *Unamuno*.

The proponents of the first theory were mostly the militaries, while falangists clearly pushed for the second one. These opposite lines made possible the criticisms and the fictitious confrontation that existed between the Army and the "*Falange*." To the middle of 1941, the phalangists' Revolutionary Nacional-Sindicalist theories were clearly undermined by the national Catholicism and Monarchial direction of the new government. The German Eastern Front Campaign was very important if their movement had any chance of surviving the reactionary push given by the Spanish Army and Franco's government.

If the German armies succeeded, the National Socialism ideas would prevail in Europe, thus making the National Syndicalism a more viable Spanish future. That was the force moving *Falange* to start the recruitment of a volunteer Unit to fight on the Eastern Front and to name it "The Blue Division" (*La Division Azul*), in remembrance of their blue uniform shirts.

Franco could not disassociate himself from the ongoing internal dispute. In order to obtain external benefits, Germany pressured him to join the fight and abandon the "neutral country" status, and internally, the conflict between the national-Catholic and the National-Sindicalist movements, he finally approved forming a Spanish Divisionary Unit composed exclusively of volunteers.

There are historians who have given a twisted Machiavellic view of the actions taken by Franco. They claim that this decision put land between the uncomfortable revolutionary units and the ideas of the Old Guard of *Falange* and Madrid. However, it was not known then that the Eastern Russian front would result in a carnage of the members.

If, on the other hand, they would have come out victorious, there is no doubt that things would have been different in Franco's Spain after the conflict. *Falange* would have had a reinforcement of their ideas with the victory, and probably a more important role in the Spanish government and cabinet.

Once the news was official, the fight commenced in earnest to see who would organize and head the Division: the *Falange* or the Army. The High Military Central Command did not want to have results presenting *Falange* as victorious in confronting communism and their return as heroes (until October 1941 all parties, including the British and the U.S., were confident of a Russian loss to the German invasion). The Army wanted to send a regular Spanish Army Division similar to the ones deployed by other Axis allies like Italy, Slovakia, and Hungary[7]; however, politically speaking, that would have had the same effect as declaring war on Russia. Therefore, it was decided to send just a Divisionary Unit composed exclusively of volunteers. The Official name would be The Spanish Volunteer Division (D.E.V.), but it would be better known as the Blue Division (*La Division Azul*).

This was not the only rivalry between the two groups. A new one started over who would be the Head of the Division. *Falange* promptly decided that the position should be given to their highly regarded and prestigious Old Shirt (*Camisa Vieja*), Jose Antonio

Capitan Alfredo Miranda Labrador, wearing a coat, with the Deposit Battalion 250 Chief, who died in the combat of February 10, 1943. Lieutenant Méndez Trigos and, in pajamas, Lieutenant Demetrio Fernandez Ochoa, died in the same day's combats. (Archives Ripoll)

The Ishora river viewed from the Spanish positions. (Archives Ripoll)

Colonel José Martinez Esparza, Chief of Infantry Regiment 269.

Fortification operations on the new Division Sector. (Archives Ripoll)

Giron de Velasco. Although not from the military Academy and carrier, he was in charge of the Castilian *Falange* Units. Under his command they had conquered the "*Alto del Leon*" with such courage and heroic assault that he received the Individual Military Medal, the highest military honor in combat for the Spanish Army. This mountain peak would be renamed popularly since then to the "*Alto de los Leones*" in remembrance of their heroic conquest.

The Military command claimed that the Unit would be better off under a military commander, proposing a popular name from the recent civil war like Moscardo.

Like Solomon in biblical times, the decision was a tie. The regular recruitment officers of the military institutions would proceed to enlist volunteers at the *Falange* designed posts and local headquarters. All Officers would need to be of military training and the rank of Captain and up, leaving the Lieutenant and Alférez with the remaining NCOs with a designation of "Temporary Officers."[8] The Commander in Chief position was reserved for General Agustin Muñoz Grandes,[9] who was a highly respected figure by both Phalangist and the Military.[10] This decision was later applauded by both sides, as General Agustin Muñoz Grandes was a man who all respected, from the military chiefs to the troops serving in his command.

Leaving aside the political maneuverings, and situating ourselves in the Spanish streets and plazas of those days, on 24 June the Gran Via street of Madrid was filled with thousand of blue shirts. The *Falange* student union group S.E.U. (*Sindicato de Estudiantes Universitarios*) ordered the suspension of academic activities and organized a demonstration with the theme "Spanish Volunteers Against Russia," asking that the rest of the population join the march.

The demonstration filled the streets on the way to the building where the F.E.T. had their offices. Serrano Suñer, the General Secretary, spoke to the people participating in the march, and finalized the speech with the famous slogan "*Rusia es Culpable*," "Russia Is Guilty." Often not mentioned is the fact that this popular demonstration was simultaneously repeated in all other Spanish locations with the SEU students as organizers.[11]

The recruitment period ran from June 26th until July 2nd. The recruitment was incredibly successful. The Spanish youth enlisted in block. Military, work force, farmers, students, political personalities, and the unemployed fought between themselves to get a position. Believe it or not, some used the old strategy of who you knew, or connections ("*enchufe*") to secure one of the openings. High military commanders finding no open position in their rank decided to enlist as NCOs, or simply as troops. The remaining of the Old Phalangists Guard went in group to the call.

To demonstrate how important enlistment was to them, and to what extreme the *Falange* was responsible for this success, we will mention a couple of examples:

The first one is the "ARRIBA" newspaper, the official journal of the FET. This was the recollection as narrated by one of those present:

"Our newspaper, the one founded by Jose Antonio, responded like any other Phalangist organization or group. The entire Publisher Section went and enlisted following their head, Comrade Echarri. Then, unfortunately, your health and fortune would determine who would participate as members of the Unit in the Blue Lines. (…)

On the way, fell those not yet recovered from the war wounds, then the old ones or those with high family commitments, leaving only those who in mere justice really deserved the honor to be part of this glorious act"[12]

Engineer Battalion Sheds at Krasny Bor, Fall 1942. (Archives Ripoll)

Legionnaires at Krottingen, Lithuania. (Archives Gregorio del Pozo)

As the final list was completed, these were the names of the newspaper volunteers that made the cut: Vicente Gaceo del Pino, Alfonso Gallego Cortés, José Caballero Palacios, Francisco Javier Goñi Sánchez, Joaquín de Alba Santizo (known by the cartoon author, "Kin"), Demetrio Castro Villacañas, Juan de Rojas Mora, Jesús Martínez Tessier (the lines previously mentioned), Salvador López de la Torre, Manuel Escamilla Crespo, Cecilio Jorquera Masa, Santiago Hernández Medina, Carlos Polonio Sánchez, Bonifacio López Andrés, Raimundo Sanz Fernández, Aurelio Sanz Bartolomé, Arturo Sola, Francisco Alba Gutiérrez, Antonio Carmena Blanco, and Manuel Hernandez Pacheco.

The first four in the list died in Russia, making the newspaper loss reach 20 per cent of their members.

Another example would be the one of the " *Centuria de Balillas de La Vieja Guardia*," the young members of the *Falange* Old Guard ("*Los Balillas*"), a name given to them after their counterparts of the Italian Fascists. During the 2nd Republic political fight, a lot of the members of this group were the object of attacks—inclusive of physical ones—by their enemies. At the beginning of the communist *Frente Popular*, six of them were assassinated and another four died during the preliminary combats of the Civil War.

The Unit had paid their dues, but the surviving members decided to join as a group. They formed their unit, and marched through the streets to the recruitment office.

In the Russian front, the Head of the Century, Miguel Alonso, the First *Falange*, Jose Calvo, and the Second *Falange* commander, Hernandez Vaquero, along with other unit members totaling thirty, died at the front.[13]

The Old Guard, nevertheless, could not contribute a human contingent sufficient to form a full Division. In fact, many of the Falangists that got recruited came from the "organizations of youth," that is to say, of the S.E.U and the Youths Front, whose militant young people wished to become worthy pupils of their old comrades that fought in the recent Civil War.

There were other groups, with their own profile, that contributed significantly to the Division. During the Civil War, a great number of militants and supporters of *Falange*, or simply anti-communists, that due to geographic reasons had been in the "Red Sector" of Spain, and some were even forced to be part of the Republican Army. These Spaniards now ran to be part of the Blue Division, to finally be able to participate in their wished fighting side.

A group with very concrete characteristics was that formed by the members that passed the Civil War in jails and the enemy concentration camps. They got ready in great number, and at the end of October 1941, approximately 35,000 people registered as "Ex-captives" in the National Delegation that fitted them within FET. A total of 2,268 would serve in the rows of the Blue Division.[14]

Falange earned with their blood that this Division be called "*La Division Azul*," the Blue Division. But realistically speaking, not all their members were sympathizers of their ideology. Some of them were *Carlists*, some just Catholics, and some others just plain patriots. The only thing that they held in common for sure was their strong anti-communist feeling.

Alferez Herrera (Archives Ripoll)

Lieutenants Mendez Trigo, Ripoll, and Alferez Nuñez. (Archives Ripoll)

Esteban Infantes. Signed photograph from Captain Jaime Ripoll. (Archives Ripoll)

The Military command who decided to volunteer for the mission were in good part the best of the best of the military units. At the conclusion of combat it showed in the Spanish military ranks, with almost all becoming Generals in the future after the conflict that had served in the Division. As it was with the German Legion Condor during our Civil War, the Divisi6n was a unique "alive military Academy." Working along with the elite of the German Army made them achieve a great level of experience.

If the excuse was the anti-communism ideal, the reality was an opportunity they could not pass to achieve military glory and a unique real conflict experience. It is a shame that no one has taken the time to make a detailed description of the Division members and to catalogue "who" went to Russia, and their achievements after the war.

The transfer of the volunteers towards Germany began 3 July, although it was only a small contingent, and it was necessary to wait until the 13th to move the first great expedition. The great public demonstration in favor of the departure of a Volunteer Unit registered in the past in Spain repeated itself on the occasion of the farewell of the Eastern Front volunteers, who were acclaimed by great multitudes even at the train steps at the stations. Around the 23rd, the Division main force was lodged in the German Military Practice range of Grafenwörh.

The Blue Division, or Spanish Division of Volunteers, was going to acquire a new identity, the "250th Infantry Division (*Spanische*)" (250th Infantry Division – The Spanish). At that time, the truth is that the Spaniards were disoriented enough on the organization of the German Army that it was necessary to reorganize the contingent that had left Spain (with four Infantry Regiments, known by the names of its colonels: *Rodrigo*, *Pimentel*, *Vierna*, and *Esparza*).

This is the moment for the development, and thus an explanation with some detail, of the structure and organization of the Blue Division, to make their scope more comprehensible, and

Lieutenants Ripoll and Mendez Trigo visit Spanish positions near Krasny Bor, September 1942. (Archives Ripoll)

the surroundings and task of our Army Interventors Corps (finance service inspectors), which is the original idea for this book.

The Command

The structure of the Blue Division was designed according to the traditional Spanish military model (in fact, the commonest in most of the western armies). This structure consisted of a Commander-in-Chief of the Unit, and a Staff General that had his own Head with four Sections (Personnel, Information, Operations, and Services). The structure of the Division command was set up differently in Germany. In spite of the German Command efforts and requests for a change, the Spaniards maintained the one that they knew best and used. Altogether, the Unit General Staff had much more personnel than its German counterpart.

In addition to the General Staff, in Headquarters there were the quarters of the different Arms, Bodies, and Services (Infantry, Artillery, Engineers, Passive Defenses, Intendance, Health, Veterinary medicine, Pharmacy, Transports, Ecclesiastic, Legal, and, of course, the Intervention). For obvious reasons Headquarters had several translator officers. To support Headquarters there were accessory sections. These sections, such as Cartographic, and a

Pedro Cuyas Ortiz, serving at the time as the Spanish Ambassador to Mauritania. He's wearing on his ambassador's uniform some of the medals he received at the Russian Front. (Archives de la Vega)

Unit of Duties and Assignments, had at their disposal the Section of Military Police of the Division Campaign (composed by members of the Spanish Civil Guard).

We can also consider as units directly tied to the Division Command the Postal Mail Section, and the Section of Press and Propaganda, which was created to publish the Division newspaper, "Leaf of Campaign." For the apparent reason that we will be seeing, the Blue Division also counted finally on a relatively ample structure in the rear lines. The position of Head of the rear Division Services was created, and held by an officer with the rank of colonel.[15]

The Infantry

This accounted for the majority of the Division forces. To the surprise (and misfortune) of the volunteers, the practical totality of the German Infantry used as means of transport ... the legs of the soldiers, and horse trailers for the baggage. In effect, it was a "hypo-mobile" Division.

The Spaniards had to readjust the group as they left from Spain, to the three typical Regiments of a German Division. The Regiment "*Rodrigo*" was dissolved. The Regiment "*Pimentel*" became the Infantry 262nd; the "*Vierna*" became the 263rd; and "*Esparza*" the 269th. Or, to be more historically precise, they should have readjusted, but in fact the volunteers never forgot or discontinued using their original Regiment names.

The original documents are many, and the texts written by the division names (articles, books) where the terminology was used to designate the Regiments was: "*Pimentel*," "*Vierna*," and "*Escarza*." Finally they used the numerical designation, with the peculiarity that is quite a rare find; for example, the expression "Regiment, two hundred sixty two" being used instead of "regiment dos-seis-dos." One case, of course, is the pure economy of the spoken language, but the shocking part is that this habit also translated to written documents as well. Even in official use in documents, you will sometimes find the literal expressions previously mentioned ("Regiment dos-seis-dos") or its numerical version ("Regiment 2-6-2").

At a certain point, the three Infantry regiments were re-baptized by order of the Germans, like Regiments of Grenadiers, without any implied modification to their structure.

The Infantry regiments, on the other hand, also had a ternary structure, with three Battalions (of four Companies), but three independent Companies, which gave a total of fifteen Companies per Regiment. A singularity of the German organization was that the fifteen Companies were numbered consecutively, with the 1st to the 15th forming a consecutive sequence. The first four corresponded to the Ist Battalion, the following four to the IInd Battalion, and the 9th to 12th formed the IIIrd Battalion. This peculiarity confuses many military students, because it is common to find a document, or a witness who says to you "I was in the 3rd Company of the IInd Battalion of such Regiment," to which one has to question one's self: is he talking about the 3rd, that belonged to Ist Battalion, or is he talking about the 7th Company that, in effect, was the 3rd of the IInd Battalion? Other times, to the contrary, documents or witnesses are unnecessarily redundant, and they inform you in which unit a

Muñoz Grandes. (Archives Ripoll)

person served, like the 8th Company of the IInd Battalion, of such named Regiment. In these cases, due to the excess of information and a reader not being warned, the conclusion that a German Battalion had, at a minimum, eight Companies might be reached.

Each one of these Battalions, always following the ternary structure, counted as three Infantry companies, plus one of Support (with machine guns and mortars). In principle, the correctly prescribed method was that Battalions designated themselves using Roman numbers, followed by a crossed bar and the number of the Regiment to which they belonged (for example, IIº/269, Iº/263, etc.). The reality, at that time, based on documents and testimonies, is very different. You may find expressions such as: "2º of the 2-6-9," "Second of *Escarza*," etc. that are more the rule than the exception. Sometimes it is even more complex, as we found papers saying "2º-269." The reader will understand that a simple, and very often made error, between (º) or (nd) and (ª) or (rd) can nevertheless change the entire sense of a phrase, because in the first case it refers to a Battalion, while in the second it refers to a Company.

The historian would be thankful, without a doubt, if those who wrote these documents had considered the official criteria to designate the units, but the reality is that it should appraise the lector of the fact.

As far as the three independent Companies, these were: the 13th, equipped with Close-Infantry support guns; 14th, equipped with antitank pieces; and the 15th, baptized officially like the Headquarters Company, which included Sections of Scouting, Combat engineers of Assault, and Transmissions. What would call the attention of a student or Spanish reader was, without a doubt, that the 13th was denominated a Company and not as a Battery Unit, since in effect it operated the cannons.

In the German organization control of these units was with infantry officers. The Spaniards, however, gave control of the seats to artillerymen.

In summary, the structure of a Regiment was:

Mendez Trigo and (unknown) on the wood planks road at Krasny Bor, 1942. (Archives Ripoll)

Volunteer in the trenches.

Reg	262nd (same as the 263rd and 269th)														
Batt	I				II				III						
Co	1st	2nd	3rd	4th	5th	6th	7th	8th	9th	10th	11th	12th	13th	14th	15th
(*)	Inf.	Inf.	Inf.	S&M	Inf.	Inf.	Inf.	S&M	Inf.	Inf.	Inf.	S&M	Can	AntiT	Mix

(*) Equipped with: Inf. Infantry rifleman; S&M: submachine and mortars; Can: Cannons; AntT: Anti Tanks; Mix : Scouting, Assault, and Transmission engineers Units

To these nine integrated Infantry Battalions in Regiments a tenth independent Battalion was added, whose composition requires explanation. The German Command had anticipated in facing the Russia campaign that, due to the gigantic distances in that theater of operations, each Division should have a Deposit Battalion following closely in their displacements that could facilitate timely replacements to the Division.

In principle such a Battalion had to include coverage for all the specialties and arms of a Division, and to have three Companies. The Spaniards organized a Battalion of this type and baptized it with the official name of the Battalion of the Deposit 250th, but it was also known as the Reserve battalion Mobil 250th or, even more frequently, by its nickname "*La Tia Bernarda*," "The Aunt Bernarda." Actually it never acted as a Deposit, but as another Battalion, and to be exact, like a front Battalion, whose commanders and troops considered themselves more as members of the Spanish Legion than members in the Blue Division.

Its structure adopted the typical one of a combat Battalion; that is to say, three Infantry companies and one of Support Arms. And finally, it is necessary to mention that, already in Russia, the climatologic conditions required the creation of a Company of Skiers (the Company of Skiers 250th) which, by the way, would carry out some of the most famous missions of the Blue Division.

Cavalry

In all the Armies of the world, the Cavalry has traditionally assumed exploration tasks. But not to be deceived, the old and glorious Cavalry had finished its days confronting the barbed wire fences, the minefields, and the machine guns of World War I. So although in the German Army, at the beginning of World War II, some units of Exploration still maintained the name of Cavalry Groups, usually they adopted the designation of Reconnaissance Groups. In an Army as poorly motorized as the German, not even these units had motor vehicles and had to be satisfied using ... bicycles. In the end, the only vestige that these units had of their origins in the Cavalry was that they maintained the designation of Group in lieu of Battalion.

This explains the confusing nomination of "Cavalry" on the Blue Division, that according to documents is the "Group of Cavalry 250," in another is "250 Reconnaissance group," and finally

Moving cavalry unit sketch.

Moving mule unit.

in others "Cycling Group 250." The originally picked group, of two squadrons and two full sections of Antitank and Transmission, ended up modifying itself by one of three squadrons. Honestly, it would be necessary to say that more than a unit of Cavalry was a unit of Infantry Riflemen, also known as light infantry.

Artillery

The Artillery was formed as a Regiment of four Groups. The first three Groups were equipped with 5 pieces of 10.5 mm, and the fourth with tubes of 150 mm. Each Group its own battery High Command, but only the Batteries of Pieces showed numeration, also correlative, from 1st to 12th (three in each Group). Each Battery counted with four guns. It is also common to find, that to the three first Groups received the qualifying adjective of "the Light" and to the IVth, "the Heavy."

Already in Russia, the Artillery Division was reinforced with materials coming from the booty taken from the French by the Germans, which allowed different organization, with three new Batteries (numbered 13th, 14th, and 15th). But the possible temporary character of these units, as well as the fact that its personnel officially remained integrated in the original Batteries from which they came, caused these three Batteries to generate very little and poor record documentation.

Another unit equipped with tubes was the Anti-tank battalion 250. This new specialty, the antitank artillery, was a very recent creation. In the case of Spain, units of this type did not exist until the Civil War, and German instructors helped with their creation. For the Germans, the anti-tank guns had to be considered part of the tank units, and as such, integrated to the tanks Corps, "the *Panzerwaffe*." For that reason, the color that identified them and their uniforms was the same; the pink, in the cases of tank destroyer tank crewmen. Nevertheless, Spanish senior officers who had control of the units of anti-tank guns came from the Artillery and, after a brief use of these units, they agreed they belonged to the Infantry Arms. The Blue Division did not wage a war of movement, but basically of position, and except for counted and very significant

Members of the 263, 3rd Section, 5th Company of the 2nd Battalion in the Chutiny sector of the Volchof Front. (Archives Dolado)

occasions, it did not fight against enemy tanks on battle. For these reasons, the reality was that in the Russia campaign the Anti-tank battalion 250° acted like an artillery unit rather than as an Infantry one, although it is not less certain that the unit commands came from the Infantry. In any case, its Composition was articulated in three Companies.

Engineers

In Spain, until very recently, this Corps included the combat engineers and the transmission engineers. However, for the Germans they were totally different bodies. The Division had individual Transmission and Combat engineer battalions, both with the 250 designation. This last one counted with individual Radio and Telephone companies.

The Combat engineers Unit originally consisted of three Companies; nevertheless, at certain moments a 4th Company was formed, like a unit of Skiers being added, that cannot be confused with the mentioned Company of Skiers 250ª. In both cases, the Battalions counted on their own light Column that brought the mobile material of the two specialties.

Medical

The Spanish Medical Unit in Russia was one of the bodies whose structure was most often modified during the campaign time. Initially articulated simply like a Medical team of the type standardized in the German Infantry divisions (in this case with the name of Medical team 250) with two Sanitary Companies, two Sections of Ambulances, and a Field hospital ("*Feldlazarette*").

Evidently, this one Field hospital could not take care of all the mutilated and wounded patients, and they had to pass to the rear lines, which possessed better facilities and means. Operations began to send Spaniards to the so-called "*Kriegslazarette*" (Hospitals military)—the name given to the German military hospitals located to the rear—in the zones of occupation, and even to "Reserves Lazarette" (Hospitals of Reserve), a name that was assigned to the military hospitals already on German ground. But in one or another case, the medical and sanitary personnel were German, which is why they were inadequate for providing care for the Spanish volunteers.

The Spaniards, after some other attempts at smaller organization and duration (like the one of the Hospital of Porchov), ended up having their own hospital facilities in Vilna (Lithuania), Riga (Latvia). In these cases, with the category of "*Kriegslazarette*," there were already facilities in Germany with the qualification of "Reserve Lazarette" in Konigsberg (at the moment Kaliningrad, and part of Russia), Berlin, and Hof.

In some of these locations not only hospital centers existed, but also Companies of Convalescent, formed by personnel who already had left the hospital and awaited their return to the front to be decided by the Commander.

We cannot leave this chapter without mentioning that the Spanish military hospitals in the second lines were staffed by Spanish doctors assisted by Spanish nurses (recruited from Ladies Auxiliaries de Military Medical and the Feminine Section of FET). Often, it was wrongfully ignored that the Spanish women also took part in the adventure of the Russian campaign. Also, they counted on the aid of German doctors and nurses, including some Russian personnel, some of Polish origin, Lothian, Lithuania, and even Jewish, and it is just to remember them, since they contributed to alleviate the penalties of our patients, the hurt and mutilated of war.

They did not lack the Medical Courts, who had to certify who had to be evacuated to Spain because of wounds or diseases that incapacitated them to return to the front. As those volunteers had the right to German pensions, the mentioned Courts were a mix of Hispanic-German.

The Blue Division counted, in its zone of actions, also a small Pharmaceutical Park, to take care of the sanitary necessities of the combatant units and their troops. Also a Veterinary Company existed, of much greater importance than it is possible to imagine because, as previously indicated, in the Division horses were used to move the artillery and other heavy pieces, like the ammunition and baggage cars, and they also drew most of the ambulances.

Intendance

The role of the Intendance Corps in the Blue Division has fortunately been the object of a recently exhaustive study, something that hopefully someday will happen with the rest of the other Corps of the Blue Division. We are talking about the work of Ricardo Recio Cardona, *The Intendance Service of the Blue Division*.[16] The Intendance Group 250th counted on individual Companies of Meat and Baking, and the Supplies Headquarters.

Transportation

Perhaps the Transportation Group 250º is the least known unit of all the Blue Division. It counted several units of trucks, one of them devoted specifically to the transport of fuels and cars (called officially, in any case, "Columns," instead of Companies). Their mission was to carry, from the great motorized parks of the Army or from the railway terminals, to the lines occupied by the Blue Division, the ammunition provisions, arms and equipment, and food and fuels. It was also comprised of the Small Repairs Service and a Mechanics Company.

When the Blue Division was operating in a static front, the Transportation group 250º would control the denominated regimental Light Columns. These columns contained the horse-drawn units that assured the regimental transport of the provisions and ammunition. In a movement war, such units would have been under the control of their respective Regiments. In a war basically of position, like the draw by the Blue Division, these regimental Columns were integrated in the Transportation group. The Infantry veterans of the Blue Division did not know that their Regiment had included this type of unit. However, the Light Columns of other units (Transmissions and Combat engineers) always formed part of their respective Battalions.

As most of the volume transported by this unit corresponded to ammunition, it is not surprising that the Transportation group 250º was named the Ammo Supply Group 250º. So that the reader gets the idea of the theoretical total of all the types of ammunition which an Infantry division must have, 51.5% was transported by the fighting forces themselves (that is to say, the set of Regiments and Battalions) for their immediate use. Approximate 9.75% would be carried by the Columns of Transport of the Regiments and Battalions, and the remaining 38.75% had to be moved by the Transportation group. Nevertheless, in the tactical mission of the Artillery regiment, the Groups transported their pieces along with 44% of the modules of assigned projectiles, and the remaining 56% were transported by the Transportation group, since the Artillery regiment lacked its own Columns of Transport. Without a doubt, now it should be better understood why it was named the Ammo Group.

Military Police

In each German Division a corresponding detachment of Military police existed ("*Feldgendarmerie*"), with an organization of Section. The movement of the hundreds of thousands of soldiers who traveled daily for the front to the rear (permits, convalescent recovered which they returned to the front, etc.) was controlled by the Army Patrol Service ("*Heeresstreifendienst*"). The Blue Division raised, of course, a very special situation, since their members evidently did not speak German and, therefore, hardly could be taken care of properly by the Army Patrol Service. For that reason, just a short time after arriving, the Spanish contingent in Russia decided to create a network of positions taken care of by members of the Spanish Civil Guard, staggered from the Franco-Spanish border and up to the zone of deployment.

This network took care of and controlled the numerous Spanish soldiers in transit between the front and the rear (Vacation permission, patients and wounded, and replacements of the Battalions of March and Repatriation). Also, in this case a monograph exists on the subject, to which we refer the reader interested in knowing more details.[17]

In order to prevent the documents or mail of soldiers revealing to the enemy data on the unit to which it belonged, in the case of its falling in their power, each operative unit had assigned a number of postal code ("*Feldpostnummer*"), that not only was used for sending and receiving the mail, but also was used in the official documents that were issued to him (certified, etc.). The list of the "*Feldpostnummer*" assigned to the Blue Division is added at the end of this introduction.

With this review of the organizational structure of the Blue Division complete we return to its operative history. As has already been indicated, the unit was quartered in the German Practice Range of Grafenwörh to receive its German equipment and instruction, beginning 28 July. The Germans considered that the minimum period of instruction for an Infantry division was 90 days. But, given the expectations that they were in the course of the war in Russia, to wait for that time would result in their arriving at the front once the war was finished. In fact, the German public opinion believed in those days that the Spanish Division would never operate against Russia, but would return to Spain to make a military assault of the British occupied Spanish territory of Gibraltar, once properly equipped and instructed for it by the Germans.[18]

The High Command of the German Army, on the other hand, also thought that by the time the Blue Division finished its instruction it would be possible to assign tasks to them for the occupation in the supposedly just defeated USSR, for which it thought that the Caucasus, which had a climate more similar to the Spanish—very continental or semi-Arctic—would be a suitable zone.[19] The Spaniards, nevertheless, had not gotten ready with any other intention than the fight against Communism and, to do it all the sooner, they convinced the Germans that the terms of instruction being used were excessive. At the end of August, the Blue Division was transported via railroad until near the old Polish-Russian border. Thence, and again to the surprise of the Spaniards, a long and tedious walking march followed to approach the front, which would not conclude until the end of September and in the zone of Smolensk.

If initially it had been anticipated to incorporate the Spanish Division in the Army Group South (in fact, a group of Spanish officials was added to a Division that operated in the Ukraine, so that it became familiar with the German procedures), the strategic necessities would have advised, already in September, to assign it to Army Group Center. And finally, the same type of considerations ended up directing it towards the Army Group North. The Spaniards were not going to fight in a tempered and sunny zone, as anticipated, but precisely the opposite. The 12 October Spaniards entered their positions in the front's first line.

The Spanish Blue Division not only was the greatest of the units of European volunteers in also starting off at the front, but also the first arriving at the front's first lines of battle. Shortly thereafter arrived the Croatian Legion (three Infantry Battalions and an Artillery Battalion), which also began to operate in October, after

To the Intervention Commands were assigned an Officer Interventor, a NCO, and three soldiers as typists. In this picture are those members in 1943. (Archives Ripoll)

Volunteer Rubio wearing his brand new coat for the picture. (Archives Ripoll)

General Headquarters, August 1942. Trying the new equipment for the winter temperatures. (Archives Ripoll)

a long walk of 1,500 kilometers. In November the *Valona* Legion (a Battalion, integrated in the German Army) and the Flamenco Legion entered into combat (also a Battalion, but integrated in this case in the *Waffen*-SS), and in December the French Legion (two Battalions, fitted in the Army).

Already in 1942, and fitted into the *Waffen*-SS, arrived at the front the Dutch Legion (with three Battalions, in January), Norway (a Battalion, in March), and the Danish (also a Battalion, in May) arrived at the front.

In the case of the four integrated foreign legions in the German Army, they received individual German High Command Communications Units ("*Deutsche Verbindugstab*"). The one assigned to the Spaniards was commanded by a captain, but given the importance of its mission it finished being commanded by a colonel. The German High Command had officials, specialist personnel, and translators, as much to assure good advising to the Spaniards in the use of equipment and material, as to ensure the perfect communication with the German grade of command. Through this Unit, all the contacts between the Spanish expeditionary unit and the German military structure were made. Nevertheless, it should be pointed out that there was an internal complete autonomy in the Spanish unit, and that the Germans never controlled the Spanish forces. The most eloquent symbol of this complete autonomy was that the Spanish Blue Division never was governed by the German Military Code, but by the Spanish one, something that did not happen in any other foreign volunteers Unit that integrated themselves with the German Armed Forces.

From 17 October the Spaniards were part of the German offensive in progress, to the east of the Voljov river, that tried to connect with the Finns between the lakes Ladoga and Onega, completing the Leningrad siege. Soon they began a series of very hard combats to the East of the Voljov, and strange names like Smeisko, Sitno, Tigoda, Dubrowka, Nikitkino, Ottensky, Possad, Schevelevo, Udarnik... became tragically familiar for that generation of enthusiastic soldiers in Russia. There, so far from its surroundings, was going to disappear a good part of the old *Falange*...

But the German offensive to the East of the Voljov not only did not reach its military objectives, but, for the first time in the course of the war, Russian armies would make the Germans retreat, forcing them to cross back west of the Voljov. It was the first time, and we repeat it, that the *Wehrmacht* made a significant retreat in the Eastern front. The Spaniards had no choice but to retreat with the Germans.

In December 1941 the great Soviet winter offensive started, with unequal results depending on the sectors on the front. In the Spaniards' operational area, a great Soviet penetration to the south of the Ilmen lake left the position of Vsvad isolated. Some reinforcements were requested to the Spaniards to help a German position. To do it, they had to cross the completely frozen lake. The mission was assigned to the Company of Skiers 250th, which went out on the mission on 10 January.

In order to carry out this order, dozens of Spaniards underwent extreme freezing temperatures that caused a large number of casualties due to frost, be they wounded or dead. When the mission concluded, only 12 of the 200 men of the unit returned alive. The holocaust sized loss caused a deep impression in the German High Command, which for the first time realized that the Spanish Division was completely loyal and dedicated to the mission regardless of the necessary sacrifices.

On 13 January the Germans also requested Spanish aid to contain the successful penetration by the Soviets north of the sector occupied by the Blue Division. From that date, and until June, different elements of the Blue Division took part in the battles to close the "pouch" on the siege of the Voljov. During the operation, the Soviet elements crossed the river towards the West where they were, little by little, surrounded and defeated.

When the spring of 1942 finally arrived, concluding the hardest winter campaign of 1941-1942, the Blue Division was a hardened by fire respected Unit. Their commander, Muñoz Grandes, received the Knight's Iron Cross, and Adolf Hitler publicly praised him before the "*Reichstag*." But the glory and prestige had been acquired at a high cost of losses. The Eastern Front Campaign, which so many had imagined as the fastest one, had become something very different. The Blue Division had to adapt its operation to a war that was beginning to appear as a long one.

From January 1942, to replace losses, battalions began to arrive from Spain with reinforcements (baptized like the Marching Battalions). And as of May 1942 some volunteers that met the criteria (younger or older than military age, seriously wounded or ill, etc., and later, the troops that already had completed their long tour of duty) began to return to Spain, forming Repatriated Battalions which, somehow, were erroneously named Relief Battalions.

The Marching Battalion forces were concentrated in the Spanish town of Logroño, from where they moved toward the German city of Hof. Here, a Deposit Battalion worked with them to be equipped and instructed while they were issued the necessary German military documents. The forces returning from the front also concentrated at Hof, where they gave back their German military equipment.

According to the "*Personalausweis*" (Personal Document of Identification) of the Spanish volunteers, this Deposit Unit was officially known as the "*Infanterie Ersatz Bataillon* 481" (481st Infantry Deposit Battalion). Nevertheless, the Spanish Deposit of Hof finished being baptized with the more appropriate name "*Ersatz Kommando Spanische Division*" (Detachment of Deposit of the Spanish Division), and because it was the unit which processed most of the documentation relative to the Spaniards, its "*Feldpost Nummer*" (39,502) appears in a great number of Spanish documents. For reasons easy to understand, this Unit of Deposit of Hof was manned by permanent German personnel.

The movement of Marching Battalions and Repatriation Battalions,[20] as well as the less numerous expeditions (vacation, convalescent, urgent relief, etc.), created the necessity to establish

Lieutenants Caraballo, Amaro, (unknown), and Paez. (Archives Ripoll)

positions covered by the Civil Guard between the Spanish border and the front. The presence of Spaniards in the rear lines and the necessity to make numerous bureaucratic proceedings before the German authorities caused the establishment of a series of offices baptized as The Representation Offices of the Spanish Division. They were as much in the territories occupied (for example, in Tallin and Riga) as in Germany (for example, in Berlin). A Representation of the Spanish Division of Volunteers was also assigned to the Undersecretary of the Ministry of the Army in Madrid.

It is typical of an expeditionary unit to inevitably generate a tremendous amount of paperwork. The established Representations of the Division in Germany and the occupied territories emitted documentation with seals that, obviously, were in German. Its official name was "*Betreuungstelle der Spanische Division*," and all of them, including the Hospitals, the "positions" of the Civil Guard, etc., were under the authority of the Rear Service Headquarters, which in documents often appears with its German designation "*Stab to der ruckwärtigen Dienste Span. Freiwilligen Div*." (High Command of the Rear Services of the Spanish Division of Volunteers).

Promptly after the conclusion of the operations in the "pouch" of the Voljov, the Blue Division received orders to leave the front of the Voljov and to transfer to the trenches that surrounded Leningrad. Facing the summer of 1942, the German High Command planned the assault of Leningrad, an operation which would have to include the Blue Division. Then things turned for the worse, the operation got delayed, and was finally cancelled.

Things were beginning to look dim for the Axis. Victory was more and more difficult to attain. In Spain, the Government began to have doubts about maintaining the Blue Division in Russia, receiving more and more pressure from the United Kingdom and the United States as allies of the USSR. On the other hand, Franco wished that the prestigious commander of the Spanish expeditionary unit Muñoz Grandes would return to Spain, to replace him with another general less friendly to the German cause.

In November, the bad auguries for the Axis took shape with the great Soviet offensive in Stalingrad and the North American disembarkation in North Africa. Until then, Spain had only a single border with one of the contenders, the Germans in the Pyrenees. Now the U.S. Army unfolded next to the border of the Spanish Protectorate in Morocco. The international situation took a decisive turn.

In December 1942 General Muñoz Grandes, already decorated with the Iron Cross with Oak Leaves (a decoration that was granted to only three non-German soldiers in the *Wehrmacht*), returned to Spain, and the General Esteban-Infantes, who since August had been the second in command of the Blue Division, assumed full command. The hardest yet winter offensive of the Soviets was approaching.

In effect, in January 1943 the Soviets broke the siege of Leningrad, perforating the German lines South of the Ladoga. The Germans moved towards the sector several additional units.

At the end of the month, the Blue Division had to send one of its better Battalions to help stop the penetration around the village of Posselok, in the epicenter of the combat. In hardly half a week the Soviet steamroller thinned the Spanish Battalion to its virtual destruction. But the worse was still to come. On 10 February 10 the Soviet offensive entered a new phase with a gigantic assault against the positions that the Blue Division occupied in the perimeter of Leningrad, concretely in Krasny Bor.

In hardly a complete day of combat the Division received 2,500 losses. However, as had happened in the combats of January to the south of the Ladoga, in Krasny Bor the Soviets could not obtain their objectives, as they were stopped in full by the Spanish soldiers. Later, the Spaniards stayed firm in their new positions by the Ishora river until the end of March. The Soviets, exhausted, cancelled their project to break the Leningrad siege for the moment.

There is no wonder why, under a direct order from Hitler in April 1943 a specific commemorative medal was created by the Germans to be granted to all the members of the Blue Division.

263 Volunteers, February 1942. (Archives Dolado)

This was an honor that never before, nor later, was given to other units of foreign volunteers integrated in the *Wehrmacht*.

In spite of the terrible blows and losses received between January and March, the Blue Division stayed firm in its positions, and the Germans renewed their confidence to such a point that they chose them for a new assault attempt on Leningrad in the summer of 1943. But this time also, the High Command project was cancelled.

Fortune was definitively adverse for the Germans in the war, and the Government of Franco continued to receive greater pressures from the allies. A symptom of the new war situation was the Anglo-American assault on Sicily, which caused the fall of Mussolini and the Italian surrender in September 1943. That same month, Franco decided to ask the Germans to retire the Blue Division, to which they agreed at the beginning of October. On the 7th of that month, the Blue Division began to abandon its positions around Leningrad.

But the majority of combatants of the Division were devoted to continue the fight, so when they learned that the Division was going to be renamed and reformed into a regimental organization, called the Blue Legion, they did not lack volunteers to fill the positions.

Esteban Infantes returned to Spain (having been awarded with the Iron Cross), and the process of the repatriation of the Division was directed by his successor, General Amado Santiago Lóriga. As far as the successive unit, the Blue Legion was left under the temporary command of Colonel Antonio Garcia Navarro.

The Blue Legion had three "Flags" (with organization of Battalion), two of them of Infantry and another mixed, with Engineer, Reconnaissance elements, Close-support guns, Health, Intendance, etc. The "*Feldpost*" numbers of this new Spanish unit are also named at the end of this text. When this unit, after its organization, arrived again at the battle lines, it was to confront the great winter Soviet offensive of 1944. What the Russians had tried time after time in vain from November 1941, to break through the encirclement that tied down Leningrad, finally appeared possible.

Engineer Battalion Soldiers at Krasny Bor, 1943.

Army Group North initiated a retreat towards the Baltic Countries. The Blue Legion fell back towards Estonia, where the news arrived that the German High Command also had acceded to Franco's request to also repatriate this unit. For those who had gone with euphoric enthusiasm to that campaign, which they considered an "Anti-communist Crusade," it was a day of mourning and sorrow. Consequently, in his last speech, the head of the Blue Legion, colonel Garcia Navarro, ordered that day the arms be carried "*a la funerala*," as is the military tradition for funeral parades.

A very reduced group, with veterans of different origins of the Division and the Blue Legion, enlisted themselves clandestinely in the German Armed Forces and continued the fight to the last days in the Bunker of Berlin, defending the City and Hitler.

If their effort contributed in any effective way to the military progress is absolutely irrelevant. Nevertheless, their gesture had a strong symbolic weight. Leaving aside the percentage of adventurers that were in this last levy, we will have to say that, in their ideal they wanted to express that Spain "did not betray" the idea of an Anti-communist Crusade in spite of the turn given by the Government of Franco when retiring the Blue Legion.

In fact, to speak of "treason" was probably an exaggeration. The international circumstances had dramatically changed, and the Government could not avoid it. From the fall of Mussolini, the different European German allies not only broke their alliance with Germany (in some cases, they tried it, but the Germans aborted that movement), but even declared war on them. Spain, as is well known, never made a similar movement, even when there was no lack of influential people suggesting Franco to join the war against Hitler.

A peculiar thing was that the proposal had been made by Stalin himself in October 1943, in a conference celebrated in Moscow between Eden and Molotov, the British and Soviet Foreign Affairs Ministers. At the meeting Stalin, who was obsessed with the idea that the Westerners would soon open a second front in Europe, and that would alleviate the pressure still exerted by the *Wehrmacht* against the Red Army, asked "Would it not be possible that Spain open the door to an Anglo-American invasion? Can we force Franco to do it?"

The British limited themselves to indicate that their pressures served to retire the Blue Division, which was of little significance for Stalin, who preferred that Franco play a similar role as King Victor Manuel and Field Marshall Badoglio in Italy, or King Miguel in Rumania. That is to say, that they would need a Copernican turn in their policy.[21]

Spain did not make it; in fact, they just limited their actions to bringing back home the troops which at that time were necessary for the Spanish defense. Also, the Germans had the same understanding, not only agreeing to the retirement of the Blue

Volunteers of the 3rd Company, Engineer Battalion: Lieutenant Paez, Captain Aramburu Topete, and Lieutenant Caraballo (died in combat February 10, 1943). (Archives Ripoll)

Division and later to the Legion, but also, for the first time since the conflict began, making delivery of military ammunition and material to the Spanish Armed Forces in Spain.

The "Crusade against Communism" that the Blue Division[22] fought on Russian soil was fought at a tremendous cost in lives and sacrifices. In November 16, 1943, when the Blue Division was in full repatriation process, the statistics department of the General Staff of the Division prepared a numerical relation of the losses since entering combat in October 1943.[23]

The figures included 3,368 dead and 752 missing in combat (many of which were, in fact, fallen, but whose bodies could not be recovered), 9,552 wounded, 1,512 frozen, and 8,398 men who had suffered diseases due to their participation in the campaign. They were not far from the definitive numbers, but the 23,552 losses registered in the document were a gigantic number in relation to the approximately 45,000 men who had been in the rows of the Blue Division.

The reader will notice that in this text, the political and diplomatic ups and downs have not been developed with the depth surrounding this particular ideological-military adventure.

It has been written over and over again, by other authors, but the narration of the combats has not occupied much space either. Who wishes to know them thoroughly should check the large existing literature on the Blue Division that can be found with the detailed story of combats, often written by the protagonists themselves. Nobody can better narrate the many episodes of sacrifice and heroic acts than they who were there.[24]

In fact, the hour arrived to raise the bar a bit more, and offer the Spanish public, from the ample existing bibliography on the Blue Division, studies of investigation specialized on each and all of its aspects: the subject of the different Arms, Bodies, and Services in the Unit; the main battles they fought, and locating them in their precise strategic context; as well as the exhaustive analysis of its recruitment. Also, the problems that were generated in maintaining such a powerful expeditionary Unit on a hard, very distant front from the mother country, etc. The pages that follow are one of the answers to this challenge.[25]

Captain Villasevil, 1942. (Archives Ripoll)

UNIT or POST Number	*Feldpost*	Notes
Division High Command	00.198	Including the Cartographic Section
Military Police	43.089	
Military Post Office	43.700	
Infantry Regimiento 262nd (Regiment "Pimentel")	05.896	Command and Joint Chiefs, including the 15th Company
IST Battalion	07.800	A, B, C, D y E, identified High Command and the four Battalion Companies
IIND Battalion	09.452	Same
IIIRD Battalion	11.371	Same
13th Company (Canons)	06.939	
14th Company (Anti tanks)	07.648	
Infantry Regiment 263rd (Regiment "Vierna")	12.747	Command and Joint Chiefs, including the 15th Company
IST Battalion	14.929	A, B, C, D and E, identified High Command and the four Battalion Companies
IIND Battalion	15.303	Same
IIIRD Battalion	15.997	Same
13th Company (Canons)	13.704	
14th Company (Anti tanks)	14.117	
Infantry Regiment 269th (Regiment "Esparza")	16.397	Command and Joint Chiefs, including the 15th Company
IST Battalion	18.125	A, B, C, D and E, identified High Command and four Battalion Companies
IIND Battalion	18.880	Same
IIIRD Battalion	19.101	Same
13th Company (Canons)	16.943	
14th Company (Anti tanks)	17.451	
Reserves Mobil Battalion 250th	31.194	A, B, C, D and E, identified the High Command and four Battalion Companies
Artillery Regiment 250th	23.863	Command and Joint Chiefs
Ist Group	24.101	A, B, C, D and E, identified High Command and four Battalion Companies
IInd Group	24.945	A, B, C, D and E, identified High Command and four Battalion Companies
IIIrd Group	25.592	
IVth Group	26.341	

UNIT or POST	*Feldpost*	
Number	Notes	
Antitank Group 250th	21.913	High Command & Transmission Section
1st Company	22.379	
2nd Company	22.800	
3rd Company	23.558	
Scouting Group 250th (or Cavalry or Cyclist)	19.798	High Command & Transmission Section
1st Squadron	20.045	
2nd Squadron	20.796	
Antitank Section	19.798	
Engineering Battalion 250th	26.994	High Command
1st Company	27.303	
2nd Company	27.938	
3rd Company	28.557	
Light Column	28.967	
Transmissions Battalion 250th	29.341	High Command
Phone Company	29.908	
Radio Company	30.397	
Light Column	30.901	
Medical 250th		
1st Company	38.936	
2nd Company	39.194	
Field Hospital	39.576	
1st Rescue Section	39.887	
2nd Rescue Section	40.159	
Veterinary Company 250th	40.883	
Intendancy Group 250th	42.413	Supply Command
Supplies Administration	38.457	
Meats Company	41.317	
Breads Company	41.953	

Transport Group 250th (or Ammunition)	31.949	High Command
1st Column (Trucks)	32.645	
2nd Column (Trucks)	32.966	
3rd Column (Trucks)	33.547	
4th Column (Hip Mobil)	34.339	
5th Column (Hip Mobil)	34.927	
6th Column (Hip Mobil)	35.295	
7th Light Column (Hip Mobil)	35.871	Belong to an Infantry Regiment by military chart
8th Light Column (Hip Mobil)	36.501	Same
9th Light Column (Hip Mobil)	36.917	Same
Fueling Mobil Column	37.176	
Work Shops Section	37.837	
Manual Labor Company	38.457	
Rear Line Command Post	03.901	
Press and Propaganda Section		
(Campaign newsletter)	23.980	
Patrol Service	40.545	
Porchov Hospital	13.797	
Sanitary services of Riga	14.105	
	25.080	Corresponding Hospital and Convalescent Unit
Sanitary Services of Vilna	27.893	
	46.630	Same
Deposit Battalion of Hof	39.502	

List of *Feldpost* numbers assigned to the Blue Legion Units:

UNIT or POST	*Feldpost* Number	Notes
Legion High Command	24.470	Including Military Police and Destinations Unit
Military Post Office Unit	43.700	
I st Flag	26.611	A, B, C, D and E, identified the High Command and four Battalion Companies
II nd Flag	25.548	Same
III rd Flag	27.893	From A to I identifying the different units of the Mix Battalion
Spanish Services at Riga	14.105	Including Hospital and Representation

The German Military Administration

If the concept of civil personnel within the Armed Forces is sometimes difficult to understand, when the personnel has a military uniform and is governed by the military codes, it is even more difficult.

Unlike Spain (which only chose the formula at the beginning of its military administrative organization), this type of civil service employee was very common in Europe, and it probably was the German Army that took it to the limit of institutionalization.

With the appearance of the first permanent active armies, the necessity that, at least, in time of campaign, the basic supplies and services be guaranteed for their smooth operation created a necessity for these functions.

The active war history in which Europe submerged itself during the XVI and XVII centuries resulted in the biggest share of the government budgetary general funds being designated to maintain their armies.

The reality was that the necessary services and provisions required during war times were an unnecessary burden in peace time. Consequently, it was for this reason that it was decided that these services be provided by personnel outside of the military circles. It was normal, for example, to demand the services of civil drivers and their oxen cars to transport the artillery pieces during the duration of the campaign, thus avoiding the cost to have to maintain animals and drivers during periods of peace.

When considering this situation, it became necessary to create a figure in charge of the communication between the troops command and their suppliers, assuring that the necessities of the units were covered in a satisfactory manner.

In most of the European armies, especially the French and the German, these civil intermediaries were nominated by a Royal Patent via which they were authorized to provide to the army all types of supplies and services.

This relation institutionalized, little by little, the figure of these intermediaries. To avoid possible conflicts with the uniformed officers, they were designated with new titles and categories that placed them in the military organization. The abuses committed by these "administrators" (fraud, corruption, bribery, etc.) forced the government to audit their activities, making of great importance the function of the surging "Commissioners."

The tier of Civil Services employees adjoined to the armies was greatly implemented by the German armed forces, surviving with all their classifications until almost the end of World War II.

These officials in administrative, legal, and technical services constituted a singular figure of the German Armed Forces. The organizational system of the German Military Administration (*Werhrmacht beamten*), due to the multitude of specialties it included and its regulation, constituted a true hierarchic nightmare.

In this chapter, it is important to notice that we will only speak about the organization of the *Heeresverwaltung* (Army

Administrative Officer Jacket, 1914. (N & T Militaria)

Assimilated to Colonel, Superior Services of Headquarters Administrative Services. The Litzen and shoulder pads. (Assoc. Retogenes)

Administration) and not of the *Werhmachtbeamten* (Armed Forces Administration). It is also important to mention, and to correct a very common mistake, when speaking about the German Army, to identify the *Wehrmacht* with the Army and not with the complete group forming the German Armed Forces. These forces were composed of the Navy, Army, and the Air Force (*Kriegsmarine*, *Heer*, and *Luftwaffe* respectively).

Basically, and by each administrative specialty, four scales of responsibility and command existed, and depending on the level of studies of the applicant they started as:

EINFACHER DIENST.- SIMPLE SERVICES.
MITTELER DIENST.- MIDDLE SERVICES.
GEHORBENER DIENST.-HIGH SERVICES.
HOEHERER DIENST.- SUPERIOR SERVICES.

To carry out Simple Services (*Eeinfacher Dienst*), the applicant needed a certificate of primary education (Elementary School); a higher education (High School) was required for Middle Services, College studies for the High Services, and a University Degree for the Superior Services.

Those belonging to the rank of the Simple Services received the military rank of NCOs, and their structure reminded one of the typical work force in private industry: the apprentice, journeyman, and the master.

The rest were officers, capable of reaching the rank of Lieutenant in the Middle Services. In the High Services the graduation was similar to the Lieutenant Colonel. In the Superior Services, the carriers could culminate at the General position. However, normally they could not accede to the Chief rank (*staboffiziere*) until having served thirty-five years.

Access to the Middle Service (*MITTELER DIENST*) was common for candidates chosen from the *Unteroffiziere mit Portepee* or NCOs (non-commissioned officers that had reached the grade of Master in their specialty), and had been two years in the Military before being promoted. In spite of its assimilation to the rank of officers, and unlike the Spanish Corps, the authority of the military civil employees was exclusive to their field of specialty; that is to say, they did not have the right to be considered soldiers, but only

German Officer and a Spanish Officer.

A pair of German officers.

to the treatment as such. Privileges and obligations corresponded to the regular officers with the same rank.

During the course of the war, it became necessary to increase the number of officers of permanent rank who filled the necessities of the administrative system. This is the reason why positions were advertised to be covered by those that, in spite of not fulfilling all the requirements nor having obtained sufficient qualifications to be *beamten*, achieved the minimum conditions to be named temporary officers, or "*Beamten auf Kriegsdauer*" (Officers for the duration of the war).

In 1944 a deep military reform began, that was frustrated with the course of the war, in which the goal was to grant total military rank to all the administrative officers, comparing them to the rest of the *Werhrmacht* officers. As a result the new figure of "*Zwoelfender*" ("The Dozen") was created due to the fact that a signed contract for twelve years was required.

Due to the lack of young candidates, an important publicity campaign was made to entice members of the old *Reichsheer* (the German Army of 1919 to 1935). It is important to emphasize that all the components of the *Heeresverwaltung* (the German Army Administration) did not have the consideration of officers, since a good portion of the administrative services were covered by personnel (men and women) contracted by the corresponding organisms.

Women could serve in the Administration, but never achieve the *Beamten* rank.

The Uniform

All the military civil employees had the right to wear a uniform that, basically, was the same as those of other officers, although it had its own characteristics that differentiated it from those used by the rest of the Army.

We will briefly try to identify those clothing elements, as well as their distinctive features and the most important variations incurred during the course of the war.

In order to be recognized, and following the typical German model, was designed a complicated palette of colors that indicated enlistment to individual specialties.

German and Spanish Administrative High Command members. The fourth, right to left, is Captain Rosón, Service Head. (Archives Rosón)

A common color unified all the administrative officers' uniforms, the dark green (*Waffenfarbe*); next to it, and to distinguish the specialty, was added a second color that defined it (*Nebenfarbe*). The hierarchic system used by the Administrative Corps was basically the same as the *Heer*, although each specialty terminology was necessary to name the branches. For example, a *Intendanturassessor* was the equivalent of a simple captain; a payer assimilated to the rank of captain was a *Stabzahlmeister*; and a legal Commander (JAG) was a *Amtsrat beim Reichskriegsgericht*.

There was such a grade of difficulty to distinguish the specialties, that in all probability most of the soldiers did not know the name or color of each specialty. They only easily recognized

<table>
<tr><td>ADMINISTRATIVE OFFICERS OF THE JOINT CHIEFS STAFF
OFFICERS INSTRUCTORS
ARMY INSPECTOR OFFICERS
ARMY LIBRARIAN OFFICERS
ARMY ARCHIVES OFFICERS
ARMY OFFICERS OF THE INSTITUTE FOR THE WAR INVESTIGATION
ARMY MUSEUM OFFICERS
ARMY METERIOLOGICAL OFFICERS
SPORT TRAINERS OFFICERS
ARMY PSYQIATRIC OFFICERS</td><td>Bright Rose
(Pink)</td></tr>
<tr><td>AREA ADMINISTRATIVE OFFICERS</td><td>Red (Hochrot)</td></tr>
<tr><td>ARMY PAYER OFFICERS</td><td rowspan="2">White
(Weiss)</td></tr>
<tr><td>OTHER QUARTERS AND SUPPLIES OFFICERS</td></tr>
<tr><td>HORSE BREEDING OFFICERS</td><td>Golden Yellow
(Goldgelb)</td></tr>
<tr><td>NON TECHNICAL INSTRUCTORS IN THE ARMY SCHOOLS OFFICERS</td><td>Light Brown
(Hellbraun)</td></tr>
<tr><td>ARMY UNIFORMS OFFICERS</td><td>Rose (Rosa)</td></tr>
<tr><td>ARMY PHARMACIST OFFICERS</td><td>Clear Green (Hellgrün)</td></tr>
<tr><td>MILITARY SUPREME JUSTICE OFFICERS</td><td>Burgundy
(Bordorot)</td></tr>
<tr><td>MEDICAL OFFICERS</td><td>Cyan Blue
(Kornblumen Blau)</td></tr>
<tr><td>JAG OFFICERS</td><td>Sky Blue (Hellblau)</td></tr>
<tr><td>TECHNICAL OFFICERS(ARCHITECTS, ENGINNERS, GUNSMITH)
SADDLE ARMY OFFICERS
CORP OF ENGINEERS</td><td>Black
(Schwarz)</td></tr>
<tr><td>RECRUITMENT OFFICES OFFICERS</td><td>Orange (Orangerot)</td></tr>
<tr><td>MILITARY PRIESTS
(MILITARY PRIESTS DID NOT USE SHOULDER PADS
NOR THE GREEN COLOR UNIFORM AS PRIMARY WAFFENFARBE)</td><td>Purple
(Violetten)</td></tr>
</table>

those that were part of their daily routines, like the payers, priests, etc.

This difficulty generalized the use, with respect to treatment, of the equivalent denomination in the regular army. The officers and NCOs wore shoulder pads with an elaborate embroider set of dark green color (*waffenfarbe*), surrounded by a live color of the specialty (*Nebenfarbe*) on which were located the cords indicating the specialty and the rank.

For the assimilated to the *Unteroffiziere* (NCOs, Fig. A) wore interlaced cords of green and silver. The equivalent to *Kompanieoffiziere*, low rank NCOs (Fig. B), had eight cords, in parallel, in silver, and between second and third, a *soutache* dark green.

For the *Stabsoffiziere* (Fig. C), assimilated campaign officers—our Chiefs in the Division—cords interlaced in silver, with *soutache* in the *waffenfarbe* color in the middle of the cord. For the equivalent to a General, they took a gold cord and, some other times, interlaced silver, and in these at intervals of 1 cm "green spots" were added.

Like the rest of the Army, they took stars (Fig. D) fabricated in metal: white for the assimilated to Generals and NCOs, and gold for the ranks of Officer and Chief.

Figs. A, B, C, and D. (N & T Militaria)

Almost all the specialties wore on the shoulder a pad with the metallic emblem, made of a monogram "*HV*" *Heeresverwaltung* (Army Administrative). The civil employees of the Postal office, or the ones in the Headquarters Administrative Services, had their own emblem. JAG did not wear any. The uniform of the Army chaplains lacked shoulder pads.

To be able to illustrate this narrative, we included the following table, and as explained before, each specialty had their own distinctive secondary color:

	Equivalent Army Rank	Denomination	
APPRENTICES	**Unteroffiziere ohne Portepee**	**Unterfeldwebel**	**Assimilated to Corporal 1st Class**
OFFICIALS	**Unteroffiziere mit Portepee**	**Feldwebel**	**Assimilated to Sergeant**
		Heeresjustizwachtmeister	NCO Assistant to the Martial Court
		Futtermeister	NCO of Animal Maintenance
		Magazinmeister	Warehouse Chief NCO
		Reichskreigsgerichtswachtmeister	NCO Assistant to Army JAG
		Oberfeldwebel- Assimilated to NCO	
		Heereswerkmeister	Army Shop NCO
		Oberfuttermeister	Mayor NCO of Animal Maintenance
MASTERS	**Unteroffiziere**	**Positions with unknown specific Rank**	
		Werkführer	Crew Chief
		Mühlenmeister	Mill Master
		Bäckermeister	Bread Master
		Regimentssattlermeister	Regiment Saddle Master
		Festungsoberwerkmeister	Fortification and Shops NCO
		Festungswerkmeister	Fortification Low Rank NCO
		Oberbotenmeister	Messenger Supervisor
		Botenmeister	Messenger
		Oberlagermeister	Warehouse NCO
		Lagermeister	Warehouse Low Rank NCO
		Ministerialoberamtsgehilfe	NCO of Ministry Administrative Office
		Ministerialamtsgehilfe	Low Rank NCO of Ministerial Administrative Office
		Amtsobergehilfe	NCO of Department Administrative Office
		Amtsgehilfe	Low Rank NCO of Department Administrative Office
		Heeresunterförster	Army Forest ranger
		Obermaschinist	Installations Chief
		Drucker	Press Worker
		Laborant	Laboratory Technician
		Heizer	Firefighter
		Hauswarte	Vigilant
		Lagerwarte	Attendant
		Wächter	Surveillance Inspector
		Arbeiter	Supervisor, Specialized Worker

Equivalent Army Rank	Denomination	
Kompanie-Officiere (Campaign Officer)	**Position of unknown Specific Rank**	
	Ministerialregistrator	Register Officer of the Ministry
	Betriebmeister	Administrative Tasks Supervisor
	Betriebsleiter	Administrative Task Chief
	Oberwerkmeister	Shops Chief Supervisor
	Heeresoberförster	Army Forest Service
	Heeresrevierförster	Army Forest Service Official
	Fachschulrektor	Technical Scholl Director
	Oberfachschullehrer	Technical School Professor
	Gewerbeoberlehrer	Commerce Professor
	Handelsoberlehrer	Commercial Business Professor
	Lehrer	University Professor
	Obersekretär der verschiedenen Laufbahnen (technisches und nichttechnisches)	Multigrade Chief Secretary of technical and non Technical
	Sekretär der verschiedenen Laufbahnen (technisches und nichttechnisches)	Multigrade Secretary of technical and non Technical
	Heeresschneidermeister	Army Master Taylor
	Heeresschuhmachermeister	Army Shoe Master
	Heeresmachinenmeister	Army Master Mechanic
	Heeressattlermeister	Army Saddle Master
	Korpssattlermeister	Army Corp Saddle Master
	Werkstättenvorsteher	Shop Supervisor Official
	Lieutenant- Assimilated to High NCOs	
	Zahlmeister	Payer
	Inspektor der verschiedenen Laufbahnen (technische and nichttechnische)	Commerce Expert Official
	Trigonometer	Trigonometry Official
	Waffenrevisor	Arms Official
	Waffenmeister	Gunsmith
	Wallmeister	Positions Official
	Oberleutnant- Assimilated to Lieutenant	
	Oberzahlmeister	Payer
	Oberinspektorr der verschiedenen Laufbahnen (technische and nichttechnische)	Commerce Specialist Official
	Kanzleivorsteher	Administrative Chief
	Obertrigonometer	Trigonometry Official
	Waffenoberrevisor	Ordinance Officer
	Oberwaffenmeister	Gunsmith
	Heeresoberwerkmeister	Army Shop Supervisor
	Kartograph	Cerographist

	Lithograph	Lithographist
	Photograph	Photographer
	Hauptmann- Assimilated to Captain	
	Studier	Army Education Officer
	Fachschulrektor	Technical School Vice Director
	Wehrmachtkriegspfarrer	Chaplain
	Kriegsgerichter	Judge of the General Branch
	Stabsapotheker	Pharmacist
	Intendanturassessor	Commissary
	Assessor (technische und nichtteknische)	Officer in Training
	Stabzahlmeister	Payer
	Ministerialkanzleivorsteher	Administrative Officer
	Heereshauptwerkmeister	Army Shop Supervisor
	Oberkartograph	Senior Cartographist

Equivalent Army Rank	Denomination	
	Position of unknown Specific Rank	
	Abteilungschef im Reichskriegs-Ministerium	Department Chief at the War Department
	Ministerialrat	Minister Advisor
	Intendant	Superintendent
	Director	Director
	Obermusikinspizient	Army Music Director
	Heeresmusikinspizient	Armed Forces Music Director
	Intendanturamtmann	Member of an Army Commissaries department
	Bibliothekar	Librarian
	Direktor bei der Heeresplan-kammer	Director of the Planning Office of the Army
	Direktor des Heerestechnischen Buros	Director Technical Office of the Army
	Heeresarchivdirektor	Army Archive Director
	Direktor bei der Heeresfeuerwerker und Panzertruppenschule	Army Director of Artillery and Panzer Troops
Stabsofiziere (Campaign Officer)	Heeresmaschinenbaudirektor	Army Director of Equipments
	Heeresbaudirektor	Army Director of Constructions Ejército
	Direktor beim Heeresarchiv Wien	Army Archives Director at Vienna
	Direktor beim Heeresmuseum Berlin-Zeughaus	Director of the Army Museum at Berlin-Zeughaus
	Regierungsdirektor (Museum Wien)	Administrative Director of the Vienna Museum
	Heeresoberpfarrer	Senior Chaplain of the Army
	Heerespfarrer	Army Chaplain

	Heeresoberforstmeister	Senior Commissary of the Army Forest service
	Heeresforstmeister	Commissary of the Army Forest service
	Heeresforstamtsmann	Administrative Official of the Army Forest Service
	Heereslandwirtschaftrat	Army Agricultural Service Advisor
	Heeressportlehrer	Army Sport Trainer
	Major- Assimilated to Commander	
	Intendanturrat	War Commissary
	Amtsrat	Senior Administration Officer
	Wehrmachtpfarrer	Armed Forces Chaplain
	Oberstabzahlmeister	Senior Payer
	Heeresjustizamtmann	Army JAG
	Kriegsgerichtsrat	Committee Member of the Martial Court
	Regierungsrat	Administration Officer
	Vermessungsamtmann	Inspection Officer
	Regierungsbaurat	Administrative Officer of Construction Services
	Technischer Oberamtsmann	Technical Administration officer
	Verwaltungsamtmann	Administration Officer
	Regierungschemiker	Chemical Administration Officer
	Oberstabsapotheker	Pharmacist
	Fachstudienrat	Technical Studies Teacher
	Heeresarchivrat	Army Archives Advisor
	Oberstleutnant-asimilated to Lieutenant Colonel	
	Oberintendanturrat	War Commissary
	Oberfeldzahlmeister	Senior Payer
	Wehrmachtoberpfarrer	Armed Forces Senior Chaplain
	Ministerialbürodirektor	Administrative Services of the Ministry Officer
	Oberstabzahlmeister	Senior Administration Officer
	Oberkriegsgerichtsrat	Committee Member of the Martial Court

	Oberregierungsrat	Senior Administration Officer
	Oberregierungsbaurat	Administrative Officer of Construction Services
	Oberregierungschemiker	Chemical Administration Officer
	Oberfeldapotheker	Pharmacist
	Studiendirektor	Army Education Official
	Oberfachschulrat	Technical School Director
	Fachstudiendirektor	Technical Studies Vice Director
	Oberlandwirtschaftsrat	Agriculture Advisor
	Oberheeresarchivrat	Army Archives Advisor
	Oberst- Assimilated to Colonel	
	Oberstkriegsgerichtsrat	Committee Member of the Martial Court
	Wermachtdekan	Army Senior Chaplain
	Oberstintendanturrat	War Commissary
	Oberstapotheker	Pharmacist
	Oberstudiendirektor	Army Education officer
	Oberfachstudiendirektor	Technical Studies Director

Equivalent Army Rank	**Denomination**	
Genérale (Generals)	**Position of unknown Specific Rank**	
	Generalintendant	General Commissary of War Commandant
	Heeresintendant	Army Commissary of War
	Ministerial Direktor	Minister, Director of Ministry
	Oberreichskrieganwalt	General JAG
	Senatspräsident	Court Martial Chairman
	Ministerialdirigent	Administrative Officer (Rank as Generalleutnant)
	Gruppenintendant	Army Croup Commissary Commandant
	Korpsintendant	Army Corp Commissary Commandant
	Ministerialrat (mit den Dienstgradabzeichen des Generales)	Ministerial Advisor General
	Oberreichskriegsanwalt	Senior Attorney of the War Office
	Senatspräsident beim Reichskriegsgericht	Court Martial Chairman
	Präsident des Heeresarchives Wien	Army Archives Director at Vienna
	Präsident	President
	Vorstand der Heeres-Plankammer	Army Planning Bureau Chief
	Generalmajor- assimilated to Brigade General	
	Feldbischof	General Chaplain of the Armed Forces
	Reichskriegsgerichtsrat	Court Martial Army Advisor

One of the elements most characteristic of the German Army uniforms were the collar tabs (*KRAGENPATTEN*), prescribed since 1915 and being used to this date. Several models existed, although we will place special attention on the three types mostly used by the *beamten*:

DOPPELLITZEN. – Best known as the "*litzen*," it consisted of embroidered double colored braid, with a live color of each one corresponding to the Army Group. Without a doubt these were the most widely and generally used.

KOLBENSTIKEREI. - An embroidered double braid, in the form of wheat ears, in silver, with fifteen "ears" for the High Command Officers, and in gold for positions in the Joint Chiefs of the Armed Forces as well as the senior officers of the *HV*. These last ones wore only seven wheat ears.

LARISCHSTIKEREI. - Patch of exclusive use for Generals. In the administrative officers the collar tabs varied according to four categories, although all the patches were sewn upon a dark green color background, with *soutache* of the secondary color (*Nebenfarbe*) on three sides of the patch.

RANK | **Collar Patch** | **Description**

Hoehere Dient (High Services)

The High Rank Officers wear the *Kolbenstikerei*,in gold with seven ears.

Administrative Corps Generals wore the same patch that the Army Generals (*Larischstikerei*) with two differences: The field was of dark green color in lieu of red, and the patch had a soutache of the secondary color (*nebenrfarbe*) as the remaining of the Administrative Officers (*Beamten*).

Gehoener dienst (High Services)

Mitteler Dienst Services)

Einfacher Dienst (Simple Services)

The two Services wore the *Doppellitzen* very similar to the one worn by the rest of the Army Officers, but with a live green color separating the double braided of the primary color (*waffenfarbe*), a live dark green and a soutache around three borders with the **(Middle** secondary color (*nebenfarbe*). There was a proposal made to differentiate the two patches of these two ranks but it was never approved by the higher authority.

For the "*Beamten auf Kriegsdauer*" (Temporary Officers of War), the *Nebenfarbe* was assigned to be of a light gray color for all specialties, maintaining the same colors for each one of the ranking levels.

RANK	Collar Patch	Description
Hoehere Dient (High Services)		*Kragenpatten* embroidered in gold broken with a live *waffenfarbe* color thread over a light gray with soutache in dark green color on three borders.
Gehoener dienst (High Services)		*Kragenpatten* embroidered in silver thread.
Mitteler Dienst (Middle Services)		
Einfacher Dienst (High Services)		*Kragenpatten* in dark gray over a light gray field.

Everything referring to uniform articles, purchase of materials, preparation, enemy captured uniforms, storage, and their distribution was the responsibility of the administrative specialties.

The *Heeresverwaltungs-amt*, Office of Administrative Affairs of the Army, was in charge of supplying the different warehouses with uniforms and other articles that would be distributed to NCOs and troops.

As was the case with the rest of the regular officers, the *beamten* had the responsibility of acquiring the diverse articles and uniform pieces every month, for which they received a "clothing stipend." Until the beginning of the war, the acquisition of articles for Officers was free and simple. They were able to buy in the Army warehouses (*Heeres-Kleiderkasse*) or in private tailor shops. Once the war started, due to the lack of raw material, it was rationed, and only those with clothing ration booklets were able to buy them.

The necessity to take proper care of the articles of clothing, including those personally owned, and the difficulty of replacement, as well as the high cost, generalized during the fight the use of articles properly tailored. There are many and very good works on the subject of the German uniform in the libraries. Recently in Spain several have been published that are excellent narratives. Without getting into a highly detailed description, we try to give a general overview of the *beamten* uniforms.

German Officer with the *Beamten* Pad detail.

The Officer Service Cap

Denominated as the *Schirmmütze*, its use was regulated for the officers, sergeant majors, and troops. Made in raincoat fabric or *feldgrau* color wool. Formed with a plate and a dark cloth *feldgrau* covered cylindrical helmet.

A. Officer Cap (Assoc. Redogenes)

B. NCO and Troops Officer Cap (Assoc. Redogenes)

In the edge of the plate, as well as both extremes of the band, was located a *soutache* with the colors of the Group, green dark in the case of the *beamten*.

The black color visor was made of vulcanized fiber, and on it rested the chin strap attached with two buttons and a braided cord of gold thread for marshals and generals, silver for the officers, and leather for sergeant majors and troops. The imperial was attached to the inside cover cap by two small buttons. In the frontal cap the silver-plated national emblem was located, and underneath it, and also in silver, were placed two crossed oak leaves in which interior was located a cap badge with the national flags (in 1943 it was authorized for use by generals, marshals, and assimilated of the gold color). The oak leaves and the eagle could be embroidered in silver or be made, as most widely used, of aluminum.

C. Cap patch.

The Uniform Jacket

Without a doubt, one of articles most significantly used in the German Army was the uniform jacket denominated the *Rock*. Of obligatory use for all the ranks several models existed, but we will comment only on a few.

DIENSTROCK (Quarters field jacket). Made in *feldgrau* heavy cloth, it had eight buttons in the front. Created in 1920 and, in spite of being a uniform article used by sergeant majors and troops, its use extended between the officers as a service uniform.

GESLLSCHAFTSROCK (Full Uniform Jacket). Regulated in 1927 was characterized by a border, with the color of the Group or Unit, and the front of the jacket (in our case dark green) and a live color cord along the cuff. Its use was obligatory for the officials and optional for sergeant majors and troops.

The generals had a similar version, the main difference being the red color border of the uniform jacket, independently of the

D. The jacket (Rock). (N & T Militaria)

Jacket sleeve button detail.

Unit or Group. However, those assimilated positions like the *Heeresverwaltung* maintained the live color of the *waffenfarbe*.

In 1928 the use of six frontal buttons instead of the original eight was ordered.

WAFFENROCK (Dress Uniform Jacket). This was the most important and proud representation of the pieces of uniform ever worn in the German Army. It was only worn in the few occasions where the importance of the occasion so required.

Created in 1935 and of mandatory use, it was part of the original clothing equipment given to the troops. The officers were required to purchase it by themselves, and it was deducted from their payroll account.

Made of raincoat fabric, it had eight buttons—gold for the Generals, and silver for the rest. The neck and sleeves were of dark green color, and like the *Gesllschaftsrock* had a cord of live color indicative of the Group or Unit. The ends of the sleeves were decorated with similar patches to the ones located at the collar.

THE WAR JACKET

In 1933 its use was regulated, and it was denominated as the *FELDBLUSE* (War Field Jacket). It was given as equipment to the troops or acquired individually. It was used generally by all ranks.

Made of *feldgrau* clothing material, the collar and shoulder pads were of dark feldgrau color, with four pockets with cover, and lateral reinforcement. It had five buttons to close the front. In the collar they wore the *kragenpatten* (collar tabs), and over the right pocket was embroidered the German National Emblem with

Silver embroidery German National Emblem. (Assoc. Redogenes)

E. The *feldbluse*. (Assoc. Redogenes)

F. The riveted *feldbluse*. (N &T Militaria)

metallic filament, gold for the Generals, and silver for the officers. NCOs and troops received a clothing patch.

In 1935 it was modified for the first time, when the color of collar and shoulder pads was changed to dark green. In 1940 the remaining pieces began to be made of the same color as the rest of the piece. In 1941 another button was added.

In 1942 the pockets were modified with the removal of the reinforcements, and in 1943 the pockets were changed to a straight cover.

The *beamten* could not wear Unit or Group numbers or emblems, not even the typical written bands used as rewards for participation in specific campaigns (i.e. AFRIKA or KRETA).

The Trousers

Two different models were worn by the Officers: the *Reithose*, or mounting model, and the *Hose,* or straight trouser. As was the case with the jackets, they could be part of the uniform received from the Army or privately purchased from the official tailors. They were made of similar materials, clothing, or the raincoat fabric.

The Hose, or straight trouser

The 1936 to 1940 models were widely worn during the campaign, and usually provided by the German Intendancy. Made of wool cloth, they differed by the grey color of the originals, then passing to be made of *feldgrau* color.

G. The Hose. (N & T Militaria)

H. The *Reithose*. (N & T Militaria)

With the use of the *Geslischaftsrock or the Waffenrock* jacket, the straight trouser had a dark green ribbon along the exterior seam. This model denominated *TUCHHOSE MIT VORSTOSS*, was of better quality, made generally in raincoat fabric, and were distinguished from the other by having the outer seam with a live color of the Unit or Group.

Mounting Trousers (H)
The mounting trousers were used widely regardless of the Unit, whether Calvary or not, and whether belonging to mounted body or not. For those units on the mounting service, they added leather pads as reinforcement.

Articles of Winter Clothing
The Cape
Its quality depended on the manufacturing process, and if they were of the Army supplies or privately acquired. Made of *feldgrau* cloth, it had two rows of six buttons. For the holidays and dress days they wore a belt named *Feldbinde*, made with aluminum filament.

The neck piece was of a dark green color until 1940, when it was replaced for the same color as the rest of the coat. The Officers did not follow the regulation.

German Officer and Soldier wearing the cape. (Assoc. Redogenes)

The Dagger

Administrative officers had the right to carry in their dress uniform a dagger similar to the one used by the military officers. In addition to the belt, for the special occasions they used a belt (*Feldbinde*) made in aluminum thread, crossed by two bands of green *feldgrau* color, similar to the one used in the rest of the Army.

Around 1935 there was a project for dagger use and regulations, including an exclusive belt for the use of the *beamten*, but this project never got final approval.

To write this chapter, we used as reference the published article "Oficiales," *by Leutenant Colonel Louis H. Brown.* Feldgendarmerie-Trupp Bulletin *(Mot.) 200, Volumen IV, Number 1 (Jan/Feb. 1994).*

German Officer with Dagger. (Assoc. Redogenes, via Ripoll)

German Officer Dagger. (Assoc. Redogenes, via Ripoll)

The Military Intervention Corps
A Brief Historical Reference

Historically, the Finance Department of the Kingdom and their Royal Properties were the primary source for covering the expenses of the King house and, particularly, those incurred by the continuous wars in which the Spanish kingdom got involved. The control of the financing, collections, and expenses was trusted in diverse royal employees ("*Oidores of Navarre comptos*"), the Rational Master, accountants, or auditors.

With the Bourbons' arrival in Spain in the beginning of the XVIII Century, and their eagerness for rationalization, which was implemented for all in the administration, there was a practical application into the profesionalization of the Army and the Navy. With being placed under the absolute and central will of the monarch came the reorganization of an Internal Revenue Department that could face the expenses of a modern state.

Through a series of Decrees, Regulations, and Instructions, Felipe V developed the foundation of what—during the XVIII Century and well into the XIX—was called the Military Finance Department, as a specialty within the Internal Revenue Department of the State. In order to direct this organism, the Intendance Institution was created in 1711 for auditing the fiscal functions of the Army and the Navy, and later to direct the Civil Internal Revenues.

This instrument of the Military Finance Department was denominated as the Military Political Corps in the Army, and the Political Body of the Ministry in the Navy. These Corps became the managers and supervisors with the functions of payer, treasurers, accountants, commissioners, auditors, comptrollers, and Intendant as much in the Army as in the Navy. They got their seeds from the Ordering and War Commissioners imported from France to guarantee the police and discipline of the troops, and to control the economic claims of their commanders.

Nevertheless, there was an important difference between the Army and the Navy; while the Political Corps of the Ministry depended on the Secretary of State for the Navy (soon a Ministry), the Political Corps of the Army depended directly on the Finance Secretary of State. Their members were auditors and comptrollers of the Military Finances, but organic and day to day operations were independent of the War Secretary, and therefore of the military high command.

The Courts of Cadiz, by the Royal Decree of February 19, 1814, established that the Political Corps had to depend for all effects on the Ministry of War. A fact that made the Army Political Corps independent of the Finance Department as was the case with the Navy.

The return of Fernando VII, and the cancellation of the approved regulations on the Courts of Cadiz brought back the previous situation, until the coup d'etat of Riego that forced the King to swear to the Spanish Constitution, inaugurating the liberal triennium (1820-1823). This caused what had already been known as the Military Administration to depend on the Ministry of Finances.

By the R.D. of May 31, 1828, a new organization of the Army was established as mentioned in Article 110, and "the military administration passed to be integrated into the Ministry of War, and the employees of the Military Finance Department were transferred to that Ministry." By R.D. of September 19, 1829, it was directed that "The Navy Military Administration would continue to be totally under the Secretary of Office of this branch, with the same Ministry Corps." In this manner was consecrated the administrative dissociation between the Military Finances and the Civil Internal Revenues.

The Accounting and Reasons Corps of Artillery continued maintaining its independence, and it would not be integrated into the Army administration until 1852.

Later, by the Law of May 15, 1902, when General Weyler was Minister of War, it was again contemplated to divide the Military Administration into two different Corps: managing Administration and Auditor. It was, however, by the R.D. of January 31, 1911, that the Administrative Corps of the Army was separated definitively into two corporations. One of which, the Military Intervention Corps, would have as function the administrative management and the accounting, and the other, the Intervention Corps, would be in charge of the auditing and control of the other.

In the Law of July 1, 1911, the Administration and Accounting Law was approved, which was implemented under Article 71, and the control powers were given to the I.G.A.E. with respect to the Military Finances.

By the Decree of June 17, 1915, the Civil Intervention of War and the Navy was created, by virtue of which the Army and Navy Interventors continued to depend on both Ministries organically, although functionally they depended on the Cabinet Presidency.

During the dictatorship of *Primo de Rivera*, by R.D. of June 19, 1924, the Supreme Court of the Public Finances was created, integrating in it the Civil Intervention of War and the Navy. This continued until the fall of the dictatorship in 1930.

With the Republic, a civil character prevailed in the Corps with the functions of intervention in the Departments of War and the Navy. Being created by the Decree of July 2, 1931, the Navy Civil Intervention became separated from the Navy Intendance branch.

After the civil war, by the Law of December 7, 1939, the Navy Intervention Corps received the "military character and category." By the decree April 5, 1940, the Intervention Corps of the Air Force was created with military category and regulation. By the Law of July 12, 1940, the Army Intervention Corps recovered its military character.

After the creation in 1977 of the Ministry of Defense, by the Law 9/1985 of 10 April the Military Intervention of the

Defense Corps was created, and unified the three existing different Intervention Corps in one.

The Military Intervention Corps (1940-1943)
The Law of July 12, 1940, in its first article indicated:

"The Army Military Intervention Corps had been re-established with the character, categories, considerations, and duties that it possessed before the Law of September 12, 1932. It depended on the Minister of this Department, as far as organization, discipline, distribution of its personnel, and normal operations, as any other Army Corps. It had advisory function in matters of a fiscal and economic nature, and the function of intervention for the military services, as it is established in the Fiscal Regulations and Laws under the powers given to them by the State General Intervention."

In 1940 the Intervention was included within the Third Section of the Logistics Services General Direction of the Ministry of the Army (this one was structured on December 20, 1939, by D.O. nº 74). According to the same regulation, the subjects of the General Intervention were the following:

- Economic Intervention in the Army as determined by Regulations and Laws.
- The Payroll Intervention of this Ministry.
- Informing whichever subjects of economic nature regarding personnel, material, and cattle the High Command needed.
- The auditing and liquidation of accounts and other documents of receivables and payables.
- The exercise of the delegated functions at the superior fiscal centers of the Nation.

The functions of each Section were:

Secretary
Registry of the Intervention, library, intervention of the budget accounting, public expenses and consignments, solutions orders given by the National Audit Tribunal, filing of insolvencies and compensations, appointment of special assignments or certificates of crossings, and finally the register of active cattle force.

Receivables
First Negotiated
Examination and liquidation of receivable documents of the Army, Civil Guard, Security and Assault, and Customs. Reporting to these departments of all activities and payments.

First Promotion of the Military Intervention Corps at Zaragoza, 1940. (Archives Ripoll)

Second Negotiated
Military Payroll. Auditing and payment of these accounts. Reporting of payroll activities to each department.

Third Negotiated
Classification in periods of extended service of the classes and enlisted men of the Army, Civil Guard, Security and Assault, and Customs. Report of these activities.

Services
First Negotiated
Auditing and Payables of the services accounts of the Intendance Corps, Equine Breeding, and Quarters. Report and filing of budgets with reference to these materials.

Second Negotiated
Auditing and Payables of the services accounts of the Artillery, Engineers, and Automobiles. Report and filing of budgets with reference to these materials.

Third Negotiated
Auditing and Payables of the services accounts of the Hospitals and Health Institutions (Medicine and Pharmacy). Report and filing of budgets with reference to these materials.

Fourth Negotiated
Auditing and Payables of the service accounts of the transports, properties, and rights of the State and Workers Compensation by Accidents, Geographic, and Cartographic Service. Report and filing of budgets with reference to these materials.

During this time, the Organic Regulation of the Intervention Corps of the Army was regulated in a Royal Order of May 19, 1913 (M° of War C.L. No. 64), in whose Article 1st was established that "the Intervention Corps of the Army was the one in exclusive charge of the economic-administrative control of the Army, guarding the interests of the State and the pursuit of the fulfillment of the laws and other dispositions directly related to the administration of Public Finances when applied to the Army."

On the other hand, Article 4th enumerated the functions that corresponded to the Corps as:

- Previous authorization of any act, document, or claim that produced any rights, obligations, money transfer, articles, and effects in the War Administration, in order to avoid contractual obligations not authorized or sanctioned by the laws.
- The intervention of the transfer of money, articles, and effects, and the verification in all the Corps, classes, services, and military facilities of the existence of personnel, cattle, cash, articles, effects, and materiel of war.
- The auditing and liquidation of payable and receivable accounts and any other related documentation.
- The legal interpretation of all rights and resolutions that may produce monetary losses.
- The exercise of the Military Notary's office.
- Delegated functions assigned by the National Audit Court of the Kingdom in the subjects of the special and exclusive jurisdiction of this Court.

In Campaigns
The Interventor had duties and analogous attributions as the ones that existed in times of peace, and was able to suppress the proceedings that were not essential, writing up documents with greater precision and clarity.

The fiscal consultant's office, in such circumstances, could verbally correct matters. In the cases of discrepancies that would originate responsibility, the orders had to be in writing.

Military Intervention in campaigns required current information of any movement of personnel and cattle, as well as of deposits and withdrawals in monetary accounts and warehouses, not only in care of the interests of the Treasury, but also to insure the rights of the personnel and the Organisms of the Army. The Intervention personnel in times of campaigns had to know and to report exactly the existence and position of the personnel, cattle, cash, and materials to the Military Administration.

All individuals of the Corps serving in campaign or maneuvers were in a permanent position, and enjoyed the same rights, such as lodging, rations, assistants, bonus, and allowances that other Army Officers and Chiefs corresponding to the same rank possessed.

In conclusion, during time of war the Interventor performed his functions in an analogous way to the ones he performed in times of peace, although they could suppress proceedings that were considered essential and, to provide fiscal advise verbally. But what received special importance during war times was the Military Notary's office, whose functions were carried to the extent of the law.

In war time, the military notary's office carried their duties as described in the Civil Code, the Law of the Notary Profession of May 28, 1862, and its Regulation of June 2, 1944, as well as the prescriptions of the Decree of September 25, 1941. These were the reasons they affected expeditionary forces while they were in campaign, and whichever particular dispositions of general character or instructions were dictated on the matter. Consequently, it included the authorization of any and all acts, documents, and contracts that integrated the notary's function in his more expanded sphere.

Within the military public faith it is possible to distinguish a legalization function derived from the notaries. In these cases, the public faith was given by the military federation instead of the notary. It was a peculiar function within the military activity.

The first one was carried out within the guidelines under private law, in time of peace or war. The second one, attributed to the Interventor of the Army, was framed so much in the scope of the private as well as the public law.

Spanish Civil Code gathers the military will between those special wills, because there are circumstances in which there is a danger of death for certain people because of war, and it is almost impossible to make a will by normal means, and the reason why it is facilitated in a simple and faster way.

This will is regulated in the 3rd Section of the I Chapter of the III Title of the III Book of the referenced legal body, that next to the Navy regulation, classifies Article 677 like a special will.

In the military will, the preeminent holder of the authorizing body is the Army Interventor, successive of the Commissioner of War mentioned in Article 717 of the Civil Code. This article makes reference to this position specifically, saying that it will exert the functions of Notary Public, and that the dispositions of Article 706 and following articles will be followed—that is to say, those that talk about the closed common will.

The military will required active military duty status and being an active duty member in a campaign. Also, they granted the military will to embarked troops when on board a ship outside the country due to military operations, since this fulfilled circumstances as indicated in Article 716 of the Civil Code.

Starting with the mentioned articles of the Civil Code, and regarding the function, the Decree of September 25, 1941, empowered the Interventor Officer or Chief of expeditionary forces to authorize all powers for services or contracts that required the Notary intervention. Due to its significance, we insert the Article for information:

Art.1 Without failing to follow the arrangements established in the Civil Code with respect to wills, the Spaniards who form part of an expeditionary force, while they are in campaign, will be able to execute all class of acts and contracts that require a notary's intervention before the Chief or Officer Interventor of the superior Unit to which they belong.

Art.2 So that the public instruments have validity in Spain, authorized or which were authorized according to the previous article, the legitimacy of copies will have to be certified by the Chief of Staff of the expeditionary troops.

Art.3 The Chief or Officer Interventor will observe, as soon as possible and in the applicable part, in addition to the dispositions contained in the Military regulations that affect the functions of the Intervention Corps, the Notary Law, its annexed Regulation, and its second and third annexes, sending at the end of year the Protocol that has been formed to the Secretary of the Registries and Notaries, by conduit of the Ministry of the Army, being understood the applicable ones to this Ministry of the Army and whichever references in favor of the notaries' legislation exist.

Art.4 The Justice Ministry is hereby authorized to dictate any additional regulation to clarify, or as a complement to the proper execution of this decree.

In accordance with the previously discussed, it is possible to reach the conclusion that the attributions and functions of the Headquarters of Intervention of the Division were: administrative review, the exercise of the notaries' faith, document legalization, and the emission of information and advisory reports in economic-administrative matters that were demanded. Also, they were in charge of the payroll functions of the German Army (Office of the Payroll of Berlin).

In order to know, in particular, what each one of these functions consisted of, we rely on the memoirs elaborated by Captain Interventor D. Jaime Ripoll Lecuona (who was Head of the Services of Intervention from 20 July 1942) as to the assignments carried out by the Intervention Headquarters of the High Command of the Division dated April 22, 1943.

Before defining each one of the functions specified in the mentioned memoirs, we will briefly review the organization and means used by the interventors during their stay in Russia.

When the Division was incorporated into the German Army, the Headquarters of Intervention consisted of a Chief, Lieutenant Colonel Gomez supported by a junior officer, Lieutenant Trigo, and the necessary subordinate personnel for the smooth operation of the Headquarters, which consisted of a sergeant major and three soldiers as writers and typists. At Grafenwörh, headquarters was located in barrack 73D.

Little changed in the organization of the intervention Services with the incorporation of the Unit to the front. Although, once the

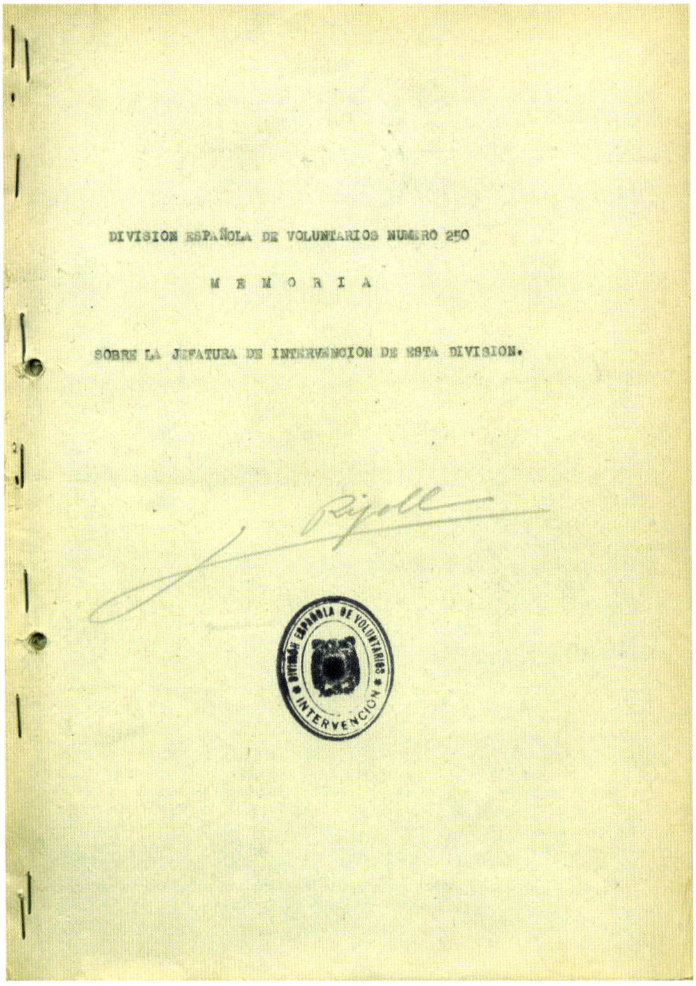
DIVISION ESPAÑOLA DE VOLUNTARIOS NUMERO 250

M E M O R I A

SOBRE LA JEFATURA DE INTERVENCION DE ESTA DIVISION.

Cover of the Review. Intervention Headquarters of the Division (Remained in a private collection, and it is the first time it has seen the light since that time). (Assoc. Retogenes, via Ripoll)

III.- REVISTA ADMINISTRATIVA

En el día de hoy, desde las dieciocho (18) horas, los Capitanes Ayudantes de las Unidades que integran la División, recogerán en la oficina del Tte. Coronel Interventor de la misma (Barraca n. 73 D.) los impresos de justificantes para la revista administrativa del mes de la fecha.

Se sobreentiende que los datos que figuran em los impresos referentes al estado civil y número de hijos, son datos jurados y, por consiguiente, sujetos a las responsabilidades por falsedad en los mismos.

Al propio tiempo se significa, que únicamente en los duplicados de las listas de revista, se acompañarán los datos q que se refiere el párrafo anterior.

El personal que sale o ha sido recientemente evacuado, figurará en la lista de revista del mes actual en sus respectivas Unidades ya que estaban presentes en las mismas el día 1. del actual.

Si algun personal no estuviera encuadrado en alguna Unidad, así como las incidencias, serán resueltas el próximo dia siete (7) en la Intervención de la División.

Review detail.

Headquarters of the Rear Services was created, two interventor centers were established: the vanguard and the rear.

It is curious to note the request done by Captain Ripoll when talking about deficiencies of material in his service:

"NECESSITIES: This office requires a typewriter in better condition, because it constantly needs to provide nominal relations of volunteers, and in its defective condition errors can result."

The exercise of the Interventor function required continuous displacements to visit the Units on the front line and in the Rear Services.

For the small displacements, the Interventor had one of the mythical BMW motorcycles. The horse-drawn character given to the Division, on many occasions and mainly depending on the station of the year, was the preferred transportation means.

For the trips to the rear positions train and airplane were the most used elements.

1. Administrative Review.

The exceptional conditions of the Spanish Division of Volunteers, the Administrative Review, and its documentation of receipts and the Review Vouchers did not have the same characteristics that they had in Spain, and was the reason why a set of Instructions were written up by Captain Interventor Ripoll, to whom the Excmo. Chief General gave his approval by order on September 15, 1942 (Annexed 1).

Office of the Corps at the Headquarters on Pokoskraia. (Archives Ripoll)

Officers at the Headquarters on Pokoskraia.

Above left: Volunteer on a bike. Above right: Volunteers on the official "vehicles." Below: Officer group on a Service Commission trip to Berlin boarding the Junkers used for travel. At the door, Lieutenant Interventor Ripoll. (Archives Ripoll)

Writer and typist soldiers assigned to the Intervention Headquarters. (Archives Ripoll)

Division Interventor desk.

The actual payment of salaries and dues to the Legionaries, the same as all the components of the Division, was independent of the original Unit in Spain, and also of the Unit of the Division in which the volunteers served. The Finance Central office of the Spanish Division of Volunteers, being located in the Ministry of the Army, was only interested in knowing the starting date of active duty and the final discharge regardless of the cause.

For that reason, the Review Voucher was numerical in nature, with the exception that Incorporation to active duty came from Spain, as did the promotion or demotion in rank within the Division. A numerical sequence was also used for the losses—the ones caused by repatriation, promotion, or demotion in rank—death, disappearance, and disappearance without right to salaries (Desertion).

If ninety days after beginning the benefit of a vacation, according to Article 1 of the General Order of November 22, 1942 (Annexed 2), they did not return to their Unit, they were definitively separated from the Division, without the right to payment of dues or salaries until they returned to the Unit. When they returned to be placed in the active duty list they were incorporated as if, at that moment, they were coming from Spain. These incorporations and discharges were part of the regular Administrative Review vouchers.

The Administrative Review vouchers extended to all the Units of the Division, as much to the front lines as to the rear, in agreement with the model that accompanied the Instructions of 15 September (Annexed 1) and the absentees' numerical relation of the Headquarters of Intervention of January 30, 1943 (Annexed 3).

The different Units would then send them to the Intervention Headquarters in the High Command so they could be stamped with the seal of "Reviewed," an operation that took place after

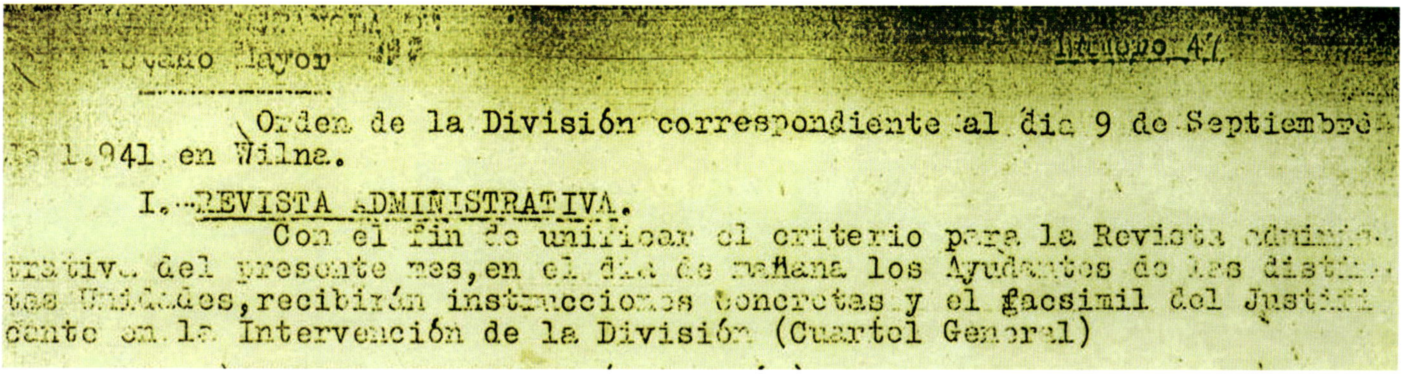

Estado Mayor — Número 47

Orden de la División correspondiente al día 9 de Septiembre de 1.941 en Wilna.

I.--REVISTA ADMINISTRATIVA.

Con el fin de unificar el criterio para la Revista administrativa del presente mes, en el día de mañana los Ayudantes de las distintas Unidades, recibirán instrucciones concretas y el facsimil del Justificante en la Intervención de la División (Cuartel General)

Division Order of September 9, 1941.

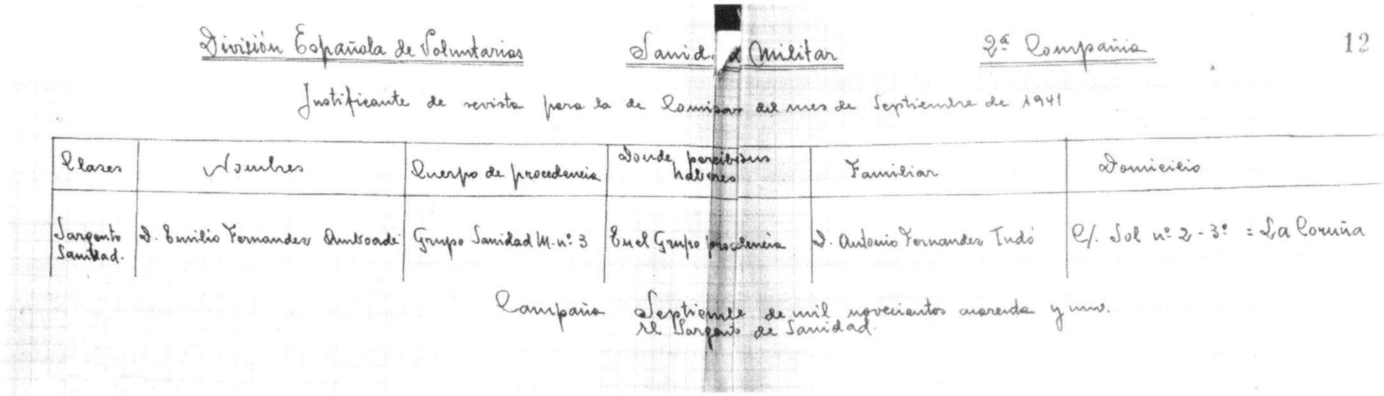

División Española de Voluntarios   Sanidad Militar   2ª Compañía   12

Justificante de revista para la de Comisario del mes de Septiembre de 1941

Clases	Nombres	Cuerpo de procedencia	Donde percibieron haberes	Familiar	Domicilio
Sargento Sanidad.	D. Emilio Fernandez Ambroade	Grupo Sanidad M. nº 3	En el Grupo procedencia	D. Antonio Fernandez Indó	C/. Sol nº 2 - 3º = La Coruña

Campaña Septiembre de mil novecientos cuarenta y uno.
El Sargento de Sanidad.

Division 2nd Company, receipt detail. (Military General Archives at Avila)

Above: Intervention Services personnel. (Archives Ripoll) Right: Personal picture of the volunteer Pedro Fernandez, dedicated to Lieutenant Ripoll. Below: Sergeant Moreno, NCO assigned to the Intervention Headquarters. (Archives Ripoll)

Sergeant Moreno, NCO assigned to the Intervention Headquarters. (Archives Ripoll)

Soldier Pedro Fernandez and Chiscano, a typist assigned to the Intervention Headquarters. (Archives Ripoll)

their examination, to verify that they were properly completed according to the mentioned orders.

Later, they were sent to the Interventor of the Representation of the Undersecretary of the Ministry of the Army, *Españoleto* 13, Madrid, which forwarded to the originating Volunteers Origin Corps the corresponding Certificates of Correspondence, communicating the discharge or active duty positions to account for the payment of salaries.

Sergeant Moreno next to Interventor Captain Ripoll in the quarters of the Intervention Headquarters, 1943. (Archives Ripoll)

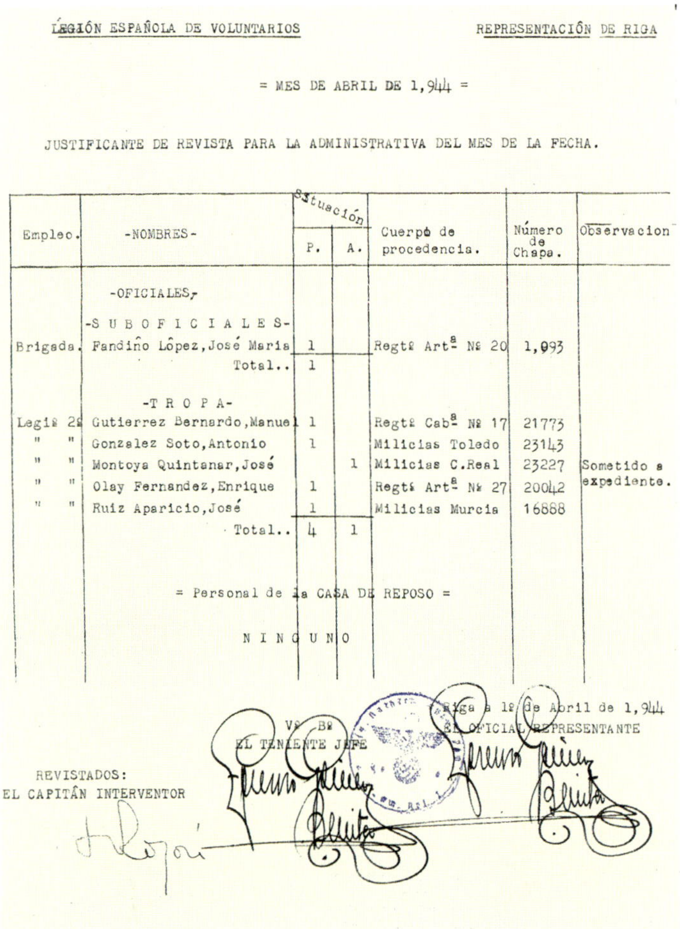

LEGIÓN ESPAÑOLA DE VOLUNTARIOS — REPRESENTACIÓN DE RIGA

= MES DE ABRIL DE 1,944 =

JUSTIFICANTE DE REVISTA PARA LA ADMINISTRATIVA DEL MES DE LA FECHA.

Empleo.	-NOMBRES-	Situación P.	Situación A.	Cuerpo de procedencia.	Número de Chapa.	Observacion
	-OFICIALES-					
	-SUBOFICIALES-					
Brigada.	Fandiño López, José María	1		Regt° Art° Nº 20	1,093	
	Total..	1				
	-TROPA-					
Legiº 2ª	Gutierrez Bernardo, Manuel	1		Regt° Cab° Nº 17	21773	
" "	Gonzalez Soto, Antonio	1		Milicias Toledo	23143	
" "	Montoya Quintanar, José		1	Milicias C.Real	23227	Sometido a expediente.
" "	Olay Fernandez, Enrique	1		Regt° Art° Nº 27	20042	
" "	Ruiz Aparicio, José	1		Milicias Murcia	16888	
	Total..	4	1			

= Personal de la CASA DE REPOSO =

NINGUNO

Riga a 1º de Abril de 1,944
EL OFICIAL REPRESENTANTE

Vº Bº
EL TENIENTE JEFE

REVISTADOS:
EL CAPITÁN INTERVENTOR

Monthly Review Report, April 1944.

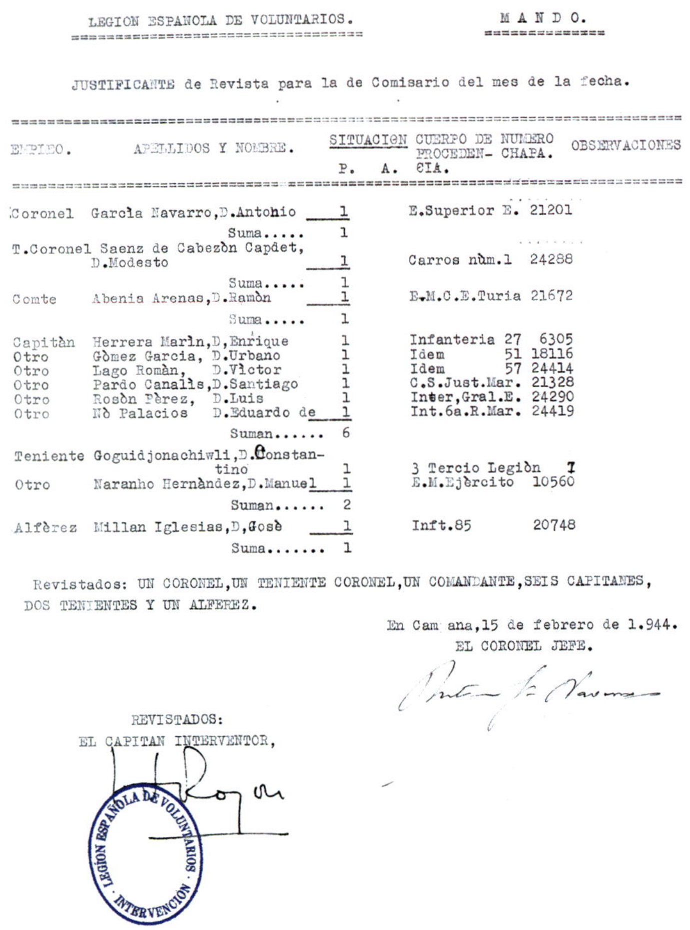

LEGION ESPAÑOLA DE VOLUNTARIOS. — MANDO.

JUSTIFICANTE de Revista para la de Comisario del mes de la fecha.

EMPLEO.	APELLIDOS Y NOMBRE.	SITUACION P. A.	CUERPO DE PROCEDENCIA.	NUMERO CHAPA.	OBSERVACIONES
Coronel	García Navarro, D.Antonio	1	E.Superior E.	21201	
	Suma.....	1			
T.Coronel	Saenz de Cabezón Capdet, D.Modesto	1	Carros núm.1	24288	
	Suma.....	1			
Comte	Abenia Arenas, D.Ramón	1	E.M.C.E.Turia	21672	
	Suma.....	1			
Capitán	Herrera Marín, D.Enrique	1	Infanteria 27	6305	
Otro	Gómez García, D.Urbano	1	Idem 51	18116	
Otro	Lago Román, D.Victor	1	Idem 57	24414	
Otro	Pardo Canalís, D.Santiago	1	C.S.Just.Mar.	21328	
Otro	Rosón Pérez, D.Luis	1	Inter,Gral.E.	24290	
Otro	Nó Palacios D.Eduardo de	1	Int.6a.R.Mar.	24419	
	Suman......	6			
Teniente	Goguidjonachiwli, D.Constantino	1	3 Tercio Legión	7	
Otro	Naranho Hernández, D.Manuel	1	E.M.Ejército	10560	
	Suman......	2			
Alférez	Millan Iglesias, D.José	1	Inft.85	20748	
	Suma.......	1			

Revistados: UN CORONEL, UN TENIENTE CORONEL, UN COMANDANTE, SEIS CAPITANES, DOS TENIENTES Y UN ALFEREZ.

En Campana, 15 de febrero de 1.944.
EL CORONEL JEFE.

REVISTADOS:
EL CAPITAN INTERVENTOR,

Commissary Monthly Review Report, February 1944. (Military General Archives at Avila)

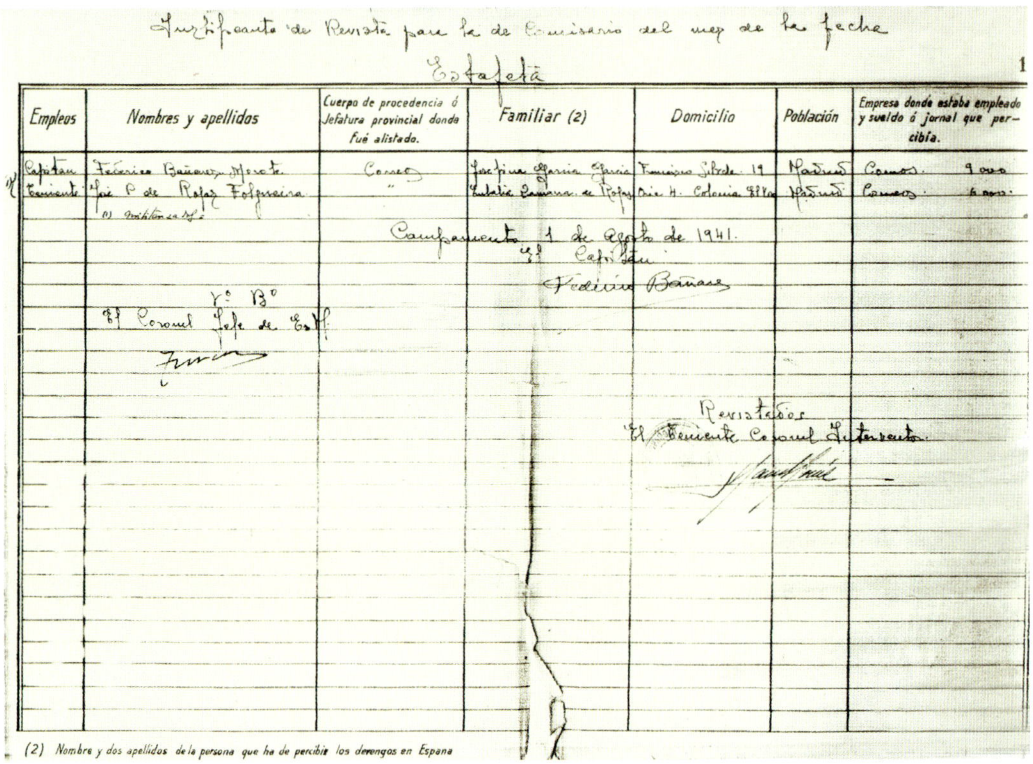

Justificante de Revista para la de Comisario del mes de la fecha

Estafeta

1

Empleos	Nombres y apellidos	Cuerpo de procedencia ó Jefatura provincial donde fué alistado.	Familiar (2)	Domicilio	Población	Empresa donde estaba empleado y sueldo ó jornal que percibía.
Capitán	Federico Bañares Moreto	Correos	Josefina García García	Francisco Silvela 19	Madrid	Correos 9000
Teniente	José P. de Rojas Folgueira	"	Eulalia Camino de Rojas	Av. 4. Colonia	Madrid	Correos 6000

Campamento 1 de Agosto de 1941.
El Capitán
Federico Bañares

Vº Bº
El Coronel Jefe de Estafeta

Revistados
El Teniente Coronel Interventor

(2) Nombre y dos apellidos de la persona que ha de percibir los devengos en España

Review Receipt, August 1941.

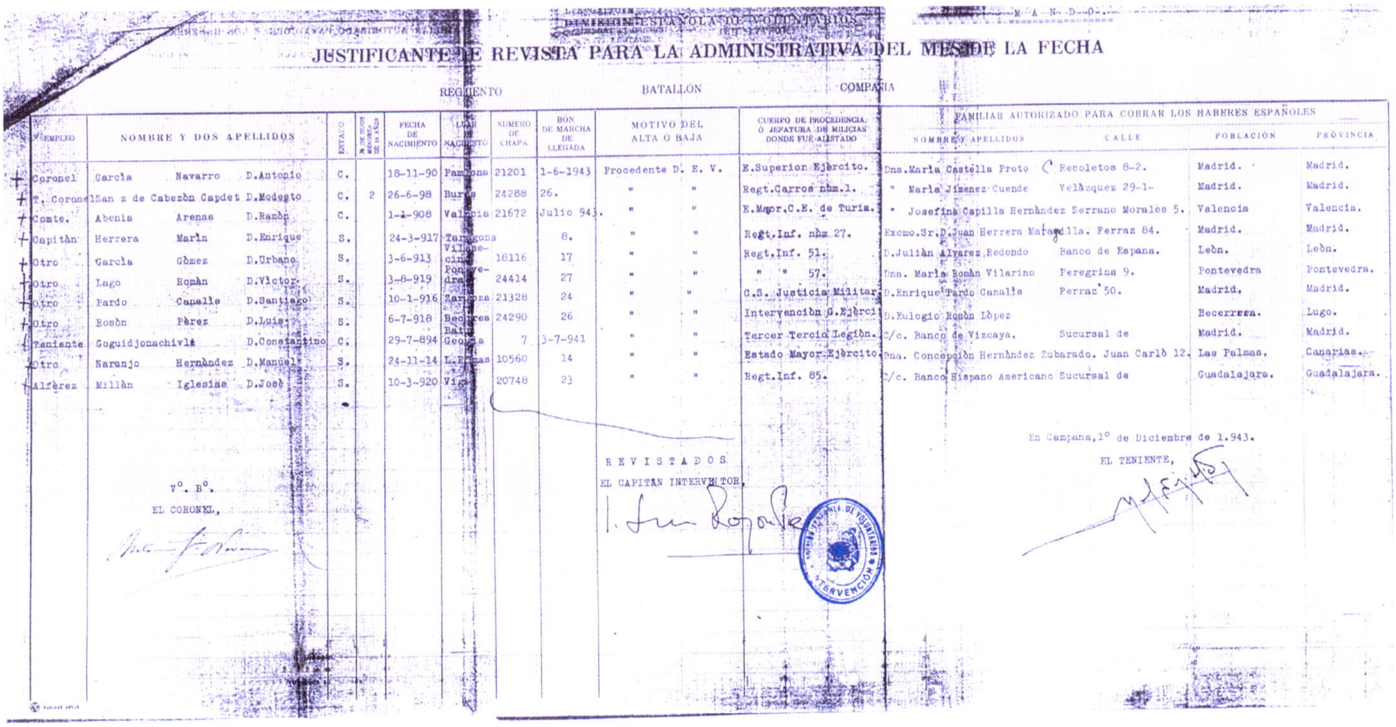

DIVISIÓN ESPAÑOLA DE VOLUNTARIOS

M A N D O

JUSTIFICANTE DE REVISTA PARA LA ADMINISTRATIVA DEL MES DE LA FECHA

REGIMIENTO BATALLON COMPAÑIA

EMPLEO	NOMBRE Y DOS APELLIDOS	ESTADO	Nº DE HIJOS MENORES DE 18 AÑOS	FECHA DE NACIMIENTO	LUGAR NACIMIENTO	NUMERO DE CHAPA	BÓN. DE MARCHA DE LLEGADA	MOTIVO DEL ALTA O BAJA	CUERPO DE PROCEDENCIA, O JEFATURA DE MILICIAS DONDE FUÉ ALISTADO	FAMILIAR AUTORIZADO PARA COBRAR LOS HABERES ESPAÑOLES: NOMBRE Y APELLIDOS	CALLE	POBLACIÓN	PROVINCIA
Coronel	García Navarro D.Antonio	C.		18-11-90	Pamplona	21201	1-6-1943	Procedente D. E. V.	E.Superior Ejèrcito.	Dna.María Castélla Proto	Recoletos 8-2.	Madrid.	Madrid.
T. Coronel	San z de Cabezòn Capdet D.Modesto	C.	2	26-6-98	Burgos	24288	26.	" "	Regt.Carros núm.1.	" María Jimenez Cuende	Velàzquez 29-1-	Madrid.	Madrid.
Comte.	Abenia Arenas D.Ramòn	C.		1-1-908	Valencia	21672	Julio 943.	" "	E.Mapr.C.E. de Turia.	" Josefina Capilla Hernàndez	Serrano Moralès 5.	Valencia	Valencia.
Capitàn	Herrera Marín D.Enrique	S.		24-3-917	Tarragona		8.	" "	Regt.Inf. nùm 27.	Excmo.Sr.D.Juan Herrera Maragdlla.	Ferraz 84.	Madrid.	Madrid.
Otro	García Gòmez D.Urbano	S.		3-6-913	Villasecino	18116	17	" "	Regt.Inf. 51.	D.Juliàn Alvarez Redondo	Banco de Espana.	Leòn.	Leòn.
Otro	Lago Romàn D.Victor	S.		3-8-919	Pontevedra	24414	27	" "	" " 57.	Dna. María Romàn Vilarino	Peregrina 9.	Pontevedra	Pontevedra.
Otro	Pardo Canalls D.Santiago	S.		10-1-916	Zaragoza	21328	24	" "	C.S. Justicia Militar.	D.Enrique Pardo Canalls	Ferraz 50.	Madrid.	Madrid.
Otro	Rosòn Pèrez D.Luis	S.		6-7-918	Becerrea	24290	26	" "	Intervenciòn G.Ejèrci	D.Eulogio Rosòn Lòpez		Becerrrea.	Lugo.
Teniente	Goguidjonachivlé D.Constantino	C.		29-7-894	Batum Georgia	7	3-7-941	" "	Tercer Tercio Legiòn.	C/c. Banco de Vizcaya.	Sucursal de	Madrid.	Madrid.
Otro	Naranjo Hernàndez D.Manuel	S.		24-11-14	L.Palmas	10560	14	" "	Estado Mayor Ejèrcito.	Dna. Concepciòn Hernàndez Zubarado.	Juan Carlò 12.	Las Palmas.	Canarias.
Alfèrez	Millàn Iglesias D.Josè	S.		10-3-920	Vigo	20748	23	" "	Regt.Inf. 85.	C/c. Banco Hispano Americano	Sucursal de	Guadalajara.	Guadalajara.

REVISTADOS
EL CAPITAN INTERVENTOR,

Vº. Bº.
EL CORONEL,

En Campaña, 1º de Diciembre de 1.943.
EL TENIENTE,

Above: Military General Archives at Ávila. Below right: Notary document No.99. (Archives Ripoll)

II. Exercise of the Notaries Faith.

The Interventor developed his notary function according to the dispositions of the Decree of September 25, 1941, authorizing to Head or Interventor Officer of the expeditionary forces to authorize all class of acts or contracts that required notary intervention.

Captain Ripoll in his place of work.

Division Notary Seals. (Archives Ripoll)

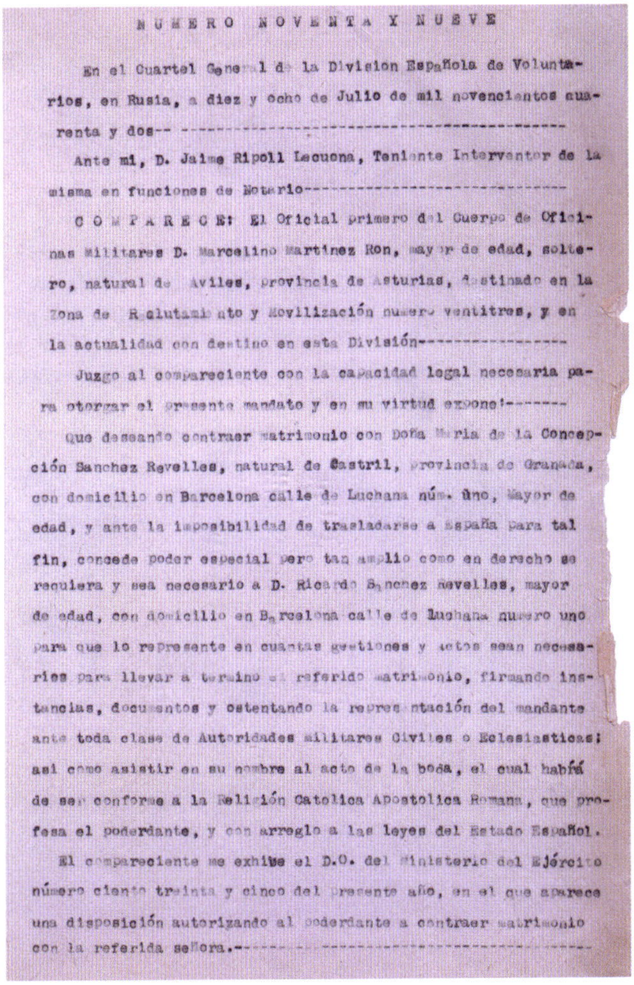

NUMERO NOVENTA Y NUEVE

En el Cuartel General de la Division Española de Voluntarios, en Rusia, a diez y ocho de Julio de mil novecientos cuarenta y dos-- --

Ante mi, D. Jaime Ripoll Lecuona, Teniente Interventor de la misma en funciones de Notario-----------------------------

C O M P A R E C E: El Oficial primero del Cuerpo de Oficinas Militares D. Marcelino Martinez Ron, mayor de edad, soltero, natural de Aviles, provincia de Asturias, destinado en la Zona de Reclutamiento y Movilización numero ventitres, y en la actualidad con destino en esta División-----------------

Juzgo al compareciente con la capacidad legal necesaria para otorgar el presente mandato y en su virtud expone:-------

Que deseando contraer matrimonio con Doña Maria de la Concepción Sanchez Revelles, natural de Castril, provincia de Granada, con domicilio en Barcelona calle de Luchana núm. uno, Mayor de edad, y ante la imposibilidad de trasladarse a España para tal fin, concede poder especial pero tan amplio como en derecho se requiera y sea necesario a D. Ricardo Sanchez Revelles, mayor de edad, con domicilio en Barcelona calle de Luchana numero uno para que lo represente en cuantas gestiones y actos sean necesarios para llevar a termino el referido matrimonio, firmando instancias, documentos y ostentando la representación del mandante ante toda clase de Autoridades militares Civiles o Eclesiasticas; asi como asistir en su nombre al acto de la boda, el cual habrá de ser conforme a la Religión Catolica Apostolica Romana, que profesa el poderdante, y con arreglo a las leyes del Estado Español.

El compareciente me exhibe el D.O. del Ministerio del Ejército número ciento treinta y cinco del presente año, en el que aparece una disposición autorizando al poderdante a contraer matrimonio con la referida señora.------------------------------------

III. Document Legalization.

At this point, the Interventor had the same functions as the rest of the members of the Military Intervention Corps, as much with the affidavit of signatures of members of the Division as with copy authentication from the originals.

IV. Payroll Office of Berlin.

When they arrived from Spain, the volunteers were placed in the general camp of the D.E.V. of Hof-Saale. They filled duplicate applications—blue and white questionnaires (Annexed 3)—that were the base for the claim and order of dues payment of the regular German military payroll, that the German State, by channel of the German Finance Office of the D.E.V. of Madrid, Plaza of Salamanca nº 4, sent to the relatives of the volunteers.

These questionnaires were sent from Hof-Saale to the Payroll Office of Berlin, which issued the order to Madrid so that the dues were paid to the relatives. These continued being sent to the beneficiaries unless a notification to suspend the payments was received.

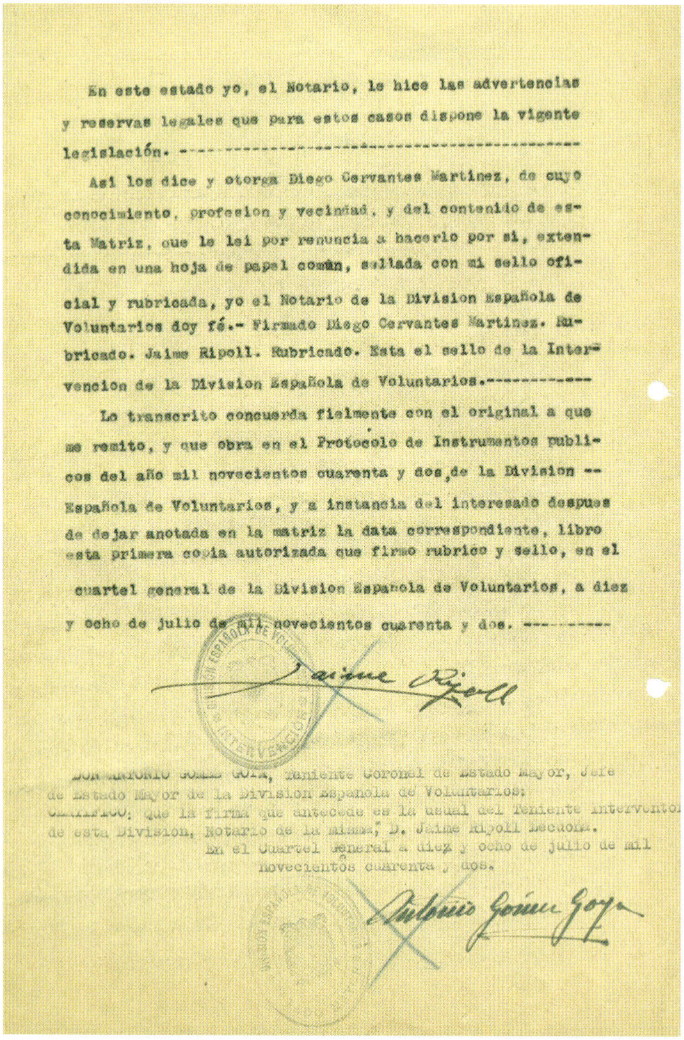

En este estado yo, el Notario, le hice las advertencias y reservas legales que para estos casos dispone la vigente legislación.--

Asi los dice y otorga Diego Cervantes Martinez, de cuyo conocimiento, profesion y vecindad, y del contenido de esta Matriz, que le lei por renuncia a hacerlo por si, extendida en una hoja de papel común, sellada con mi sello oficial y rubricada, yo el Notario de la Division Española de Voluntarios doy fé.- Firmado Diego Cervantes Martinez. Rubricado. Jaime Ripoll. Rubricado. Esta el sello de la Intervencion de la Division Española de Voluntarios.------------

Lo transcrito concuerda fielmente con el original a que me remito, y que obra en el Protocolo de Instrumentos publicos del año mil novecientos cuarenta y dos, de la Division -- Española de Voluntarios, y a instancia del interesado despues de dejar anotada en la matriz la data correspondiente, libro esta primera copia autorizada que firmo rubrico y sello, en el cuartel general de la Division Española de Voluntarios, a diez y ocho de julio de mil novecientos cuarenta y dos. ----------

Jaime Ripoll

DON ANTONIO GOMEZ GOYA, Teniente Coronel de Estado Mayor, Jefe de Estado Mayor de la Division Española de Voluntarios:

CERTIFICO; que la firma que antecede es la usual del Teniente Interventor de esta Division, Notario de la misma, D. Jaime Ripoll [illegible].

En el Cuartel General a diez y ocho de julio de mil novecientos cuarenta y dos.

Antonio Gómez Goya

Above: Notary document. (Archives Ripoll) Right: Metal German Seal. (Archives Retogenes)

Friendly lunch with the German Administrative Service. Fourth from the left, Captain Interventor Ripoll. (Archives Ripoll)

When a volunteer was considered definitively out of service in the Division, the Unit had the obligation as soon as possible to communicate it to Berlin by means of a correction of the salary card. These cards were filled according to variations and documents that appeared in the regulations of the Intervention Headquarters of February 16, 1943, written up in Berlin in agreement with the Payroll Office (Annexed 4).

When these correction cards referred to volunteers who were repatriated, missing, or deceased, as the volunteer could not sign this document, an agreement was reached with the Payroll Office and the competent German authorities from the O.K.W. so that the data of the volunteers could be matched with the one from the General Interventor and the Head of Chiefs Staff. This agreement was ratified by the General (Annex 5).

With the object of clarifying the Units and the obligations that they had in this respect, two General Orders were dictated regarding administrative instructions. (Annex 6, 7, and 8).

V. Reports and Advisories in Economic-Administrative matters.
The Headquarters of Intervention fulfilled the advisory assignment whenever it was required, compiling also reports on matters and subjects that needed regulation or modifications to the existing ones, and forwarding them for approval by the Exc. General.

-BALANCE DE FUERZA-

-EXPRESION-	Comandantes.	Capitanes.	Tenientes.	Alfereces.	C.A.S.E. M.A.	C.A.S.E. M.H.	Brigadas.	Sargentos.	Cabos de 1ª.	Cabos.	Legionarios 1ª	Legionarios.	TOTAL
Fuerza presente en el mes anterior.........							1					4	5
ALTAS...												1	1
Suman...							1					5	6
BAJAS....													
Quedan en revista el 1º del mes de la fecha							1					5	6

Forces Summary. (Archives Ripoll)

Salaries

By Instruction of July 4, 1941, emitted by the General Joint Chiefs of Staff of the Spanish Army, instructions were given for the Division members to receive two salaries.

One would be for the corresponding service as a member of the German Army, and the other would be in accordance with the amounts that the Spanish Government had anticipated to give in the mentioned Instruction (the pay that the Spanish Government would satisfy to each member would be based on the rank and the branch origin of the volunteer). Thus, the personnel coming from the ranks of the Army and the Officers and the NCO members of the Militia would receive payment just like the military members of the Legion. Whereas the troops recruited in the Enlistment Pennants that did not have work assignment would perceive equal wage as the troop personnel of the Army, and if they had work assignments, they would obtain the pay specified to them in their contract.

In both cases, the money would be paid in Madrid to the relatives of the volunteers, since the economic legislation of the Third Reich prohibited currency leaving Germany. This is the reason why the payment of the German salaries by the Spanish government was considered as an advance payment against the debit account, which Germany had to compensate by means of the liquidation of the part of the military debt that Franco had contracted with the Third Reich during the Civil War.

Since the salaries were paid to the relatives of the volunteers, the Division personnel got a per diem for their necessities and Bonus of Campaign and Clothing, which the German Army gave to them.

In this respect the Interventor, with the monthly nominal relation of men enlisted in the Unit, received from each Company or Battery information, and made the reports of the entire Spanish Division, which were transmitted to the Intendance headquarters, with the intention of obtaining from the German counterpart the money necessary to pay the Bonus and Per Diem.

Once they received the money, the Division Finance Office and the Paymaster of each Battalion or Group made the withdrawal of the money corresponding to its Unit and gave it personally in hand to each of the members of the Division.

The Division Finance Office had a paymaster, an Intendance officer, and an Interventor. It depended on the Service of Intendance, being assigned to the Headquarters of the Division, and was in charge of all the subjects related to payroll.

Regarding those functions, it is important to mention the following rules and regulations:

Regulation of salaries of the Spanish Division of Volunteers, approved by the Spanish Cabinet. (November 10, 1941) (Blue Division Funds Foundation).

The German Government will pay to the personnel of the Spanish Division:

- Expenses for the provisions, clothes and lodging.
- Campaign Bonus.
- The Additional front line payments.
- The normal salaries.

The first line of expenses is not the object of these normative. The second and third is given, in different quantities according to the cases, to the Chiefs, Officers, NCOs, and troops.

The quarterly salary was normally given in the German Army to the families, since it was prohibited that the amount of the payments be spent in the combat or occupation sites.

This modality could not be used in the case of the Spanish Division because the German currency could not leave the Reich, as was the case with the Spanish currencies of Spain.

In order to solve this difficulty, it was agreed:

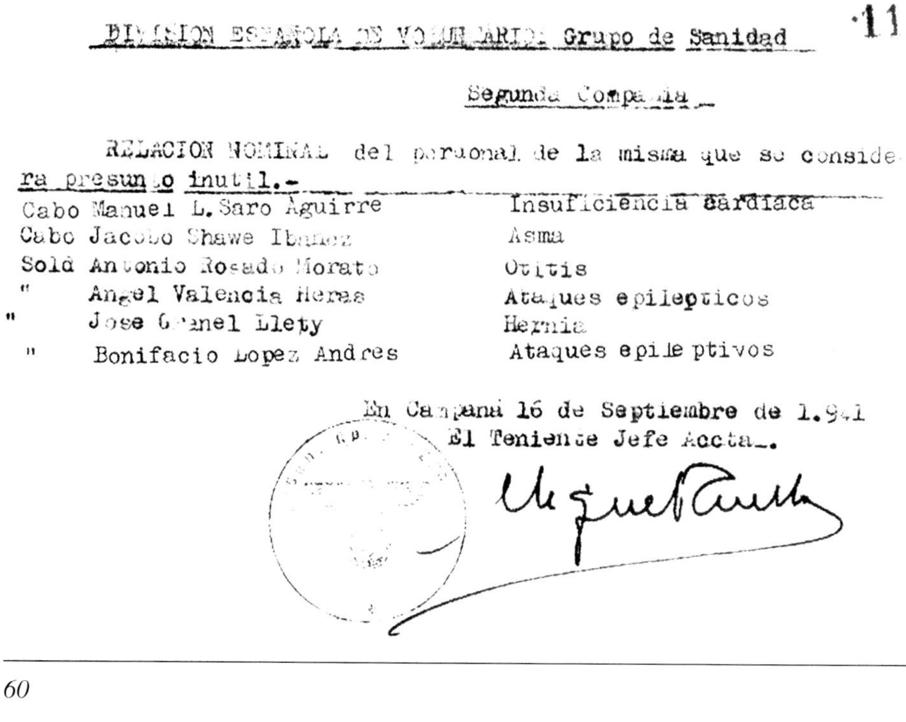

DIVISION ESPAÑOLA DE VOLUNTARIOS Grupo de Sanidad ·11

Segunda Compañia

RELACION NOMINAL del personal de la misma que se considera presunto inutil.-

Cabo Manuel L. Saro Aguirre — Insuficiencia cardiaca
Cabo Jacobo Shawe Ibañez — Asma
Sold Antonio Rosado Morato — Otitis
" Angel Valencia Heras — Ataques epilepticos
" Jose G.anel Llety — Hernia
" Bonifacio Lopez Andres — Ataques epileptivos

En Campaña 16 de Septiembre de 1.941
El Teniente Jefe Accta.-

Loss Report, 2nd Company, September 16, 1941. (Military General Archives at Ávila)

1. The Spanish Government delivered, in *pesetas,* the monthly amount that corresponded to the sum of the normal payments of the Spanish Division. This sum, which was determined by means of liquidation between Spain and Germany by the Connection and Information Bureau, according to the calculations, was twelve and a half million *pesetas* monthly.

Like the Spanish Corps that they belonged to, the volunteers demanded that the fixed salaries be sent to their families, and the previous sum was given to these Corps according to their liquidation. This way, the families received in the same check bonus and salaries, with the German salary converted to *pesetas*.

2. At the same time, the German Government credited in the account of the Spanish Government the amount in RM of the delivery made by the Spanish Government for normal salaries (approximately twelve and a half million).

General Instruction Num. 4,117 of the General Joint Chiefs Staff, of April 15,1942 (Blue Division Funds Foundation)

Subject: Instructions to be followed for the checking accounts in German banks, and the use of funds in the Savings Postal Accounts.

In my Headquarters, April 15, 1942:

1. The Payer Brigade of the Companies, Batteries, or Squadrons will request from their personnel that wish to open checking accounts in any German Bank, to clearly complete the Annex 2, which will be sent by the conduit of the Paymaster of their Unit to the Division Finance Office, the next April 15.

Once that requirement was completed, they would follow the same method used to send funds to Spain, to receive the amounts, filling with all clarity Annex 1, and providing it, by duplicate, to the Paymaster of their Unit, who would provide a signed receipt. This Official would prepare the totals of the Companies in a duplicated manner, similar to the ordered totals for the remittances to Spain. These would be given to the Division Finance Office with the seal of approval.

They received amounts for their personnel in a similar paperwork, but independently of the one used for the funds sent to Spain.

The receipts of the amounts sent, which the banks issued to the account holders, were returned to this Payer Office. They, in turn, would send it to the Payer Master of each Unit.

As the opening of an account was a prerequisite, until the account numbers were received no money could be sent. The dates of direct deposit were available in the Division Payer Master once they were received from the Payer Officers of the Units.

2. If they decide to make use of the Postal Savings Accounts, the deliveries of funds will be done in the Division Finance office the 8th and the 23rd of every month, using the same normative as the opening of Checking Accounts in the banks.

Annex 1

General Instructions for the vouchers in the Administrative Report, September 15, 1942. *(Personal File of the Captain Ripoll Inspector).*

Having observed that the vouchers of Administrative Reports do not correspond in all their points to the requisites of the D.E.V., the following norms need to be implemented immediately:

FIRST: The Voucher for the Report, in duplicate, will be as the model that is enclosed, and it will be due at the Headquarters of Intervention before the 5th of every month.

SECOND: The force will be reported NUMERICALLY, on the first of the previous month.

THIRD: In the New Positions will also be reported NUMERICALLY the force moved from other Units of the Division, and NUMERICALLY reported those that are New Members in the Division coming from Spain (that is, on this form they will only be counted in the Voucher of the First Administrative Report passed, once the numbers of the Units of the Division are added), and those due to promotion within the Division.

FOURTH: In the decreased numbers or casualties will be reported NUMERICALLY those transferred to other Units of the Division, and NOMINALLY only those that are definitive in nature, such as the repatriated, promotions, and the deceased by any concept, including POWs, MIA, and deserters.

FITH: The members of the Division that pass due to wounds or disease to the Military Hospitals of Vanguard or Rear Lines will be dropped from the rolls in their Units. These Losses will occur NUMERICALLY.

SIXTH: As to new members or drops from the rolls transfer from or to other Units of the Division, it will be noted in successive lines those that come or go to each Unit, and the reason for new members being added or dropped in the Unit from which they come or to which they are going.

SEVENTH: Of all the new members or drops that occur, NOMINALLY, it will be necessary to print the following data: reason for the discharge or loss, Corps or Headquarters of Militia, relatives, and address and town.

EIGHTH: The members of the Division that move in service commission will not drop from the rolls in their Units. Neither will those that travel with permission to Spain. If, on the first day of any month, they are as much in as outside of their Units, we must send to them the corresponding Report Voucher.

NINTH: When some Chief, Officer, NCO, Sergeant major, private, or corporal is behind schedule for his granted leave to Spain for more than sixty days, he will be dropped NOMINALLY from the rolls in the first Report Voucher, specifying that the loss has been motivated by lack of incorporation in this term.

When the sixty days are up, without carrying out this incorporation, the Units will communicate by memorandum to this Headquarters Office. Also, they will announce their incorporation when this takes place after the term of the sixty days.

TENTH: The Military Hospitals of vanguard or rear lines will report monthly, in accordance with the previous norms to their personnel, as to the members of the Division that are hospitalized in them.

ELEVENTH: The members of the Division that are hospitalized in the German Lazaretos will send, on a monthly basis to this Headquarters, the corresponding Report Vouchers.

TWELFTH: The Hospitals will consider that, according to the Ministerial Order of August 28, 1941, the personnel who is evacuated to Spain as a patient will have to be taken out of the count NOMINALLY. Those that are wounded will continue comprising the Division while they remain in this situation, having to send to the Representation of the D.E.V. of the Undersecretary of the Ministry of the Army, from the hospitals in which they are, the corresponding Report Voucher. Once they are evacuated, the Military Hospitals of the D.E.V. will terminate them in their Report Vouchers, NOMINALLY, specifying the reason as to their transfer to the Hospitals in Spain to continue their treatment.

Annex 2

General order of the Division corresponding to day 22 of November 1942. - In campaign. *(Personal File of the Captain Interventor Ripoll)*

ART. 1: The term for dropping NOMINALLY from the rolls, in the Report Vouchers to personnel of the Division that enjoys permission in the rear lines or Spain, is increased to NINETY days.

"Lack of incorporation of permission" would be used as the reason for the loss.

The Unit commanders would communicate to the Intervention Headquarters when this period was completed, and the name of the soldiers in these conditions. Also, the incorporation would be notified when it took place after the term of NINETY days.

The first Voucher completed after their incorporation would register them NOMINALLY (in case that in a previous Voucher

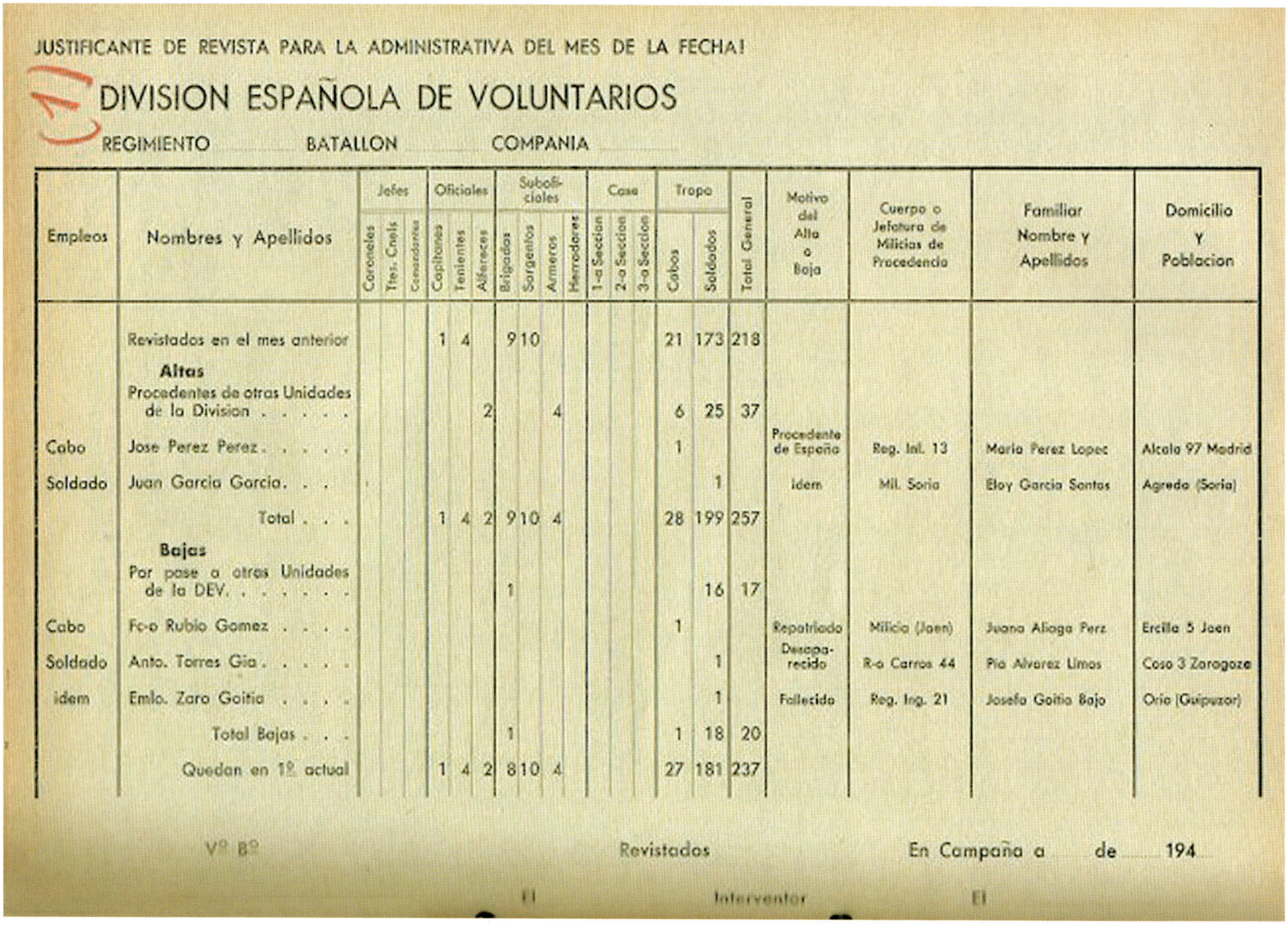

JUSTIFICANTE DE REVISTA PARA LA ADMINISTRATIVA DEL MES DE LA FECHA!

DIVISION ESPAÑOLA DE VOLUNTARIOS

REGIMIENTO .... BATALLON .... COMPANIA ....

Empleos	Nombres y Apellidos	Jefes: Coroneles	Tres. Cnels	Comandantes	Oficiales: Capitanes	Tenientes	Alfereces	Suboficiales: Brigadas	Sargentos	Armeros	Herradores	Case: 1-a Seccion	2-a Seccion	3-a Seccion	Tropa: Cabos	Soldados	Total General	Motivo del Alta o Baja	Cuerpo o Jefatura de Milicias de Procedencia	Familiar Nombre y Apellidos	Domicilio y Poblacion
	Revistados en el mes anterior				1	4		9	10						21	173	218				
	Altas Procedentes de otras Unidades de la Division						2			4					6	25	37				
Cabo	Jose Perez Perez														1			Procedente de España	Reg. Inf. 13	Maria Perez Lopez	Alcala 97 Madrid
Soldado	Juan Garcia Garcia. . .															1		idem	Mil. Soria	Eloy Garcia Santos	Agreda (Soria)
	Total . . .				1	4	2	9	10	4					28	199	257				
	Bajas Por pase a otras Unidades de la DEV.							1								16	17				
Cabo	Fc-o Rubio Gomez														1			Repatriado	Milicia (Jaen)	Juana Aliaga Perez	Ercilla 5 Jaen
Soldado	Anto. Torres Gia															1		Desaparecido	R-o Carros 44	Pio Alvarez Limos	Coso 3 Zaragoza
idem	Emlo. Zaro Goitia															1		Fallecido	Reg. Ing. 21	Josefa Goitia Bajo	Orio (Guipuzcoa)
	Total Bajas . . .							1							1	18	20				
	Quedan en 1º actual				1	4	2	8	10	4					27	181	237				

Vº Bº ... Revistados ... En Campaña a ... de ... 194

El ... Interventor ... El

Monthly Review Report Receipt. (Archives Ripoll)

they had been considered as a loss), indicating as the reason "Incorporated from permission at the .... days."

New members and losses given for these reasons would specify the Spanish Corps which they came from, as well as all their family information.

Annex 3
General order of the Division corresponding to day 24 of March 1943. *(Personal File of Captain Interventor Ripoll)*
Subject: Instructions of administrative order.

FIRST ARTICLE: In relation to the norms reference to cards of rectifications of salaries, of February 16, 1943, the Units will observe the following:

In the rectifications due to promotions, the German symbols of the new rank will be indicated, and will be shown as of the day of the promotion Order, regardless of whether it was by Ministerial or Division Order.

SECOND ARTICLE: All the correspondence, rectification cards, blue and white questionnaires (in case that there is a need to extend them), etc. would be transmitted to the Payroll Office of Berlin (Dienstelle Feldpostnummer 40 545) via this Headquarters (Headquarters of Intervention). When this office sent a Communication to the Office of Payroll to the Corps, it would be returned to be filed at the Headquarters, together with the answer.

THIRD ARTICLE: The Units will make all the necessary efforts to answer in an expeditious manner any communications received from the Office of Payroll, with the intention to expedite the payment to the components of the Division the German salaries.

FOURTH ARTICLE: As soon as there is some definitive loss in the Division, by repatriation, death, disappearance, disappearance without right to compensation, etc., the Units will extend the corresponding cards for correction of salaries according to the Normative of 16 February, and they will send them to this Headquarters.

FIFTH ARTICLE: When the Units need blue and white questionnaires, they will request them from the Headquarters of Intervention, it being understood that absent said request of the Office of Payrolls, or an Order of this Headquarters, it would not be issued.

SIXTH ARTICLE: Every fifth day of the month a nominal list of the personnel coming from Spain will be sent to the Office of Payroll via the Headquarters incorporated to each Unit during the previous month, and a nominal list of the disappeared or deceased during that month.

SEVENTH ARTICLE: When it is known that some volunteer is not receiving the German salary it will be communicated to this Headquarters, indicating the rank, full name, dog tag number, date of border crossing, march Battalion, and name and address of the authorized person to receive the salary.

EIGHTH ARTICLE: When exceeding the ninety days of departure given in a permission, without returning to the Unit, a card of rectification indicating a loss would be sent. When he was incorporated, another one would be needed to put him back on payroll, indicating the days that it took to incorporate.

NINTH ARTICLE: The first Chiefs of the Corps, Dependencies, and Units will give the orders necessary to assure that the report vouchers get extended without mistakes, in agreement with the regulations of the Instructions of 15 September, General Order of the Division of November 22, 1942, and memorandum of Headquarters of Intervention of 30 January referring the last numerical relation of absentees.

TENTH ARTICLE: As much in the vouchers of administrative reports as in cards of correction of salaries, when one is to terminate a deserter the written reason will be "DISAPPEARED WITHOUT RIGHT TO SALARY FROM THE DAY OF ....," without the word "deserter" appearing in any case.

ELEVENTH ARTICLE: In each Unit, it will be necessary to have the daily average of all the personnel that are in the Unit.

TWELFTH ARTICLE: Whenever there is reason to send to this Headquarters some nominal relation of personnel of the Division, the list will be prepared following the rank order, and thus organized by the rigorous alphabetical order of the last names.

THIRTEENTH ARTICLE: The Units will put special care that all names and last names are written without any errors. The lettering must be clear, so that there is no interruption of payroll caused by spelling mistakes.

Annex 4
Normative reference to cards for correction of salaries during the German campaign of February 16, 1943. *(Personal File of Captain Interventor Ripoll).*

In case it is necessary to correct in the questionnaire for German payment, it will be communicated from today according to the sample correction card that is enclosed, with the following variations:

1) Rectification by Promotion: In the card will be noted the new rank of the person with the date of the Order of promotion. In

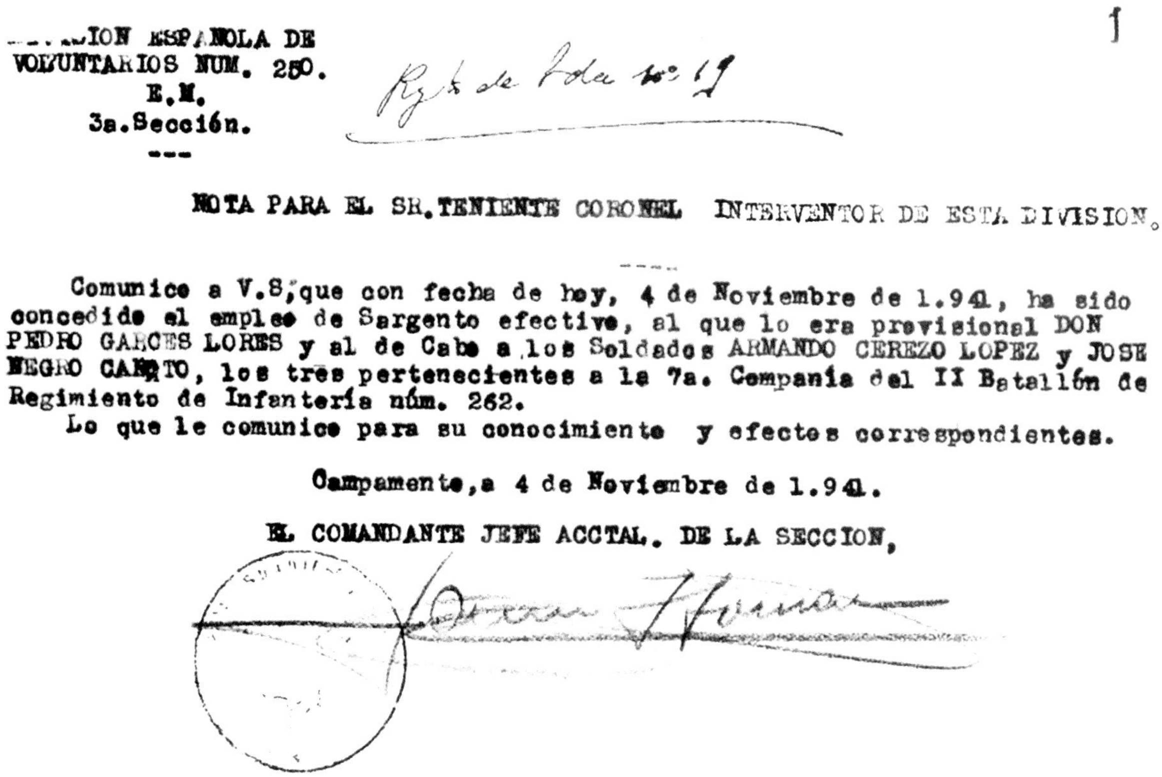

...CION ESPAÑOLA DE VOLUNTARIOS NUM. 250.
E.M.
3a.Sección.

1

NOTA PARA EL SR.TENIENTE CORONEL INTERVENTOR DE ESTA DIVISION.

Comunico a V.S, que con fecha de hoy, 4 de Noviembre de 1.941, ha sido concedido el empleo de Sargento efectivo, al que lo era provisional DON PEDRO GARCES LORES y al de Cabo a los Soldados ARMANDO CEREZO LOPEZ y JOSE NEGRO CAMPTO, los tres pertenecientes a la 7a. Compañía del II Batallón de Regimiento de Infantería núm. 262.

Lo que le comunico para su conocimiento y efectos correspondientes.

Campamento, a 4 de Noviembre de 1.941.

EL COMANDANTE JEFE ACCTAL. DE LA SECCION,

Above: Promotion memorandum. (Archives Ripoll) Below: Personal Information Page. (Archives Ripoll)

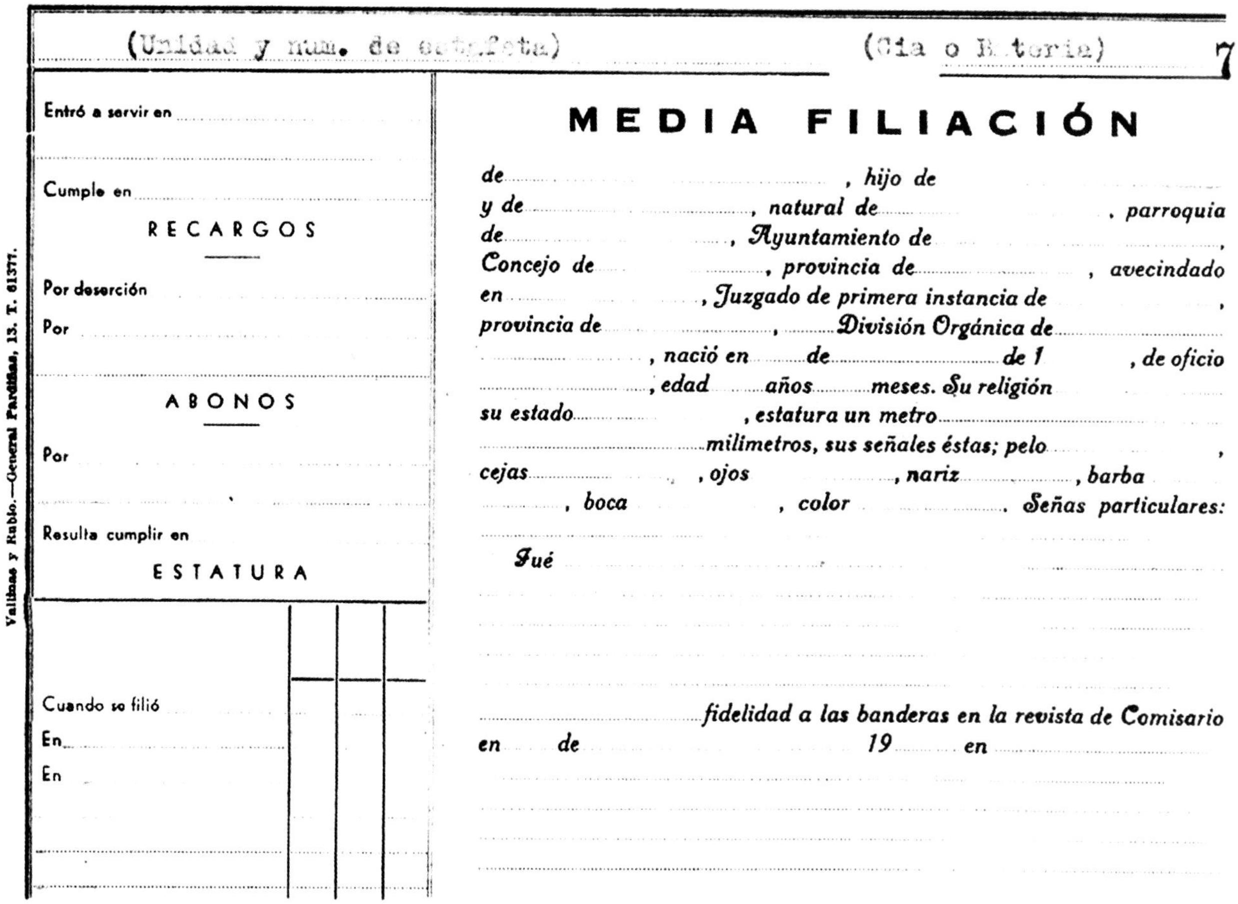

(Unidad y núm. de estafeta) (Cía o Batería) 7

Entró a servir en

Cumple en

RECARGOS

Por deserción

Por

ABONOS

Por

Resulta cumplir en

ESTATURA

Cuando se filió

En

En

Valllinas y Rubio.—General Pardiñas, 13. T. 61377.

MEDIA FILIACIÓN

de , hijo de y de , natural de , parroquia de , Ayuntamiento de , Concejo de , provincia de , avecindado en , Juzgado de primera instancia de , provincia de , División Orgánica de , nació en de de 1 , de oficio , edad años meses. Su religión su estado , estatura un metro milímetros, sus señales éstas; pelo , cejas , ojos , nariz , barba , boca , color . Señas particulares:

Fué

fidelidad a las banderas en la revista de Comisario en de 19 en

addition, a certified copy of this Order will be enclosed that clearly indicates the date as of which the volunteer will wear the German symbols of the new rank.

2) Rectification by loss of ranking: In this case, it is necessary to observe the same dispositions as in the case of promotions. Also a copy of the Order must be enclosed that expresses clearly the date from which the volunteer no longer has the right to show the German symbols of the previous rank.

3) Rectification in case of death or disappearance: In this case, the date will be indicated in which the mentioned events happened.

4) Rectification in case of marriage or birth of a boy of the volunteer, or in case of death of the wife or of a son: In case of marriage or the birth of a son of the volunteer, the date of the marriage or the birth will be indicated in the card, and will enclose a Court authorized certification. In case of the death of the wife or a son of the volunteer, a rectification card is necessary that clearly indicates the date of the death, enclosing a certified copy of the death certificate.

5) Rectification by change of collection of authorized person, or change of address: The name to whom is authorized last names, address, town, and province will be indicated with all exactitude. If the salaries must be directly deposited to a bank checking account or savings, it is precise to indicate the account number or the bank identification.

6) Rectification in case of repatriation: The date of the loss of the Unit will be indicated and, in addition, it will be noted if the volunteer has been transferred to the Hof Camp, or if he is concentrated to be repatriated, without leaving the Division.

7) Rectification in case of desertion of the volunteer: It will be indicated with the card "Disappeared without right to have salaries from the day...."

8) IN NO CASE WILL NEW QUESTIONNAIRES BE ISSUED (printed white and blue) WHENEVER RECTIFICATIONS AS ABOVE MENTIONED OR ANY OTHER WHICH MAY BE NECESSARY.

9) Attention is called to the memorandum of the Official Center Mail: 40 545 of 15,1,1943 - A-z.: L -. In the answers to letters or offices of this Official Center Mail: 40 545, the negotiated of the mentioned dependency will be indicated (A-z. : ...), which will appear in the right upper corner of the paper.

10) The Units receive with this instruction orders advising the volunteers who return to Spain that the payment of their salaries corresponds only to them, and until the end of the month in which they cross the French-Spanish border. The people authorized for the collection of the salaries indicated in the questionnaire (letter "D") will be notified by the volunteers themselves immediately of the fact that any salaries received after the crossing of the border must be given back to the Military Central Finance office of the D.E.V. in Madrid, with the observation: "The volunteer has returned to Spain the day ...... and therefore the salaries of Campaign do not correspond to him."

11) It is expected the Units will implement in the future these arrangements, with the purpose of guaranteeing the volunteers receive their salaries in the least amount of time, and with no one being overpaid.

Annex 5

General Order No. 2 of the Headquarters of Intervention, April 16, 1943. *(Personal File of Captain Interventor Ripoll).*

FIRST ARTICLE: Frequently, the administrative agencies of the German Army contact this Division, making notice that because of the delays in the communications of the losses of salaries, or by lacking these communications, considerable upheavals and damages occur that are impossible to correct in most of the cases. Every time, the volunteers that continue receiving the

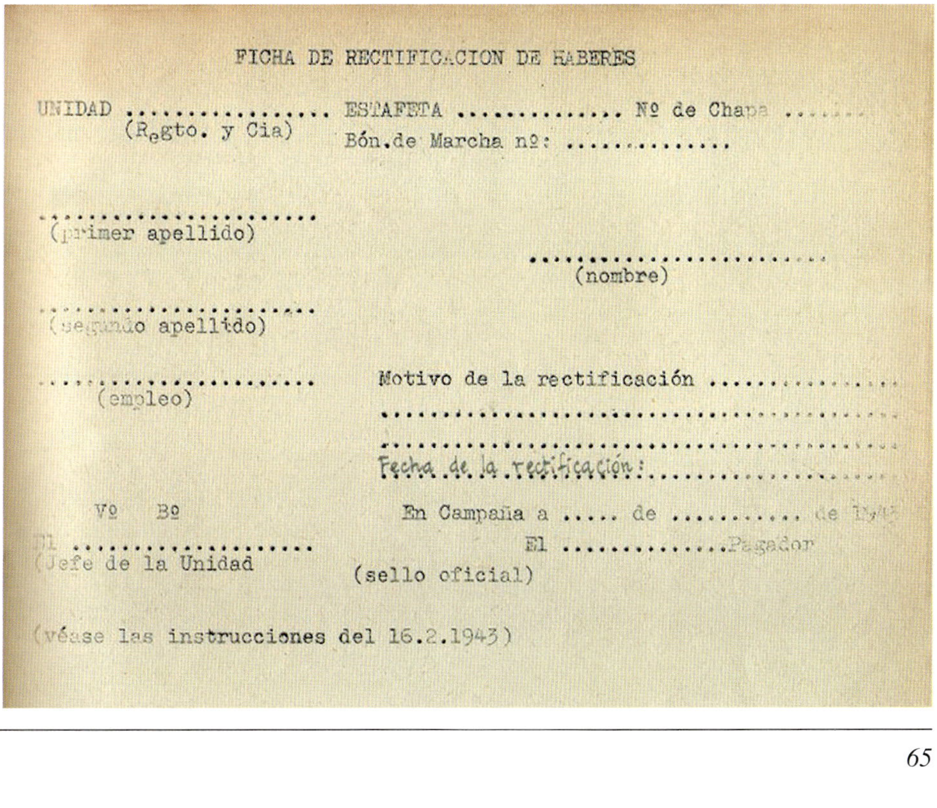

FICHA DE RECTIFICACION DE HABERES

UNIDAD .... ESTAFETA .... Nº de Chapa ....
(Regto. y Cia) Bón.de Marcha nº: ....

....
(primer apellido)

....
(nombre)

....
(segundo apellido)

....
(empleo)

Motivo de la rectificación ....
....
....
Fecha de la rectificación: ....

Vº Bº
El ....
(Jefe de la Unidad)

En Campaña a ..... de .... de 194
El ....Pagador
(sello oficial)

(véase las instrucciones del 16.2.1943)

Payroll Adjustment Note. (Archives Ripoll)

German salaries after repatriation are more numerous, and when it is requested back, they do not have the money that needs to be returned.

Recently I received a memorandum from the Administration of the XVIII Military District, in which it was documented that they are registering great losses to the German finances due to the previously stated reasons.

For that reason, and with the object of avoiding the shame that such facts bring not only to our Division, but also to our Mother Country, each Unit Commander, Dependency, and Independent Unit, immediately after knowing the definitive loss in the Division of some component of the Unit under his control, will send to the Office of Payroll of Berlin, via this Headquarters, and according to Orders and Instructions previously given, the Personnel losses of the military German salaries.

Special care will be taken to insure that the full name and other data of the volunteers is present in the documents with exactitude, without abbreviations of any class, since these can induce errors. The orders and instructions of administrative character will be fulfilled in all their points, having understood that the responsibility for the errors or other mentioned mistakes will be demanded from them, and untimely from the Unit commanders, according to the instructions received from the German High Command of the Army in its Decree on Withdraws.

SECOND ARTICLE: When the Office of Payroll requests the issuance of a blue and white questionnaire of some volunteer who has passed away, disappeared, or is repatriated, the Units will extend these questionnaires, but without signing it, as is required to be fulfilled in the Headquarters. In these cases a card of rectification will be attached giving the permanent administrative loss and the date in which happened the death, disappearance, or repatriation.

THIRD ARTICLE: The lists of variations of salaries that were ordered every month in T.F. of last 15 January are hereby cancelled, due to the requirements of the request in the Instructions of 16 February, and General Order of last 24 March.

Annex 6

General order of the Division, of July 30, 1943, No. 24. *(Personal File of Captain Interventor Ripoll).*

FIRST ARTICLE: In the General Order of November 22, 1942, it was established that for the 90 days of permission granted it was necessary to place the personnel in the loss listing, since all the effects this loss had occurred in the Report Voucher because of "Lack of incorporation from a permit."

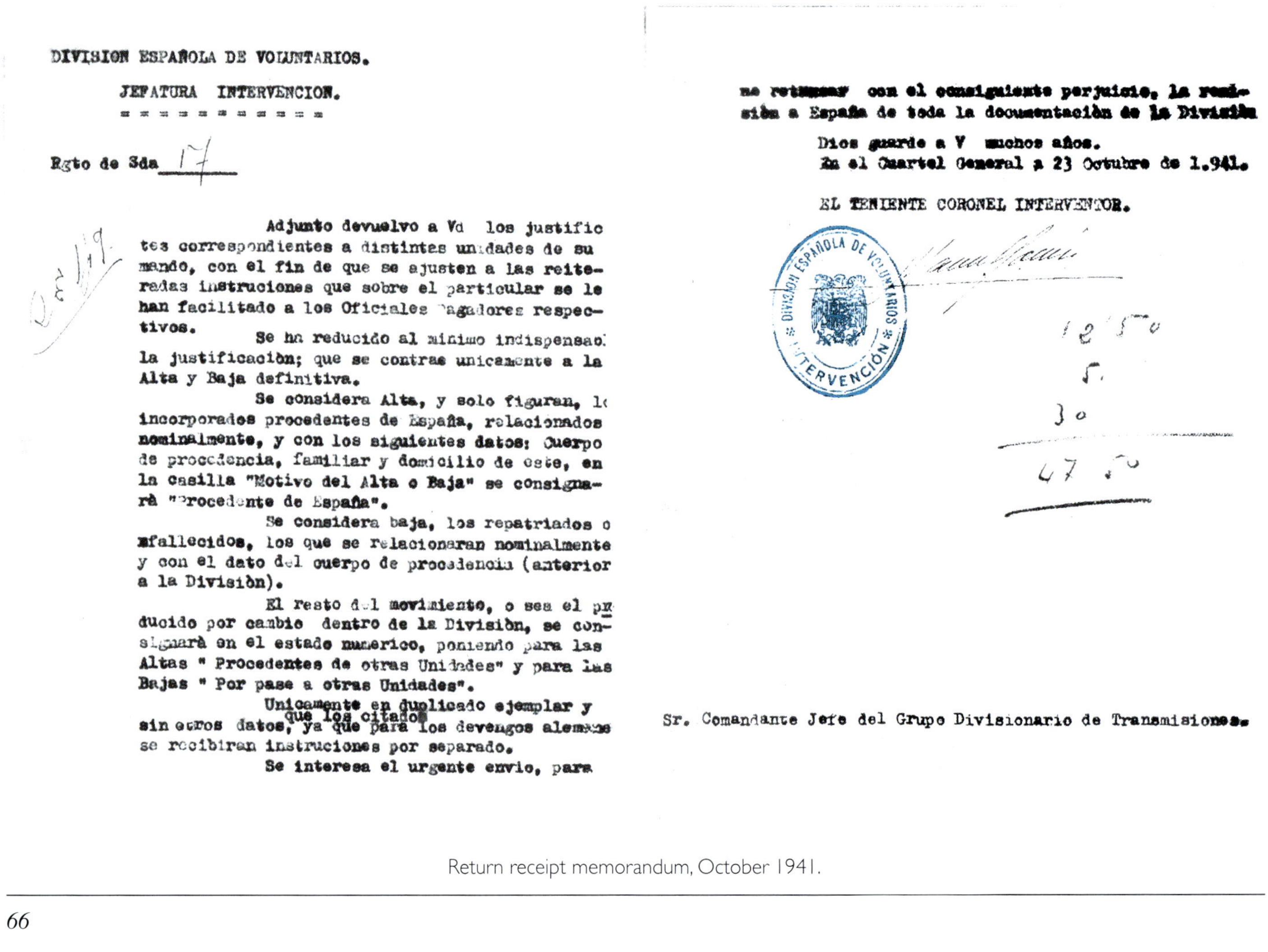

DIVISION ESPAÑOLA DE VOLUNTARIOS.

JEFATURA INTERVENCION.

Rgto de Sda 17

Adjunto devuelvo a Vd los justificantes correspondientes a distintas unidades de su mando, con el fin de que se ajusten a las reiteradas instrucciones que sobre el particular se le han facilitado a los Oficiales Pagadores respectivos.

Se ha reducido al mínimo indispensable la justificación; que se contrae únicamente a la Alta y Baja definitiva.

Se considera Alta, y solo figuran, los incorporados procedentes de España, relacionados nominalmente, y con los siguientes datos: Cuerpo de procedencia, familiar y domicilio de este, en la casilla "Motivo del Alta o Baja" se consignará "Procedente de España".

Se considera baja, los repatriados o fallecidos, los que se relacionaran nominalmente y con el dato del cuerpo de procedencia (anterior a la División).

El resto del movimiento, o sea el producido por cambio dentro de la División, se consignará en el estado numerico, poniendo para las Altas " Procedentes de otras Unidades" y para las Bajas " Por pase a otras Unidades".

Unicamente en duplicado ejemplar y sin otros datos, ya que para los citados devengos alemanes se recibiran instrucciones por separado.

Se interesa el urgente envio, para no retrasar con el consiguiente perjuicio, la remisión a España de toda la documentación de la División.

Dios guarde a V muchos años.
En el Cuartel General a 23 Octubre de 1.941.

EL TENIENTE CORONEL INTERVENTOR.

Sr. Comandante Jefe del Grupo Divisionario de Transmisiones.

Return receipt memorandum, October 1941.

In art. 8th of the General Order of last 24 March, it was also arranged that if the 90 days passed without the officer returning, a card of rectification giving him as a loss in the German salary would be extended for the same reason.

It is generally known that a few volunteers who took absentee leave for more than that time continue receiving the German and Spanish salaries as if they continued being active in the Division. In order to avoid these cases in all the Units, it will be necessary to make a new count of volunteers who are in these conditions, verifying if they were placed in the loss status and holding German and Spaniard salaries. If deficiencies are found, they must be corrected and notified immediately to this Headquarters.

SECOND ARTICLE: With the 13 Battalion of Repatriation, there have been volunteers licensed who arrived at the Division on March 17, 1942 (date of the crossing of border of 4° Batt. in March).

It is necessary to know with exactitude the personnel that crossed the border prior to this date and remain active in the Division. High Staff Commanders, Regiments, independent Battalions, Groups, and Units will send by 5 August a nominal relation of Chiefs, Officers, Sergeant majors, and Troops who are in these conditions listing them by ranks and alphabetical order of last names, indicating date of border crossing and dog tag number.

THIRD ARTICLE: Find enclosed the instructions of the Administrative Order for all the Units of this Division for general knowledge and fulfillment.

FOURTH ARTICLE: In the High Staff First Section are, available to the Units, blank personnel cards that they can complete and file for all those that depend on the Division.

Annex 7
Instructions of Administrative Order of the Headquarters of Intervention of July 28, 1943. *(Personal Archives of Captain Interventor Ripoll).*

ART. I : Considering that the volunteers who are FIRST CORPORALS in Spain received a higher salary than the simple corporals, the corporals of the Division who possess said rank will receive in payment No. 14 an additional increase in the amount of 17´50 R.M. because of surpluses.

ART. II: The first Chiefs of Corps, Centers, and Dependencies will send to this Headquarters (Headquarters of Intervention) before the 5th of next month, of August, nominal relations of the First Corporals that exist in their Units indicating in each one of them the following data: Date and birthplace, Corps of origin, family status, relatives and address of them, dog tag number, date of border crossing or March Battalion of arrival, and finally, the date of the order and number of the D.O. by which they got promoted to the position.

ART. III: In case of preventive prison, provisional detention, destitution of the position, or to undergoing sentence imposed by Court Martial, the volunteers of the Division will receive the third part of the surpluses only, from the day following the one when they got detained or destitute. The two third parts of the surpluses not paid during a preventive prison, provisional detention, or destitution will be paid later in case of dismissal, or of not receiving a sentence with imprisonment.

The arrested are not including in this Article. Those under this concept, and if forming part of a Punishment Squad, will perceive their surpluses from the Company of Manual labor. The combat bonus will not be paid to them.

ART. IV: The prisoners passing to the *Gendarmerie* Jails of Headquarters will perceive their corresponding proportion of surpluses from the Finance office of Headquarters.

ART. V: To the components of the Spanish Division who are suspected of having acquired disease or, having been hurt deliberately to leave the service, will be paid the third part of their surpluses. If found free of these charges they will receive the entire amount of the surplus.

ART. VI: In case of moving away without permission from the Unit, and in case of Desertion, the right to surpluses is lost from the day following the leave. From the day of the presentation or the detention, they will be paid the surpluses in the corresponding amount.

ART. VII: It has been noticed that too often the volunteers change the authorized person for collection of the German salaries in Spain. For that reason, the Unit commanders will try to restrict these changes as much as possible, not giving course to rectification cards for this reason unless there appears to be a good cause.

ART. VIII: Whenever the white and blue questionnaires get extended for any volunteer of the Division they must be printed with the dog tag always.

ART. IX: All the Units are reminded that when the white and blue questionnaires of the personnel are extended because the member has passed away, disappeared, been repatriated, or another analogous cause, sections E and F should be left blank. In addition, a rectification card must be attached indicating the reason and date of the Loss. When the volunteers are present in the Unit they must sign section E, and the Commander of the Unit should sign the F section.

ART. X.: Whenever a definitive Loss happens in the Division by repatriation, death, or disappearance excess of the term of permission, one must send to the Headquarters of Intervention the corresponding cards of rectification as soon as possible.

ART. XI: The Units will have to ensure that of all the documents sent to the Office of Payroll are sealed with the corresponding

Official seal. Those received without the stamp will be returned by this Dependency. If there is no seal available, please submit your requisition to obtain one. This is an Order to be known and followed by all Units.

Annex 8
General order of the Division of August 4, 1943. No. 27. *(Personal File of the Captain Interventor Ripoll).*

ARTICLE FIRST. - As further explanation in article XIII of the Administrative Instructions of 28 July, it should be known that duplicate cards of rectification are only required when it is a promotion of Chiefs and Officers, and always attaching copies of the corresponding Orders.

One of the cards and copies of the Order will be sent directly to the Office of Payroll of Berlin Dienststelle 405 45 Feldportnummer Turmstrasse 25/26, and the other to the Headquarters of Intervention of this High Command for its submission to the German Connection Chief of Staff.

The Intervention of the Spanish Division of Volunteers in its Documents.

Division Order of August 1, 1941, in Grafenwohr, from the High Command, No. 16. *(Fund of the Foundation Blue Division).*

IV. PERSONAL SALARIES.
The Corps and Units of all the Division will communicate to the Troops that the daily marc that is given to them in hand is mainly destined for care of cleanliness necessities, hygiene, and maintenance of their personal gear and equipment, which is the reason why it is requested that they should watch how it is expended.

Division Order of August 4, 1941, in Grafenwohr, from the High Command, No. 19. *(Fund of the Foundation Blue Division).*

III: Administrative Report
Effective today at (1800) hours, the Assistants Captains of the Units that integrate the Division will pick up in the office of the Lieutenant Colonel Interventor of the same (Cabin # 73 D) the voucher forms for the administrative report of this month.

It is understood that data that appears referenced to their civil status, and number of children, are sworn data and, therefore, subject to the responsibilities of falsification or fraud in documents.

At the same time, only in the duplicates of the master rolls will data accompany as referenced in the previous paragraph.

The personnel who possibly leaves because they are evacuated will appear in the master roll of the present month in their respective Units since they were also present in the 1st day report.

For those not fitted yet in any Unit, as well as their incidences, resolution will take place on the seven (7th) in the Division Intervention.

Division Order of August 5, 1941, in Grafenwohr, from the High Command, No. 20. *(Fund of the Foundation Blue Division).*

SALARIES:
The salaries of surplus Officers and those attached to other Corps will be posted with their Units.

The German Intendance has modified the scale of combat salaries for the NCOs and troops as follows:

Brigades, Gunsmiths and fitters	60 RM month
Master leather and horseshoers	54 RM month
Sergeants	45 RM month
Corporals	36 RM month
Welders of 1st and 2nd class	30 RM month

Division Order of August 11, 1941, in Grafenwohr, from the High Command, No. 26. *(Fund of the Foundation Blue Division).*

I. **NEW and LOSS**.
Effective tomorrow, Corps and Services will send daily reports of New and Loss personnel to the 1st Section of the High command nominally and following the attached model.

They will be starting from the force appearing in the general reviews of Section II of Order number twenty-four (24).

Every 1st and 16th of the month they will send forces report, in accordance with the model that is enclosed, with the situation as of these days.

Division Order of September 9, 1941, in Wilna, from the High Command, No. 47. *(Fund of the Foundation Blue Division).*

I.- ADMINISTRATIVE REPORT.
With the purpose of unifying criterion for the monthly Administrative Report, tomorrow, the Assistants of the different Units will receive concrete instructions and the copy of the voucher in the Division Intervention (Headquarters).

II SPECIAL SALARIES (4th Section)
All the forces that as of the 1st of the present month were in territory belonging to Russia and occupied by Germany, i.e. they crossed the border located near Augustow, will have the right to an increase of 25% on their combat pay or clothing allotment after the tenth of the month.

Those that on this day have not arrived at the Russian territory, and doing so at a later date, will enjoy this benefit from the second tenth of the month.

Division Order of August 7, 1943, from the High Command, No. 30. *(Fund of the Foundation Blue Division).*

Ist ARTICLE:
The Administration of the General Camp of this Great Unit in Hof-Saale had the powers for final payments for the repatriated, having become the claims office for the filing of claims of salaries not received. In addition, moneys could be transferred from Spain to the position.

With the object that the Orders on restrictions of transfers of money be followed, and to avoid constant questioning of the Units, as of today, all the personnel that march repatriated to Spain as part of an expedition, or individually, will be provided with a document, according to the attached model, subscribed by the Paymaster or corresponding payer, with the OK of the Unit Commander.

In this document will be reflected until which date the surpluses and the bonus have been paid to him, and the total amount in R.M. that they have perceived by all concepts from the time of crossing the Hispanic-French Border to getting incorporated to this Great Unit, adding a note with all the money transferred to Spain.

The Unit commanders will be careful to follow all the directives given previously. To achieve it, each Payer will keep a list of all Decennial Transfers corresponding, opening an account for each volunteer.

When some volunteer happens to render services to another Unit, they will send to this unit a list of all documents of reference with all the data for himself.

In order to facilitate the fulfillment of this Order, forms will be provided to the Units in a near date. In the meantime, they will need to give typed ones.

DIVISION ESPAÑOLA DE VOLUNTARIOS

Rgt.................... Batallòn............... Cia...............

Pagaduria.

El Voluntario...................... ....
(empleo) (Nombre y dos apellidos)

....

ha percibido sus Sobras hasta el dia ....de................de 1.94

Ha percibido sus Pluses de Frente hasta el dia.........de.............

.................de 1.94

Ha sido abastecido hasta el dia...........de.............de 194

ha percibido durante su permanencia en la Divisiòn un total de R.M.....

....
(en letra y cifra)

Ha girado un total de R.M...
(en letra y cifra)

El citado Oficial ha percibido su gratificaciòn de Vestuario hasta el dia............de...........de 194
(Si el Voluntario no es Oficial se dejarà sin llenar)

En Campaña a.......................194

El.................Pagador

V.B.
El......................
(Jefe de la Unidad)

Payroll Bonus receipt.

Division Order of August 22, 1943, from the High Command, No. 36. *(Fund of the Foundation Blue Division).*

SECOND ARTICLE: The German High Command Chief Staffs communicate new regulations as to the amounts of money that volunteers will be able to exchange at the French-Spanish border during their trips from vacations, services, or return to Spain.

They are allowed to take with them the amounts corresponding to Combat pay and per diem that correspond to them during the trip of permission, return, etc., and an additional amount of 30 RM.

According to this, the maximum amounts that will be exchanged at the Spanish border for the diverse categories are as follows:

Colonel	255.00RM	Brigades	105.00RM
Leut. Colonel	217.50RM	M.Horseshoers	97.50RM
Commanders	202.50RM	Sergeants	86.25RM
Captain	187.50RM	First corporals	82.50RM
Lieutenant	168.90RM	Corporal	75.00RM
Alferez	157.50RM	Soldiers	67.50RM

Those that go to Spain on vacation will, in addition, have the right to exchange the abovementioned amounts, and the amount of RM equivalent to the total of their food daily ration allowance during their permanence in Spain. The daily indemnification provided for meals during the permission ascended to 2.10 RM, not only for married, but also for the single members.

For example: assuming a period of vacation of 30 days in Spain, for a Captain, he would be entitled to 250.50 RM, which would be the sum of 187.50 plus the amount of rations allowed during the permission, 63 RM.

For those traveling back to Spain while in Commission they could exchange the abovementioned amounts, in addition to any amounts they had the right to receive by day for indemnifications during their permanence in Spain. The amount of the indemnifications would depend on the number of days and duration of the trip. It could reach 3.00 RM for married soldiers, and for single ones up to 2.10 RM.

For those that were entitled to receive the complete diets, it was as follows:

General	14.00 RM
From Division General to Colonel	12.00 RM
Lieutenant Colonel to Captain	10.00 RM
Lieutenant, Alferez	8.00 RM
Brigade	6.50 RM
Sergeant to Soldier	5.50 RM

If the home address corresponded with their official business, their payment got reduced to 2.10 RM, regardless of whether married or not.

All exchanges would be in German currencies.

For the period of permanence in Germany, a reasonable amount in RM could be exchanged in the German offices of the *Wehrmacht*.

Each volunteer who went to Spain with permission, or in a Service Commission, would receive from the Payer a certificate with the OK of the Commander of the Unit, indicating the amount authorized to be exchanged at the border.

The amounts exceeding the authorized ones for exchange in this Order would have to be transferred to Spain, from the Units, or the General Camp at Hof.

Division Order of August 25, 1943, from the High Command, No. 33. *(Personal File of the Captain Interventor Ripoll).*

ONLY ARTICLE: His Excellence, the Chief General of the High Command of the Army, in the memorandum No. 1.386-J., of the 24th of last month, communicated that as a result of difficulties experienced by the Chiefs, Officers, and Sergeant majors of the Spanish Division of Volunteers, when requesting assignments of normal provision, due in part to the late arrival of the advertised positions in the Official Newspapers have, in many cases, arrived at this Great Unit when the term granted in the dispositions was already exhausted. Hereby:

The Minister has decided that these personnel may ask for, at any time, by card or instance, election of duties and assignments, aid, or provisional position that they may wish, without waiting for a vacancy announcement.

The requests, when received in the respective Centers, will be considered for the vacancies requested when they become available.

Division Order of September 3, 1943, from the High Command, No. 41. *(Fund of the Foundation Blue Division).*

FIRST ARTICLE: From the publication of this order, all the Corps, Centers, and Dependencies of this Division, will point out in their respective memorandums related with personnel, in addition to the full name, the dog tag number, as much if it is a Senior Chief or Officers, as the NCOs, C.A.S.E., and troops.

SECOND ARTICLE: As a result of the General Order of the Division, No. 36, of 22 August ppdo. As to money which the volunteers of this Great Unit can take back to Spain; the different units can obtain from the Division Finance office some pamphlets (one for each individual) sent by the M.P.s, in which the norms for this subject are defined, with the objective that nobody can allege ignorance on the effective dispositions in this matter.

These sheets say "Prescriptions about the transactions of German circulating currency to Spain by the volunteers of the Spanish Division"

1) Each volunteer can take:

a) Reichsmark 10.00 - in German metallic currency or tickets of the Rentenbank Rm 1. - or RM.

b) The military pay as well as the corresponding food allowance corresponding to the vacation time, in tickets of the Savings Bank of the Reich (Reich-Kredik-Kassencheine).

c) In addition, at the most, for each volunteer, RM. 30.00 - Also solely in tickets of the Savings Bank of the Reich (Reich-Kredik-Kassencheine).

2) Regarding the abovementioned amounts under the numbers 1b) and 1c), each volunteer must take a written certificate of explanation. The Irun Office of exchanges will exchange tickets of the Savings Bank of the Reich for circulating Spanish currency only with delivery of this certificate.

3) If, in addition to the amounts mentioned under number 1), some quantity of money would be exceeded, each volunteer must surrender it, with the purpose of transferring it to Spain to the Paymaster, indicating the wished delivery address in Spain. The remittance will be made according to the procedures already in place as soon as possible.

4) The exportation of the banknotes of the Reich Bank is expressly prohibited (*Reichsbanknoten*).

Division Order of August 25, 1943, from the High Command, No. 51. *(Personal File of the Captain Interventor Ripoll).*

ARTICLE FIRST. – All Units of the Division are reminded that it is only necessary to submit duplicate cards of rectification for the promotion of the Chief and Officers. Any other submission should go in original only.

Instructions regarding personal dossiers. Headquarters, October 1, 1943. Intervention Head Office *(Personal File of the Captain Interventor Ripoll).*

The forms and extracts or personal dossiers will serve in the successive as the information instrument for the pension files that the German State grants to the relatives of the deceased or disappeared volunteers, and those that correspond to volunteers mutilated or handicapped as a result of military action, or by disease acquired during the campaign.

All the Units of the Division will then complete them with extreme urgency, considering that they need to be printed clearly and legibly, since they are destined to the German Authorities.

Once extended, and with the objective to avoid as far as possible that they undergo capture or destruction due to the enemy operations, they will be deposited in the High Command Offices of the Regiments or Independent Units.

The Commanding officers will communicate to the Headquarters on the date in which they are completed and delivered all the personnel at the present time that it are in the Unit's control.

To these personnel will be extended the data of the present Unit and relative on file, without considering that before they may have belonged to other Units, or their civil state may have changed during their permanence in the Division.

In SECTION TWO, the mail number of each Regiment High Command or their independent Unit. Next, the dog tag number.

In SECTION THREE the rank that the volunteer had when incorporated to the Division must be indicated.

In SECTION FIFTEEN will be indicated the successive promotions until reaching the present rank. For the Officers and Sergeant majors the date of the Ministerial Order will be used as the date of promotion. For the troops, the date of the Order of the Division by which the new rank was obtained. If the promotion was due to military merits, it will have to be pointed out.

SECTION TWELVE will be used only for loss caused by transfer to another Regiment or independent Unit, or to the hospital. THE NEW AND LOSSES WITHIN THE REGIMENT OR INDEPENDENT UNIT DO NOT HAVE TO BE ACCOUNTED FOR WITH THE OBJECT OF CLOSING EXTRACTS AND OPENING NEW ONES.

In SECTION THIRTEEN, the originating thing will be indicated by the loss due to another cause. If the loss is by repatriation, it will put "by repatriation leaving the Unit literally....on ..... of 194.." If it is for another reason (wound, disease, disappearance, disappearance without right of salaries, death, etc.) it would be indicated in the epigraph, and the corresponding paragraph would be filled. The word "*mortally*" of the second paragraph of the reference section must be erased in all the extracts. In the paragraph "communicated the loss to" will be substituted by "To the Headquarters."

In SECTION FOURTEEN would be indicated the Unit and if the wound, injury, death, or disappearance took place as a result of military action, in fulfillment of an ordered service, accident in act of service, etc. Or, if on the contrary it was due to negligence, improper use, or was intentionally caused, it would be answered with a rude "Yes" or "No."

SECTION SEVENTEEN would be completed at the moment at which the corrective measures were applied.

In SECTION EIGHTEEN it will be filled with the previous stays in hospitals of the volunteers once they had been checked and verified by these hospitals before pointing them out.

SECTION NINETEEN would be left blank until the High Command of the Army communicated the denominations of the combats. In their day these denominations would be sent to the Units.

Opening, Closing, and Course of the Extracts

When the volunteer is considered a loss in the Regiment or independent Unit, regardless of the reason for that, the pertinent data would be indicated in sections TWELVE AND THIRTEEN, and after making mention in SECTION TWENTY-ONE of the conduct that the volunteer deserved. It will be closed, signed by the Assistant of the Unit with the Approval of the Corps Chief or Unit, sealed, and sent to the Headquarters for later course to the German Office of Admission of the General Cam at Hof-Saale.

When they became losses as a group of volunteers in some Unit, when forming part of repatriation expeditions, the extracts of connection of all of them would be sent together.

When causing a discharge of a volunteer in a Regiment or independent Unit coming from another Unit of the Division, a new will page will be opened for him, with the data of rank and the day in which he became a New, indicating in the TENTH SECTION his previous Unit. Also the same procedure will be followed for hospitalized volunteers, in SECTION TEN noted with "of hospital" and in SECTION EIGHTEEN, referring to the last stay in the hospital.

For the volunteers getting incorporated into the Division from Spain after this, the extracts will be opened in the German Office of Admission of Hof-Saale, which will send it to the Headquarter Units for distribution.

When they are received in these positions, a postal number of mail as well as the date of the discharge from the Unit will be posted.

Division Order of October 2,1943, from the High Command, No. 55. *(Fund of the Foundation Blue Division).*

SECOND ARTICLE: In a five day term, all High Commands of Regiments and Independent Units will pick up from the Intervention Headquarters upon signing their receipt enough printed formularies of "Extract of Personal Information" for their personnel as Chiefs, Officers, NCOs, and troops. They will also receive instruction manuals for their use in each Company or Unit.

Division Order of October 25, 1943, No. 63. *(Personal File of the Captain Interventor Ripoll).*

ARTICLE FIRST. – As a continuation to the General Order of 7 August, establishing a document to be provided to all the personnel who repatriate, forming part of an expedition or individually in which is indicated, among other data, the amount of R.M. that he has perceived by all concepts since the crossing at the France-Spanish border, to become a part of this Great Unit, as well as the total amount transferred to Spain.

It is ordered that from this date, this document has to be given in duplicate according to the model that accompanied the mentioned Order. The original is to be sent to the volunteer, and the duplicate is to be sent to the Headquarters of Intervention of this Division for transaction to the same Representation in Madrid.

ARTICLE SECOND. - As of today, the different Units will stop issuing Cards of Rectification by the Office of Payroll of Berlin in the following cases:

a) When they are referencing personnel who are repatriated definitively.
b) When is due to pass the authorized 90 days of permission.

The Cards of rectification in both cases will be extended by the Office of the General Camp of the D.E.V. at Hof-Saale.

Specifically it is clarified that such modification does not affect the remaining reasons for a rectification of salaries (promotions. descents, death, disappearance, change of authorized person, birth of a son, marriage, etc.,), which cards will continue to be extended by the Units.

Detail photo of Captain Ripoll's desk. (Archives Ripoll)

DIVISION ESPAÑOLA DE VOLUNTARIOS

GRUPO DE TRANSMISIONES 250 JEFATURA. 8

Justificante de Revista para 1º de Comisario del mes de la fecha.

NOMBRES.	Jefes.	Ofic.	Subf.	Trop.	Motivos del alta o baja		Cuerpo de procedencia anterior a la Div.	Familiar que ha de percibir	Domicilio	Poblacion	Empresa y sueldo	Est.Civil	Numero de hijos menores 17
ALTAS.													
D.Fernando Fresno Moro		/ /			Procedente	Espana	Academia Sanidad	D.Fernanda Fresno Moro	Pola de Lena	(Oviedo)	——	soltero	——
D.Jose Menendez Arce		/ /			id	id	Bon.Trans.79 C.E.	D.Teresa Arce Rivero	Covadonga 15	(Gijon)	——	soltero	
D.Manuel Fernendez Arguelles		/ /			id	id	Bon.Trans.4º C.E.	D.Pepita Sabas de Fernandez	Pasaje Marimon 6.	(Barcelona	——	casado	——
D.Leonardo Urra Chasco			/ /		id	id	Rgto.Inf.51	D.Pedro Urra	Murieta	(Navarra)	——	soltero	——
Francisco Villanueva Rubio				/ /	id	id	Rgto.Art.16	D.Javier Villanueva Martin	Real 21	Padul (Granada)	——	soltero	——
Manuel Valades Pajuelo				/ /	id	id	Bon.Trans.2º C.E.	D.Diego Valades Duran	Martin Vazques 4	(Huelva)	——	soltero	——
Benjamin Garcia Sierra				/ /	id	id	Bon.Trans.7º C.E.	D.Francisco Garcia Braga	Virgen Cabesa numero 3	Ciano (Asturias)	——	soltero	——
Florencio Castellote Bueno				/ /	id	id	Centro Electrotecnico Ing.	D.Valentin Castellote Fraile	Benito Hernando 39	(Guadalajara)	——	soltero	——
Jose Suares Solis				/ /	id	id	idem idem	D.Francisco Suares Luque	Alonso Cano numero 9	(Madrid)	——	soltero	——
Suman......		2 1 3	1 1	1 4 5									
BAJAS.													
D.Fernando Fresno Moro		/ /			Pasa al 262 Bon.Inf.								
Suman		/ /	/ /	/ 4									
Existencia en Revista.		1 1 2	1 1	1 4 5									

Vº Bº
El Comandante Jefe

En Campana a 21 Septiembre 1941
El Comandante Jefe.

Above: Monthly Review Receipt, September 1941. (Military General Archives at Avila) Below: Officers Force Active Count. (Archives Ripoll)

	CORONEL	TTE.CORONEL	COMTE.	CAPITAN	TENIENTE	ALFEREZ
Revistados en el mes anterior.........	1	1	1	6	2	1
ALTAS.........						
BAJAS.........						
Quedan en Revista el dia primero.........	1	1	1	6	2	1

ESTADO DE ALTAS Y BAJAS.

ALTAS.

N I N G U N A.

BAJAS.

N I N G U N A.

En Campana, 15 de febrero de 1.944.

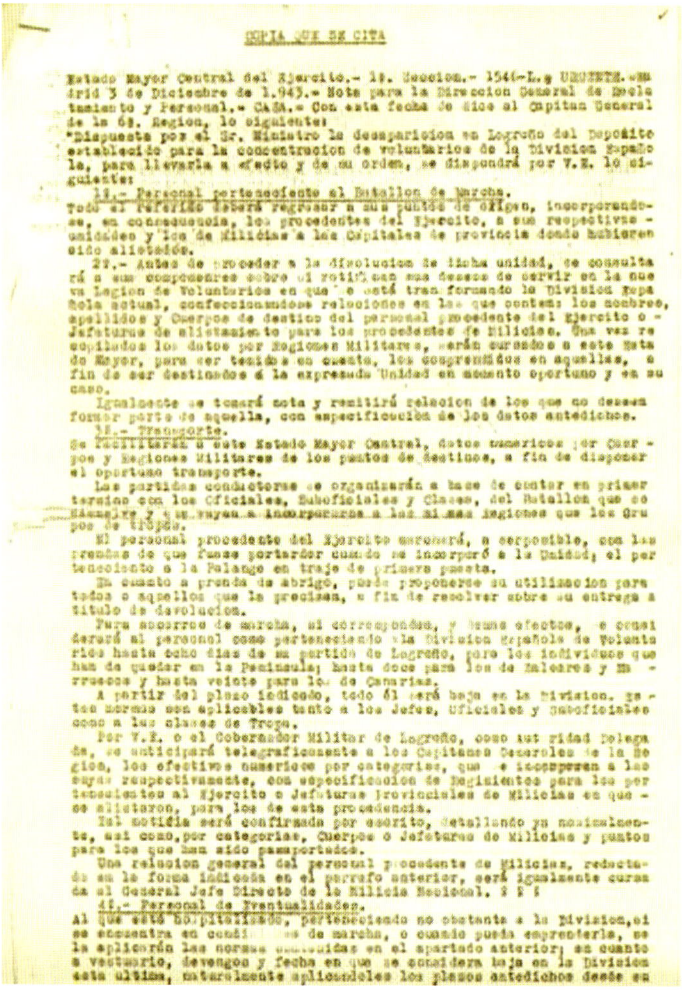

COPIA QUE SE CITA

Estado Mayor Central del Ejercito.- 1ª. Seccion.- 1546-L.ª URGENTE.-Madrid 3 de Diciembre de 1.943.- Nota para la Direccion General de Reclutamiento y Personal.- CASA.- Con esta fecha se dice al Capitan General de la 6ª. Region, lo siguiente:

"Dispuesta por el Sr. Ministro la desaparicion en Logroño del Deposito establecido para la concentracion de voluntarios de la Division Española, para llevarla a efecto y de su orden, se dispondrá por V.E. lo siguiente:

1º.- Personal perteneciente al Batallon de Marcha.

Todo el Personal deberá regresar a sus puntos de origen, incorporandose, en consecuencia, los procedentes del Ejercito, a sus respectivas unidades y los de Milicias a las Capitales de provincia donde hubieren sido alistados.

2º.- Antes de proceder a la disolucion de dicha unidad, se consultará a sus componentes sobre si ratifican sus deseos de servir en la nueva Legion de Voluntarios en que se está transformando la Division Española actual, confeccionandose relaciones en las que consten: los nombres, apellidos y Cuerpos de destino del personal procedente del Ejercito o Jefaturas de alistamiento para los procedentes de Milicias. Una vez recopilados los datos por Regiones Militares, serán cursados a este Estado Mayor, para ser tenidos en cuenta, los comprendidos en aquellas, a fin de ser destinados á la expresada Unidad en momento oportuno y en su caso.

Igualmente se tomará nota y remitirá relacion de los que no deseen formar parte de aquella, con especificacion de los datos antedichos.

3º.- Transporte.

Se facilitarán a este Estado Mayor Central, datos numericos por Cuerpos y Regiones Militares de los puntos de destinos, a fin de disponer el oportuno transporte.

Las partidas conductoras se organizarán a base de contar en primer termino con los Oficiales, Suboficiales y Clases, del Batallon que se [illegible] y que vayan a incorporarse a las mismas Regiones que los Grupos de tropas.

El personal procedente del Ejercito marchará, a ser posible, con las prendas de que fuese portador cuando se incorporó a la Unidad; el perteneciente a la Falange en traje de primera puesta.

En cuanto a prenda de abrigo, puede proponerse su utilizacion para todos o aquellos que la precisen, a fin de resolver sobre su entrega a titulo de devolucion.

Para socorros de marcha, si corresponden, y demas efectos, se considerará al personal como perteneciendo a la Division Española de Voluntarios hasta ocho dias de su partida de Logroño, para los individuos que han de quedar en la Peninsula; hasta doce para los de Baleares y Marruecos y hasta veinte para los de Canarias.

A partir del plazo indicado, todo él será baja en la Division. Estas normas son aplicables tanto a los Jefes, Oficiales y Suboficiales como a las clases de Tropa.

Por V.E. o el Gobernador Militar de Logroño, como autoridad Delegada, se anticipará telegraficamente a los Capitanes Generales de la Region, los efectivos numericos por categorias, que se incorporen a las suyas respectivamente, con especificacion de Regimientos para los pertenecientes al Ejercito o Jefaturas Provinciales de Milicias en que se alistaron, para los de esta procedencia.

Tal noticia será confirmada por escrito, detallando yo nominalmente, asi como, por categorias, Cuerpos o Jefaturas de Milicias y puntos para los que han sido pasaportados.

Una relacion general del personal procedente de Milicias, redactada en la forma indicada en el parrafo anterior, será igualmente cursada al General Jefe Directo de la Milicia Nacional.

4º.- Personal de Eventualidades.

Al que esté hospitalizado, perteneciendo no obstante a la Division, si se encuentra en condiciones de marcha, o cuando pueda emprenderla, se le aplicarán las normas contenidas en el apartado anterior; en cuanto a vestuario, devengos y fecha en que se considera baja en la Division esta ultima, naturalmente aplicandoles los plazos antedichos desde su

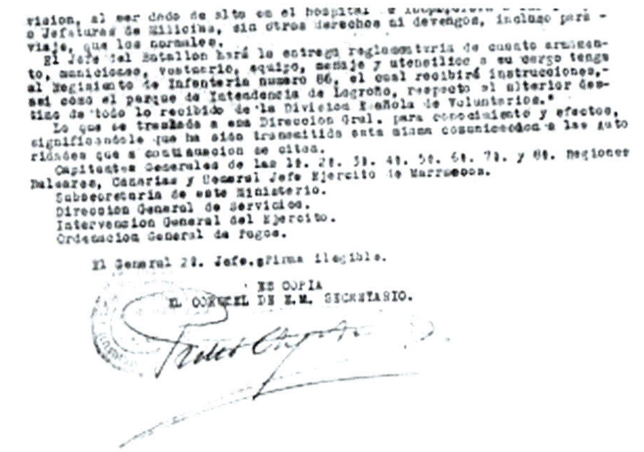

vision, al ser dado de alta en el hospital [illegible] o Jefaturas de Milicias, sin otros derechos ni devengos, incluso para viaje, que los normales.

El Jefe del Batallon hará la entrega reglamentaria de cuanto armamento, municiones, vestuario, equipo, menaje y utensilios a su cargo tenga al Regimiento de Infanteria numero 86, el cual recibirá instrucciones, asi como el parque de Intendencia de Logroño, respecto al ulterior destino de todo lo recibido de la Division Española de Voluntarios."

Lo que se traslada a esa Direccion Gral. para conocimiento y efectos, significandole que ha sido transmitida esta misma comunicacion a las Autoridades que a continuacion se citan.

Capitanes Generales de las 1ª. 2ª. 3ª. 4ª. 5ª. 6ª. 7ª. y 8ª. Regiones Baleares, Canarias y General Jefe Ejercito de Marruecos.

Subsecretaria de este Ministerio.

Direccion General de Servicios.

Intervencion General del Ejercito.

Ordenacion General de Pagos.

El General 2º. Jefe.=Firma ilegible.

ES COPIA

EL CORONEL DE E.M. SECRETARIO.

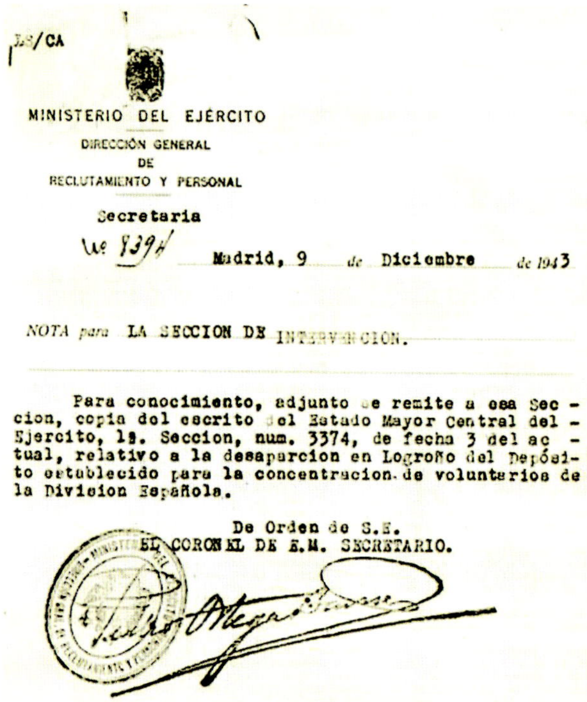

LS/CA

MINISTERIO DEL EJÉRCITO

DIRECCIÓN GENERAL DE RECLUTAMIENTO Y PERSONAL

Secretaria

Nº 9394 Madrid, 9 de Diciembre de 1943

NOTA para LA SECCION DE INTERVENCION.

Para conocimiento, adjunto se remite a esa Seccion, copia del escrito del Estado Mayor Central del Ejercito, 1ª. Seccion, num. 3374, de fecha 3 del actual, relativo a la desaparcion en Logroño del Depósito establecido para la concentracion de voluntarios de la Division Española.

De Orden de S.E.

EL CORONEL DE E.M. SECRETARIO.

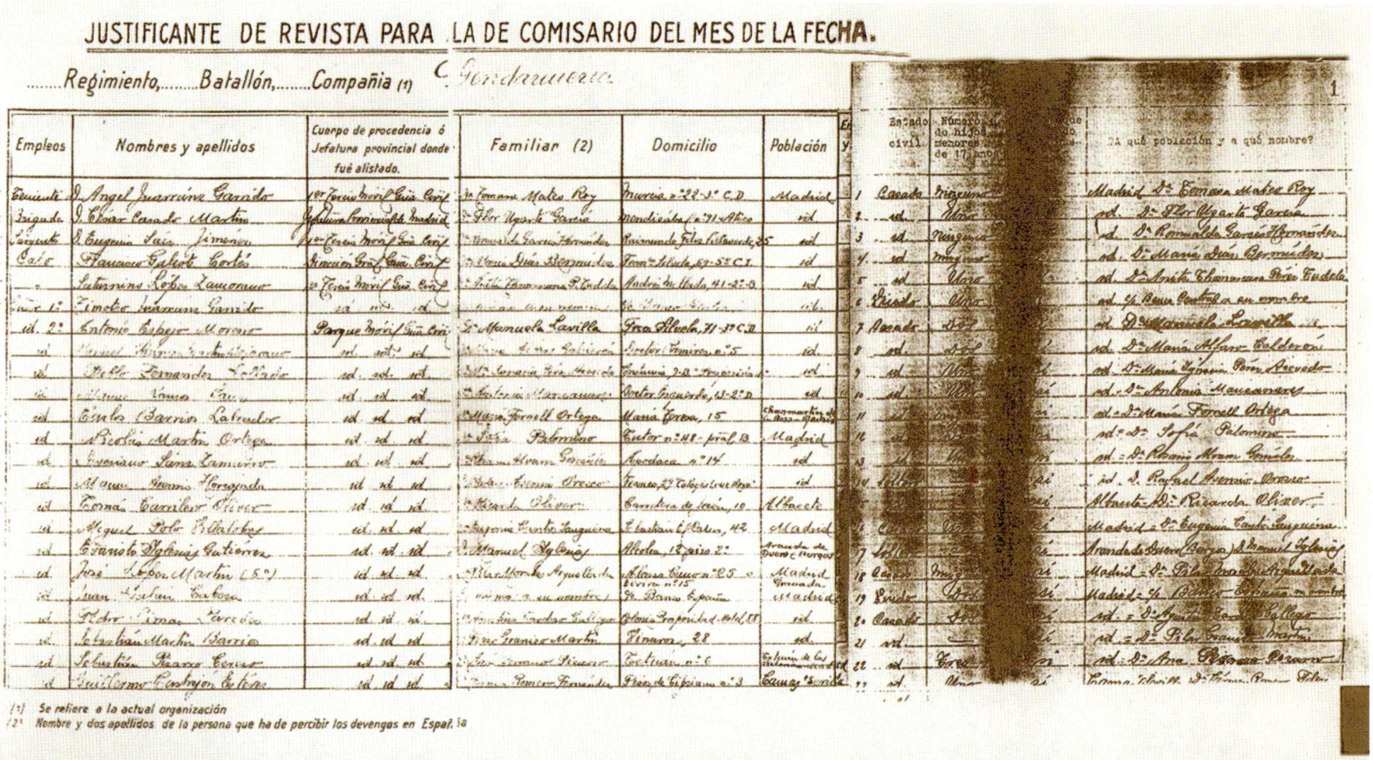

JUSTIFICANTE DE REVISTA PARA LA DE COMISARIO DEL MES DE LA FECHA.

........Regimiento,........Batallón,........Compañia (1) Gendarmería.

Empleos	Nombres y apellidos	Cuerpo de procedencia ó Jefatura provincial donde fué alistado.	Familiar (2)	Domicilio	Población
Teniente	D. Angel Juarrùna Garrido	1er Tercio Móvil Guía Civil	Dª Tomasa Mateo Rey	Murcia nº 22-3º C.D.	Madrid
Brigada	D. Elixir Casado Martín	Jefatura Provincial de Madrid	Dª Flor Ugarte García	Mendizábal nº 71 Ático	id
Sargento	D. Eugenio Saiz Jimenez	1er Tercio Móvil Guía Civil	[illegible] García Hernández	Raimundo [illegible] 25	id
Cabo	Francisco Galeote Cortés	[illegible]	Dª María Díaz Bermúdez	[illegible] 69-5º C.I.	id
"	Saturnino López Zamorano	1er Tercio Móvil Guía Civil	[illegible]	[illegible] 41-2º D.	id
[illegible] 1º	Timoteo Juarrùna Garrido	id id id	[illegible]	[illegible]	id
id. 2º	Antonio Esteyo Moreno	Parque Móvil Guía Civil	Dª Manuela Lavilla	[illegible] 71-3º C.D.	id
id	[illegible]	id id id	[illegible]	[illegible] nº 5	id.
id	Pablo Fernandez [illegible]	id. id. id.	[illegible]	[illegible]	id.
id	[illegible]	id id id	[illegible]	Doctor Esquerdo, 13-2º D	id.
id	Carlos Barrios Labrador	id id id	Dª María Fornell Ortega	María Teresa, 15	Chamartín de la Rosa-Madrid
id	Nicolás Martín Ortega	id id id	Dª Sofía Palomino	Tutor nº 48- pral. B.	Madrid
id	[illegible] Sanz Zamorano	id id id	[illegible]	[illegible] nº 14	id
id	[illegible]	id id id	[illegible]	[illegible]	id
id	Tomás Carrilero Oliver	id id id	Dª Ricarda Oliver	Carretera de Jaén, 10	Albacete
id	Miguel Polo Villalobos	id id id	Dª Eugenia [illegible]	[illegible] 42	Madrid
id	Ernesto Iglesias Gutierrez	id id id	D. Manuel Iglesias	Alcolea, 12 piso 2º	Aranda de Duero (Burgos)
id	José López Martín (5º)	id id id	[illegible]	[illegible] nº 25	Madrid
id	Juan Galán Cabezas	id id id	[illegible]	[illegible] Banco España	Madrid
id	Pedro [illegible]	id id id	[illegible]	[illegible]	id
id	Sebastián Martín Barrios	id id id	[illegible] Martín	[illegible] 28	id
id	Sebastián [illegible]	id id id	[illegible]	Tetuán nº 6	[illegible]
id	Guillermo [illegible]	id id id	[illegible] Fernández	[illegible] nº 3	[illegible]

(1) Se refiere a la actual organización

(2) Nombre y dos apellidos de la persona que ha de percibir los devengos en España

MOH/MG

MINISTERIO DEL EJÉRCITO

DIRECCION GENERAL
RECLUTAMIENTO Y PERSONAL

Madrid, 30 de Junio de 1941

Sección Secretaría

NOTA PARA la SECCION DE INTERVENCION

El General Subsecretario, en escrito de 27, me dice:

"El Estado Mayor del Ejército, en escrito "RESERVADO", Sección 1ª, de 26 del actual, comunica lo siguiente:

"Con esta fecha se dice a los Capitanes Generales y Jefe del Ejército de Marruecos, lo que sigue: "Remita urgencia telégrafo relación nominal Generales Brigada, Jefes, Oficiales, Suboficiales y C.A.S.E. Estado Mayor, Infantería, Caballería, Artillería, Ingenieros, Intendencia, Sanidad, Veterinaria y por correo aéreo o en mano, por procedimiento más rápido, de tropa que sean voluntarios para ir luchar contra comunismo, debiendo tener tropa garantía político-social, aptitud física, siendo preferible condición excombatientes.- Lo digo a V.E. a los mismos efectos."

Lo que se comunica a esa Sección para que antes de las doce horas remita relación del personal de esa Sección, que hallándose comprendido en el escrito antes mencionado, quiera figurar en la que esta Dirección entregará antes de las trece, en Subsecretaría, significándole que con relación a Cabos y soldados no debe hacer ninguna exploración de sus deseos, pues pertenece hacerlo al Batallón del Ministerio, del cual dependen.

De orden de S.E.
El Coronel de E.M., Secretario,

LEGION ESPANOLA DE
VOLUNTARIOS

PLANA MAYOR ADMINISTRATIVA
INTERVENCIÓN

Núm. 18

Adjunto le remito los Justificantes de Revista del mes de Diciembre actual en el que constan todos los componentes de esta Legión, incorporados desde la disuelta División Española de Voluntarios, que son reflejo exacto de la Revista de Presente que se ha pasado por el que suscribe a todas las Unidades de esta Legión el día 1º., y que deben considerarse como la base de los antecedentes personales que se abren a todos los componentes de aquella.

El personal que excepcionalmente no lleva los datos completos, según el modelo de los impresos utilizados, es el que no estuvo presente en la Revista por disfrutar de permiso o por otro motivo justificado.- Con la brevedad posible serán completados los datos de dicho personal.

Próximamente le serán remitidas las instrucciones que aprobadas por el Mando de esta Región están pendientes de publicación, en las cuales se regula la forma de redactar los Justificantes de la misma y el reflejo que en ellos han de tener las diversas situaciones del personal destinado en aquella.

En todo caso, es indispensable que la inteligencia recíproca entre esa Intervención y la Plana Mayor administrativa de esta Unidad, que ostenta el que suscribe, y en la que está incluida la Intervención de la misma, haga posible el deseo del Mando de que todo el personal legionario encuentre el máximo de facilidades para solventar las incidencias que en la reclamación y percibo de haberes se provoquen, así como que aquellas se resuelvan con la mayor urgencia.

Dios guarde a V. muchos años.
En Campaña, 3 de Diciembre de 1943.
EL CAPITÁN INTERVENTOR, JEFE DE LA PLANA MAYOR ADMINISTRATIVA,

Sr. Interventor de la Representación de la División Española de Voluntarios. MADRID

LEGIÓN ESPAÑOLA DE VOLUNTARIOS. Intervención.

NOTA aclaratoria y de reparos a los Justificantes de la 1a. Bandera de esta Legión, correspondientes al mes de Febrero de 1944.

En el Justificante de la P. M. está incluído indebidamente el Cabo MANUEL MARQUEZ FERNANDEZ, que en la fecha de los Justificantes estaba hospitalizado en Riga.

En el justificante de la 1a. Cía., está incluído indebidamente el Legionario CRUZ FEIJOO MARTIN, que ha justificado en la Secc. de Intendencia de esta Legión, a la que pertenece efectivamente, y en la que estaba presente el día de la Revista.

En dicho justificante está incluído también indebidamente el Legionario MANUEL RODRIGUEZ PARDO, que está destinado en la P. M. de esta Bandera en cuyo justificante aparece.

En el justificante de la 2a. Cía., debe de considerarse incluído el Legionario SEBERINO ALLER GARCIA, que aún cuando no estaba incorporado a su Unidad en el momento de la Revista, había sido dado de alta en el Hospital de Riga el día 4, siendo debido su retraso en la incorporación a la imposibilidad de localizar su Unidad. Efectuó su incorporación a ésta el día 23 de los corrientes.

DESAPARECIDOS:

A consecuencia de las operaciones en que ha tomado parte activamente esta Legión en el mes de Enero ppdo., y de las marchas simultáneas y subsiguientes, aparecen justificados como desaparecidos una serie de personal que el día 15 de los corrientes (Febrero), no estaban todavía incorporados a su Unidad, habiendo hecho su presentación a la misma entre el 15 y 29 de dicho mes.

Deben de considerarse presentes, por lo tanto, los siguientes:

1a. Cía. Cabo ROBLES ROBLES, JESUS.
" Legionario GONZALEZ DURAN, JESUS.- Hospitalizado en Riga el día 17-II-44.
" id. RUIZ CORDERO, ANTONIO.
2a. Cía. id. ANDUJAR GALVEZ, NICOLAS.
" id. CUBERO JIMENEZ, FRANCISCO.
" id. DIAZ GONZALEZ, HILARIO.
" id. INIGUEZ RODRIGUEZ, EMILIO.
4a. Cía. Cabo MAS OJEITOS, JOSÈ.
" id. ROQUE VERA, ANGEL.
" id. RIVAS CASTILLO, JUAN.
" id. RODRIGUEZ VIVÒ, ESTEBAN.
" Legionario CARRION VIVAR, JOSÈ.
" id. ORTI IRIGOYEN, ERNESTO.
" id. RUEDA MAYA, RAFAEL.
" id. VEGA ANTUNA, JOSÈ.

El personal que continúa en situación de desaparecido el día 29 de Febrero es el siguiente:

2a. Cía. Legionario DUENAS PEREZ, ANTONIO.
3a. Cía. id. RODRIGUEZ RODRIGUEZ, RAMÒN.
3a." id. PEREZ FERNÀNDEZ, FLORENTINO.
4a. Cía. id. MARTINEZ URÌA, JUAN MANUEL.

La desaparición de este personal no debe de tener trasdendencia sobre sus haberes ni comunicarse al Cuerpo de procedencia ni a los familiares, porque actualmente se está pendiente de que los Hospitales alemanes comuniquen los nombres de personal español hospitalizado en los mismos, siendo presumible que la mayoría de los desaparecidos aparezcan en situación de hospitalizados.

Durante el actual mes de Marzo se harán las gestiones pertinentes para determinar la situación del personal que todavia continúa desaparecido en este momento.

En Campaña, 1 de Marzo de 1944.

EL CAPITAN INTERVENTOR,

Firmado: Luis Rosón Pérez.

LEGIÓN ESPAÑOLA DE VOLUNTARIOS · INTERVENCIÓN

REGIMIENTO DE TRANSMISIONES

Division Espanola de Voluntarios 250

Grupo de Transmisiones

Cia de Radio

Núm. 46

Adjunto tengo el honor de remitir a Vd. los Justificante de Revista para la de Comisario del mes de la fecha, segun su escrito num. 242 del 14 del corriente.

Dios guarde a Vd muchos anos.

Campamento 15 de Setiembre de 1941.

El Capitan

DIVISION ESPAÑOLA DE VOLUNTARIOS · Cª RADIO · Grupo Transmisiones

SR. Capitan Jefe del Grupo. Campamento

DIVISION ESPAÑOLA DE VOLUNTARIOS 250"

REGIMIENTO "VIERNA" 263"

MANDO

número 1319

2do nº 29

Consecuente a su escrito número 22, fecha 26 de los corrientes, remito a V.S. adjuntos duplicados justificantes de revista para la de Comisario del mes actual, de las unidades que componen este Regimiento.-

Dios guarde a V.S. muchos años

En mi Puesto de Mando 29 de octubre 1941

EL CORONEL JEFE

RESERVADO

MINISTERIO DEL EJÉRCITO

DA/VF.

DIRECCIÓN GENERAL DE RECLUTAMIENTO Y PERSONAL

Secretaria.

1.077 Madrid, 22 de Octubre de 1943

NOTA para la Sección de INTERVENCION.

El Estado Mayor del Ejército, en nota 1ª Sección, reservada, de fecha 14 del actual, dice lo siguiente: "Para el debido conocimiento, adjunto se remiten copia de escritos dirigidos a los Capitanes Generales de las 8 Regiones, Baleares y Canarias, General Jefe del Ejército de Marruecos y General Jefe directo de Milicias, relativos a que por el momento cese la incorporación del personal de todas clases y categorias á las Unidades en organización en España para la División Española de Voluntarios.

En cuanto a las normas a aplicar al personal que perteneciente a la División se encuentra actualmente en España por cualquier concepto, le serán comunicadas en cuanto se redacten".

Lo que se traslada a esa Sección para conocimiento y efectos.

De Orden de S.E.

El Tte. Coronel del S.E.M. Secretario Accdtal,

The Division Interventors

War Comissary, 1st Class
D. Manuel Gomez Garcia.

Infantry Cadet Manuel García Gomez, 1910. (Archives Dolado)

Born in Malaga on March 11, 1893. He was admitted as Cadet to the Infantry Academy on July 4, 1910, where he started on 30 August.

He swore alliance to the flag, and commenced his studies in the Toledo center. He would continue until June 23, 1913, when he was promoted to the position of 2nd Lieutenant of the Army and received the orders of duty in the quarters located at the *Castillo de San Fernando of Figueras*.

He moved to a new position on 23 August in the King's Infantry Regiment No. 1 (*Regimiento de Infantería del Rey nº 1*), with headquarters in Madrid, where he would remain on duty until March 26, 1914, when he traveled to Melilla. In this African post he was assimilated to the Infantry regiment Africa No. 68 (*Regimiento de Infantería África nº 68*), being an active participant in all actions that were required from his Unit. His Battalion was congratulated by the War Ministry and the Commander in Chief of the Army Operations in Morocco. He received personal recognition in the Territorial Order (*Orden del Territorio*) after recovering the Bucherit position.

He will be mentioned again and congratulated in the Order of 23 June for his participation in the combats of Karus Aüillas where "*he distinguished himself following promptly and correctly all the command orders....*"

He was declared candidate to the 1st Lieutenant position with a tenure to 24 June because of being named again in the ROC of 29 June due to "*his expressed gallantry while commanding his section in the battle of Tikermur*."

In the ROC of 29 September (DO nº 218) he was assigned to the position of "while available" in commission to the Intervention Section of the War Ministry of Morocco (*Sección de Intervención del Ministerio de Guerra en Marruecos*), where he was promoted to Official 2ª of the Intervention Corps, and with tenure to the first day of September once he passed with honors the practice portion of the Entrance to the Corps course.

In 1918, and by direct personal Order of the Minister of War, he was assigned to duties in the Postal Savings Bank (*Caja Postal de Ahorros*). The government decided to militarize all the personnel working in the Postal and Telegraph Services. Once the militarization ended, he returned to his previous position.

He was declared a candidate for the position of Official 1ª by the RO of 2 April.

That same year he married *Dª Maria de la Luz Cepeda y Picón*.

At the beginning of September, he was part of the High Commission empowered with the rearrangement of the Kingdom's Accounting Tribunal (*Tribunal del Cuentas del Reino*), and the reform of the Northern Spain Railroad Company (*Compañía de Ferrocarriles del Norte de España*) to transport Army troops and material from 1871-72 to 1888-89.

In 1922 he was promoted to the position of War Commissary 2ª, and duties to the War Ministry.

In 1925 he traveled as Inspection Commission to the post on the Occidental Sahara, Cape Juby, Villa Cisneros, and the Agüera.

In 1926 and 1927 he was a member of the codification and legislation reform of the Ministry of War. In 1928 he was also named a member of the *Cooperativa del Ministerio*, being part of the Commission in charge of the reorganization of the Services of Arabic and Berber.

In 1929 he actively participated in the writing of the new Procurement Rules for the War Branches.

On May 11, 1931, he was declared a candidate to the immediate position. At that time he was transferred to the Services of Intervention of the Air Force High Command, where he was

Morocco Campaign Medal. (Assoc. Retogenes)

in charge of the purchase and reception of new material and equipment to the Air Force services.

In 1932 he was nominated as the Kingdom's Accounting Tribunal auditor to oversee the investigative findings and return of 2,564,514.61 *pesetas* that disappeared from the account of the Air Force Service.

In the same year, without the prejudice of the previous assignments, he was assigned Interventor for the Naval Bases inspection. By the Order of 7 November he received the assignment of service commission to travel to England to receive the helicopter (*autogiro*) purchased by the Air Force La Cierva Autogiro Company Limited.

In DO nº 39 of February 15, 1933, was created the War Civil Intervention Corps (*Cuerpo de Intervención Civil de Guerra*), which replaced the Military Intervention Corps (*Cuerpo de Intervención Militar*) and modified the chain of command from the Subsecretary of the War Ministry (*Subsecretaría del Ministerio de la Guerra*) to the General Administration of Intervention (*Intervención General de la Administración del Estado*).

During this year he traveled representing the Ministry of War to France, Germany, Czechoslovakia, and Holland. He returned to Spain to begin a new trip to England to purchase four small "Tiger Moth" airplanes, and to Holland to receive a new Fokker F VII airplane.

In 1934 he participated in writing the general conditions of the procurement procedures for the bids of new machine guns and automatic air defense cannons.

In 1936 he was assigned as a Delegate with Commissary 2ª Enrique Navasa Pérez and Carlos Alfaro del Pueyo of the Interventor of the Joint Chiefs of Aviation (*Intervención de la Jefatura de Aviación*).

After the uprising of the Nationalist forces (*Alzamiento*), these three interventors refused to turn in the documentation under their care obstructing the popular militia actions. As a result of this act, Commissary Alfaro de Pueyo was assassinated (after being arrested and moved to the Army Ministry "*checa*" in the month of November). Arrest orders were issued for Navasa Pérez for being considered "dangerous" and for Gomez García for his "recognized right wing tendencies." The two started a life in the shadows and away from any official center.

The republican government placed him in the scale of "TBD by the Government." His family was given asylum in the Norwegian embassy in November.

In September 1937 DO nº 233 declared him an insurrect to the regimen with the resulting loss of employment and all benefits.

In March 29, 1939, the Nationalist Army entered Madrid (*Ejército Nacional*). He abandoned the safe heaven of the embassy to present himself to the military authorities, where he was placed in the "TBD pending investigation" and proven innocent.

On January 10, 1940, he received an absolutory sentence for the charges presented against him under cause nº 156.

Once the sentence was signed, he was assigned as an Interventor to the Chemical Products factory, thereby being promoted to the position of Commissary of War 1ª (*Comisario de Guerra*).

In June 12, 1941, by Reserved Order, he was assigned to serve in the *División Española de Voluntarios*, relocating on the same date to the Unit General Headquarters.

On the 20th he began the trip to Germany, crossing at the town of Irun, on the Hispanic-French border. He arrived at Grafenwörh Camp, in Bavaria, the 24th. This was the location of the Intervention High Command (*Jefatura de Intervención*).

In addition to the proper functions of intervention, the Spanish command assigned to him a variety of tasks, one of which was the receipt of all war material from the German Army.

Die Richtigkeit der Angaben und der eigenhändigen Unterschrift bescheinigt
(Testifico la exactitud de los datos anteriores y la autenticidad de la firma)
Representación Estafeta 39502
Datum (Fecha)
Truppenteil (Unidad)
Name (Nombre y apellido)
Dienstsiegel (Sello)
Teniente Coronel Interventor
Dienststellung (Función)

Left: German Postal zip code. Below: Arrival in Germany; Spanish and German Officers at the Wagner palace. In the center is General Munoz Grandes, at his right (unknown), and War Commissary Manuel Garcia Martin. (Assoc. Retogenes)

After becoming acquainted with the German organization and systems, the Division moved to the front lines on 21 August.

They arrived at Treiburg on the 23rd, where they remained until the 29th. They moved to Grodno, where they camped until 8 September, at which time they were relocated again to the town of Wilma.

They traveled to Minks on the 14th, and were once again moved towards the Mignon Camp. On the 27th they arrived at Witebs, where they camped until 4 October, when the Division was ordered to move to Dno, and then to Shinks and Telemets, arriving finally at the Camp of Grigorovo, in Nowgorod, on 11 October.

He was assigned to the Headquarter, to the functions proper of his rank and experience.

On 20 October the division General ordered him to move to Porchovv. He was directed to organize the administration of the Spanish military hospital of this town.

On 24 November 24 he was assigned duties on the service commission to the German High Command in Berlin.

He returned to Russia in December, where he remained in the General Headquarter until May 1942, when he was assigned Chief of the West Overbach Camp, and later to the de Hof.

In this Camp he was in charge of the arrival of the transfer battalions, their training, education, loyalty swearing ceremonies, and their assignment into the German Army. In addition, he assisted the returning battalions that started their trip back home.

On 3 August he was replaced, as the Chief of the Camp by the War Commissary 2ª (*Comisario de Guerra de Segunda*) *D. Alfredo Guedea Millán- Astray*.

He crossed the border and returned to Spain on the 5th. He was assigned to the General Industry and Material Group (*Dirección General de Industria y Material*) upon his return.

He received the following awards during his tenure in the Division:

On February 11, 1942, he was awarded the *Cruz del Mérito de Guerra Alemana con espadas*. By Certificate of 15 February, the band of the *Medalla conmemorativa del invierno de 1941-42 en el Este*.

On September 30, 1943, he received the High Command of the Division (*Cuartel General de la División*) Award of the *Cruz de la Orden del Mérito Militar de 2ª clase con distintivo blanco*; on 27 November he was awarded two *Cruces Rojas del Mérito Militar* as a reward for his heroic acts. On December 19, 1944, he was allowed the use on his uniform of the *Medalla Conmemorativa de la Campaña de Rusia*.

Parade after the oath swearing ceremony, headed by lieutenant Colonel Gomez Garcia, Camp Chief at Hof, May 1943.

Colonel Gomez Garcia cartoon made by his fellow officer, Sabino Fernandez Campos.

2nd Officer - D. Manuel Trigo Cabrerizo
Unknown date of birth.

The 18 July uprising surprised him in the town of Zaragoza, where he was undertaking Law studies.

He joined the *Banderín de Enganche de las Milicias de Falange Española* on August 2, 1936, and volunteered to the *Cuartel de Castillejos de Zaragoza*, being assigned to the *Primera Bandera de Aragón*, with destination to the front in the area of Cariñena to reinforce the troops in Huelva, Las Cotas, Racién, and Portabella. He remained in this location until 21 December, when he was transferred to the front at Almodóvar.

In December 1937 he was assigned to the Gualadajara front lines where he joined the 4th flag of Navarre (*Cuarta Bandera de Navarra*), assisting with communications services with the Headquarters of the 61st Division headed by his uncle D. Agustín Muñoz Grandes. He is moved after 29 December to the Teruel front, where he participated in the extremely hard combats of the Muela conquest.

He joined the Temporary Officials Academy of Avila on February 22, 1938, where he was promoted to the Alférez Provisional position on 20 April and assigned duties with the 52 División.

In 28 May he was called to serve as the Order Assistant in the 150th Moroccan Division, where he participated in operations at Tremp (Lérida), and was active in the conquest of the locations of Paus, Solsona, and Verga. Once the summer started he was returned to the Guadalajara front, where he remained until the end of the conflict. Due to his activities he received *La Medalla de la Campaña* with the front distinctive, two *Cruz Roja del Mérito Militar*, and one *Cruz de Guerra*.

At the beginning of 1940 he was assigned duties with the 42 Infantry Regiment, based in the *Plaza de Leganés* of Madrid. September 4th he returned after graduating from Law School and receiving the assignment of Secretary of the Military Tribunal Number 27 of Special Contra espionage.

On April 5, 1941, he registered as an alumnus of the *Academia de Intervención Militar*, receiving his first promotion after the war to the position of Lieutenant Interventor with an effective date of 15 November, and with duties in the Intervention Office of the 4a Military Region.

Lieutenants Buron, Pascual, Trigo Cabrerizo Mendez, Amaro (?), and Alferez Herrera.

Lieutenant Interventor Trigo Cabrerizo, Commandant Tena, Guedea Millan Astray, and Lieutenant Zubiaurre. Grigorovo, July 1942.

By Order of the Army on 22 January he was assigned to the duties of Assistant Official to the Interventor of the Spanish Volunteers Division.

On 28 January, after crossing the Spanish-French border he joined the Intervention Headquarters in Grigorovo, under the orders of the Commissary Gómez García. In April, due to the Commissary receiving a new assignment to the Hof Camp, he assumed the head position of the Intervention Services until mid-June, when he was substituted by the War Commissary 2a Alfredo Guedea Millán-Astray.

Once the Services were filled he requested assignment to the General Headquarters of the Division, where he was placed in fortification services.

In September he was assigned to the position of Orders Official of the General.

He returned to Spain at the beginning of January 1943. He received a promotion to Captain on 15 February and duties to the Intervention General of the Army. He served as attaché to the Division representation of the Spanish Volunteers Division in Madrid.

He received the German Cross of War (*la Cruz de Guerra alemana*), the first winter medal (*la Medalla del primer Invierno*), and one *Cruz al Mérito Militar* with red ribbon.

He finalized his military career as Colonel of the Military Intervention Corps.

(Left to Right) Commandant Interventor Guedea, Commandant Tena, Lieutenant Interventor Trigo Cabrerizo, and seated is Lieutenant Interventor Ripoll Lecuona. Grigorovo, July 1942.

(Left to Right) Lieutenant Interventor Trigo Cabrerizo, Lieutenant Rose, Commandant Martinel, Lieutenant Romo, Lieutenant Otero, Commandant Sainz, Captain Muñoz, Lieutenant Herrera, Commandant Serra, and Lieutenant Ackermann. General headquarters at Proprowaskaya, September 1942.2

War Comissary, 2nd Class
D. Alfredo Guedea Millán-Astray.
Unknown place and birth date

He began as a first grade Cadet in the Infantry Academy on September 2, 1925. He attended the required studies until June 9, 1928, when he was promoted to the position of *Alférez*, and received commission duties in the Infantry Regiment of *Tenerife nº 64*.

On 2 December he moved to Madrid to receive instruction in the fly school *Escuela Superior de Aeronáutica*. He returned to the Canary Islands on January 24, 1929.

On 9 March he moved to the *Grupo de Fuerzas Regulares Indígenas de Ceuta nº 3*, where he served in the 3rd Cia. of *2 Tabor*. On July 9, 1930, he received a promotion to Infantry lieutenant.

By the R.O.C. of 10 December (D.O. nº 297) he was nominated to second official of the *Cuerpo de Intervención Militar*, being placed in the list of TBD by the Central Payroll office until he reached his statutory training and practices in the *Sección de Intervención Militar del Ministerio del Ejército*. He remained there until July 29, 1931, when he received a promotion to the grade of Official 2ª of the *Cuerpo de Intervención* with commission assignment to the *Intervención General*.

On 19 November he was again promoted to the grade of Official 1°, arriving at his new post in Valladolid, where he remained until May, when he moved to Segovia to the *Intervención de los Servicios de Guerra*.

In December he was reassigned again, to Madrid. He again joined the *Intervencion Central de Guerra*, where he stayed until March 23, 1936, at which time he traveled to *Ecija* as the Commission Interventor to buy mustangs for the Division.

On the day of the *Alzamiento* he reported to the Military Command and stayed under their Military command. He participated actively in the operation and maneuvers of the pacification of the towns and farms of the region.

On 3 August, in the civilian town of Osuna he was singled out for his bravery and aggressiveness during the combat to take this position. He was also congratulated for his heroic valor during the combats to conquer Fuente-Carretero. He was commanding the infantry troops and a cavalry platoon that forced the retreat of all enemy forces.

On 27 August, after the combat and victory at the *Cordoba* town of *Poleno del Rio*, he was congratulated by the Unit Commander as follows:

"This officer distinguished himself for his acts of bravery while at risk and for the moral encouragement he gave to the troops. He was always at the most ferocious combat positions, and for that I need to congratulate him for his exemplary and patriotic behavior demonstrated in all operations where he participated, and for being well above and beyond the duties with a proven command leadership, discipline, and extraordinary aggressiveness even when he belonged to a non-combatant Corps."

On 1 September, by Order of the Division Interventor he moved to Badajoz, where he assumed the duties of Services of Intervention of the quarter. He remained at this position until July 1938, when he was moved to the *Intervención de Fuerzas Militares de Marruecos*.

On June 28, 1940, he was promoted to the position of Commissary 2ª.

In 1942 he vacated his position of *Intervención de los Servicios de Tánger*, leaving with a TBD position towards Madrid.

On 25 June he was called to report to San Sebastian Camp, from which he traveled in Germany's direction the next day, arriving at the Hof quarters on the 30th.

After receiving the adaptation courses he was sent to the Russian front as part of the *12º Batallón de Marcha*. He arrived and reported to the Headquarters of Grigorovo on 18 July.

On 28 August, and by Order of the General Muñoz Grandes, he received the assignment of Chief Commander of the West Camp of Overbach (Hof). The functions he performed while Chief Commander were:

Lieutenant Interventor Amaro Lasheras, Commandant Interventor Guedea Millan Astray, Jacqueline, Captain (?), and Lieutenant Pulido. Hof-Saale, June 1942. (Archives Ripoll)

Lieutenant Interventor Amaro Lasheras, Commandant Guedea Millan Astray, Lieutenant Gascón, Lieutenant Checa, and Blesa. Grigorovo, July 1942. (Archives Ripoll)

Intendant Commander Parra, Lieutenant Interventor Ripoll, and Commandant Interventor Guedea at the presentation acts, General Muñoz Grandes headquarters, July 1942. (Archives Ripoll)

Above: Commandant Interventor Guedea. Below: Soldier Pedro Fernandez, Commandant Interventor Guedea, and Intendant Commander Tena, Hof, 1942.

- To receive the troops from Spain and the returning units from the front.
- Organize and supply the troops in the units with the necessary training adaptation plans and uniforms, and to prepare all of them for the swearing ceremony of loyalty to the *Führer*.
- Administrative functions for all the second lines.
- To serve as the liaison and the representative of the Major General with the German High Command.

On February 4, 1943, he traveled under a Service Commission to the new headquarters in Proprowaskaya. He arrived on the 11th

during the grand soviet offensive to Krasny-Bor that had started on the 10th. Due to the extreme gravity of the situation he received the orders, along with Lieutenant Colonel Oranjo, to visit all the units at the front, and prepare the official report of the casualties and units needed. On 11 March, once the situation was normalized, he received orders from General Esteban Infantes to return to the post at Hof.

He moved to Spain by Direct Order of the General on 18 March.

He later returned to Germany and remained at his post until 9 August, when his Unit returned to Spain.

He was awarded the medal of *La Cruz del Mérito de Guerra con espadas*.

He retired as the Director of the Corps Academy in 1969 as Colonel Interventor.

Lieutenant Interventor Jaime Ripoll Lecuona, November 1941.

PRISION PROVISIONAL DE HOMBRES NUM.3. ENFERMERIA.

El recluso Jaime Ripoll Lecuona queda autorizado a tomar el sol en el patio de 10 a 12.

Madrid 20 de marzo de 1.938

El Médico Oficial.

Ripoll document.

2nd Officer - D. Jaime Ripoll Lecuona.

He was born on September 5, 1916, in Zaragoza from a family of military heritage. They moved to Madrid, where he attended law studies at the beginning of the Spanish Civil War .

On September 6, 1936, he was detained and jailed in the *Cárcel Celular de Madrid* along with his father, the artillery Commander D. Francisco Ripoll Álvarez, his mother Da. Rosa Lecuona Hardisson, and his sister María Rosa. On 7 November his father was taken out of jail by the red militia and assassinated in the town of Paracuellos del Jarama.

Upon the evacuation of the jail, the rest of the family was moved to the Prison de Portlier.

On November 8, 1937, he was declared a rebel against the Regime (Communist Popular Front), and charged with the following:

"*...founding documents, like a segment of harangue to the black shirts Italians, a manifest of the group JONS, radicalizing poetry against the previous President of the Spanish Republic referring to Sres. Prieto y Largo Caballero and correspondence from his friends from Arenas y El Escorial, where they mentioned the assassination of Calvo Sotelo...*"

He was sentenced for these charges by the Popular Tribunal to three years in jail.

The surviving family would not see each other until March 9, 1939, the date of the liberation of Madrid by the National Forces.

Once Madrid was liberated he requested and was granted leave to form part of the *1a Centurial de la 8a Bandera de Militias de F.E.T y de las JONS* to the military command. He was assigned duties in the headquarters of the Central Region of the Air Force as Official 3° Honorary of the Judicial Corps under the authority of the General Director of Personnel and Enlistment of the Army. He was then part of the Judicial Counsel of the Air Force.

In 1940, compliant with the requirements specified in the 1st Article of the Order of May 25, 1939, he received two medals of *Sufrimiento por la Patria*.

In 1941, by O.C. January 15th (*B.O. del Ejército del Aire nº 7*), he was included in the initial Complementary Scale in the Judicial Corps of the Air Force, with the grade of Alférez recognizing his tenure to November 13, 1939. He was then removed from the Army listing.

On 17 January he was promoted to Honorary 2° Official.

By O.C. on April 5th he was admitted to the Academy of *Intervention Militar*, where he entered on 15 April.

On 15 September he went to the General Army Academy of Zaragoza. He swore allegiance to the flag on 15 November and received his promotion to Lieutenant *Interventor*, with tenure to March 31, 1939.

He assumed his new duties in the General Intervention of the Army High Command. He joined *La División Española de Voluntarios* by Order of May 16, 1942. He crossed the border as *Agregado* on 26 June as a member of the 12th Marching Battalion. He arrived on the 30th at the Division Camp located on Hof-Saale.

After the change in uniform and the swearing in ceremony to the *Führer*, he departed on a military train to the Eastern Front. He arrived on the 15th at Grigorovo, where he received immediately the position of Chief of Intervention on the High Command by General Order of the Division on 20 July.

The 250 Division was moved to the Leningrad Front by train on 11 August to be apart of the "Northern Light" operation.

Lieutenant Ripoll traveled to the towns of Novvolosimo, Winpa, and Krekbreewo, finally arriving on 8 September at Proprowaskaya, where the General Headquarters had been moved.

Due to his Interventor duties he continuously had to visit all the front units, where he experienced first hand all the combat and aerial and artillery bombardments scenes.

By the Order of January 29, 1943, he received the promotion to Captain Interventor. As part of a Service commission he left the front lines on 4 February to go to Unit positions at Riga, Konigsberg, Berlin, and Hof, returning to the front line 11 March.

On 24 August he flew to Berlin, from where he traveled to Landsberg Erfurt, Salbuzburg, Innsbruck, and Hof, returning to the front again on 20 September.

By the General Order of the Division of 2 October, due to the arrival of the Commander Interventor D. Francisco Ponce González, he was relieved of his duties as Chief of the Intervention Services. On 7 October the General Esteban Infantes ordered him to move to Berlin, naming him as the Second Line Interventor of Services and of the General Camp of Hof-Saale, adding the duties of the Office of Censure Chief.

He was impressed by the results achieved by the Anglo-American bombardments on the German cities and civil objectives, defining these acts as "terrorist actions," and he put these denominations on his daily Service Reports.

On October 12, 1943, General Lindemann informed Esteban Infantes of the decision to repatriate the Division.

Due to that political decision he received the order to return home. In accordance with the resolution he was relieved of duties on 21 December from the Hof headquarters. He traveled to Berlin, Paris, and Hendaya, crossing the border on 21 December.

After enjoying his vacation time, he traveled to Ceuta at the beginning of 1944 to take command of the Intervention Services of the quart of Alcazarquivir.

On April 5, 1943, he received the *Cruz Roja del Mérito Militar*, and on the 20th received the *Cruz del Mérito de Guerra de 2ª clase*. On 20 November he achieved the *Cruz del Mérito de Guerra de 1ª clase con espadas*. On 20 December he received the *Cruz Roja*.

He received permission to use the medals on his uniform of the *Medalla Conmemorativa de los Voluntarios Españoles en la lucha contra el bolchevismo* and the *Medalla Conmemorativa de la Campaña*.

He retired as a Colonel Interventor in 1981.

Above: Military passport. Left: Studio picture of Lieutenant Interventor Jaime Ripoll at the arrival at Hof, dressed in the regulation uniform of a German Infantry Officer. July 1942.

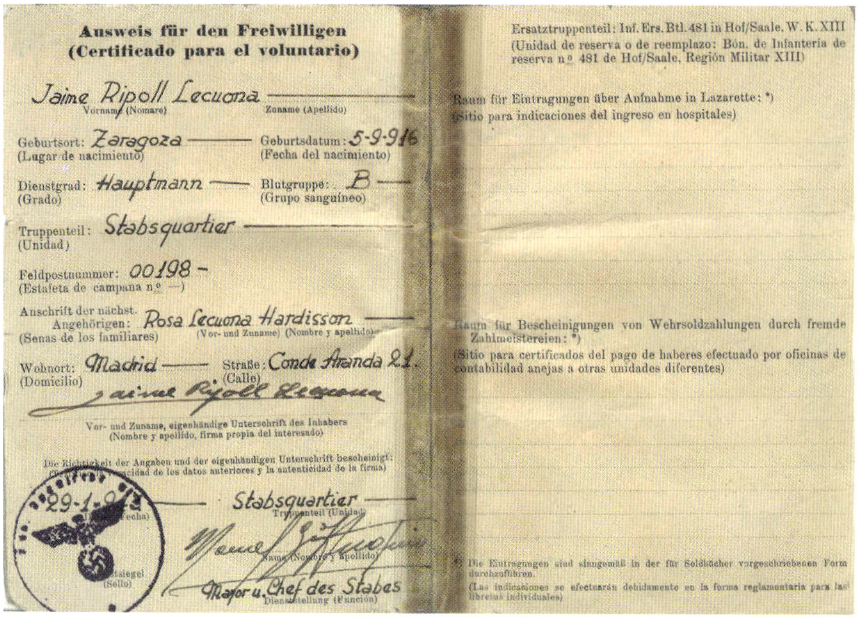

Ausweis für den Freiwilligen
(Certificado para el voluntario)

Jaime Ripoll Lecuona
Vorname (Nomare) — Zuname (Apellido)

Geburtsort: Zaragoza (Lugar de nacimiento) — Geburtsdatum: 5-9-916 (Fecha del nacimiento)

Dienstgrad: Hauptmann (Grado) — Blutgruppe: B (Grupo sanguíneo)

Truppenteil: Stabsquartier (Unidad)

Feldpostnummer: 00198 - (Estafeta de campana nº —)

Anschrift der nächst. Angehörigen: Rosa Lecuona Hardisson (Senas de los familiares) (Vor- und Zuname) (Nombre y apellido)

Wohnort: Madrid (Domicilio) — Straße: Conde Aranda 21. (Calle)

Jaime Ripoll Lecuona
Vor- und Zuname, eigenhändige Unterschrift des Inhabers
(Nombre y apellido, firma propia del interesado)

Die Richtigkeit der Angaben und der eigenhändigen Unterschrift bescheinigt:
(...cidad de los datos anteriores y la autenticidad de la firma)

29-1-942 (Fecha) — Stabsquartier Truppenteil (Unidad)

...siegel (Sello) — Name (Nombre y apellido)

Major u. Chef des Stabes
Dienststellung (Función)

Ersatztruppenteil: Inf. Ers. Btl. 481 in Hof/Saale. W. K. XIII
(Unidad de reserva o de reemplazo: Bón. de Infantería de reserva nº 481 de Hof/Saale, Región Militar XIII)

Raum für Eintragungen über Aufnahme in Lazarette: *)
(Sitio para indicaciones del ingreso en hospitales)

Raum für Bescheinigungen von Wehrsoldzahlungen durch fremde Zahlmeistereien: *)
(Sitio para certificados del pago de haberes efectuado por oficinas de contabilidad anejas a otras unidades diferentes)

*) Die Eintragungen sind sinngemäß in der für Soldbücher vorgeschriebenen Form durchzuführen.
(Las indicaciones se efectuarán debidamente en la forma reglamentaria para las libretas individuales)

Clockwise from top left: Back in Spain, wearing the 1943 model of the Iron Cross first class; Military ID papers; Medal of suffering for the Mother country; General Division headquarters, Grigorovo, July 1942; Interventor Ripoll and Artillery Lieutenant Ackermman; Lieutenant Interventor Ripoll dressed with the model 1940 regular uniform; Trip stop while getting to the Hof camp as a member of the 12th March Battalion, May 1942.

Lieutenant Ripoll and German Lieutenant Natus, Connection High Command member.

JAG Captain Pardo, Captain Villasevil, and Lieutenant Ripoll.

2nd Officer - Maximiliano Amaro Lasheras

Joaquin Amaro Lasheras. (Archives Amaro)

Joaquin Amaro Perez and wife. (Archives Amaro)

He was born in *Linea de La Concepcion*, in a middle-class catholic family on August 10, 1917, the son of Mr. Jose Amaro (doctor, surgeon) and Dª Trinidad Lasheras. The fruit of this marriage were six children.

He was a militant of the University Spanish Union (S.E.U.) since its inception. By coincidence, the Spanish Civil War surprised him in his native city. At nineteen years of age he enlisted in a Century of the Phalange, participating in the liberation of Guadiaro, San Enrique, Manilva, Estepona, Marbella, and Ojén.

His first services in the war were as a driver, without a driver license, of the Government Delegate Mr. Grufill,. His mission was to establish communication between this authority and the General Queipo de Llano, with whom he would become close and have a great friendship. As an anecdote of that time, he remembers that due to his short stature, his automobile was well known as the ghost car, since it was practically impossible to distinguish its driver from the outside.

At the beginning of 1937, while participating in the taking of Malaga, he was stationed at the *Tercio of Zamacola*, with headquarters in the front of Cordova.

On 1 April he moved to Seville, where he enrolled in the Academy of Provisional Alfereces of Infantry, rendering oath of allegiance to the flag. He left for duty on the 31st with the rank of Provisional Alferez to the Infantry Regiment Pavía nº 7. He incorporated to his new Unit in the town of Algeciras.

On 20 June he requested permission to go to the III Tambor of the Regular Forces Indigenous of Larache nº 4. Destiny wanted the brothers on the same front in the same Unit. The four of them: Jose (military doctor who would reach the rank of Major General), Luis (Odontólogist and Provisional Alférez), Joaquin (student of Pharmacy), and Maximiliano were distinguished by their bravery in combat.

There is no better proof of this spirit than their own blood. Jose was wounded five times, and Joaquin fell in military action on June 19, 1938, during the hardest combats of the Pedroches, in the mountain range of Santa Ines. He was wounded by shrapnel in both legs and refused to be evacuated, so as not to leave his company without a leader, due to the highest loss of life suffered by his Unit.

On 10 July, while continuing with the interim control of his company, he left for the front of Extremadura, acting in the Sector of Cabeza del Buey. In this destiny, and by Order of 23 August, it was communicated to him that he had been promoted to Provisional Lieutenant of Infantry.

Jose, Luis, and Joaquín Amaro Lasheras next to their father, José Amaro Perez. (Archives Amaro)

Lieutenant Interventor Amaro Lasheras, first from the left, at a stop on his way to the Hof Camp. (Archives Ripoll)

From here he was moved back to the Sector of Cordova, where he took part in the breakthrough of the front, finishing the fight while he was near the locality of Andújar.

On 6 April he moved with his Tambor to Africa, fortifying the locality of Alcazarquivir.

He received the following awards and medals: medal of the Campaign with band of Vanguard, two Red Cross to the Military Merit, and a Military Cross.

On May 8, 1940, he entered the Officer Retraining Infantry School in Zaragoza, to follow the prescribed course. To his own surprise, he did not remain in the mentioned center for more than twenty days. The reason once more was he did not reach the minimum height. Returning to his Regiment seated in Granada, he was named, with temporary character, Judge Provincial Instructor of Political Responsibilities.

He went back to studying Law, and upon graduating decided to participate in the advertised position of the newly formed Military Intervention Service. He was accepted, with 59 others, to what would be the first class. They needed to get to the Corps Academy, located down the street known as Areneros, and owned by the Jesuits. He finished his academic period in Zaragoza, emphasizing in gymnastics and horse riding. On November 15, 1941, and with seniority to March 31, 1939, he was promoted to the position of Lieutenant Interventor with the number 45.

His first duty: the Offices of Military Intervention of the X Army Corps in Melilla. He went with his two closest friends, Lieutenants Guillermo Sierra Garcia and Daniel Lerena Nájera.

By communication of June 12, 1942, he was destined to the Spanish Division of Volunteers. On June 26, 1942, he crossed the Spanish-French border via train with Commander Interventor Alfredo Guedea Millán-Astray and his companion of promotion, Lieutenant Jaime Ripoll Lecuona, arriving at Hof on 3 July. There, they were moved to Novgorod, where they presented themselves to the Headquarters of Muñoz Grandes, requesting a first line of combat position to the General.

They are assigned to the Third Company of the Assault Combat Engineer Battalion.

The Battalion quickly occupied its position at Lapolgen, on the sector of the Volchof. This battalion such frequent movements in front of enemy fire reaching the point that their unit was reduced by 50% of their members.

On October 10, 1942, on the Leningrad front, he was assigned to release the detachment of their company destined for the sector of the 269th grenadiers, placing two minefields and making six patrols between the enemy lines. This action was officially congratulated by the Colonel of the Regiment, as well as by the Division General.

On 30 December 30 he entered with a patrol in the enemy field, managing to blow their wire fence, as well as to install another minefield.

On January 1, 1943, he was destined for the sector of Krasny-VOR, in which they placed more than two thousand mines.

On February 10, 1943, at 06:30 AM, after receiving heavy attacks of artillerymen, the Russian Army mounted a great offensive attack with the objective to free the surrounded city of Leningrad. Lieutenant Amaro, with his company, was trenched along the Moscow-Leningrad highway, a key point in the offensive.

They received orders to try to stop the advance of the KV1 and T34 enemy tanks. With two young volunteers, and with no antitank equipment, they used the advantage of the frozen slopes of the highway, and started to throw their mines as if they were playing a bowling game.

A tank moving towards them opened fire, and an impact reached the Spanish position, killing the two volunteers, and leaving the Lieutenant seriously hurt.

"That 10 February I was born again; still today, at night, when I am closing my eyes, appear before me those two young falangists. Why them, and not myself? ... Definitively, I was born again."

He remembers with bitterness and admiration a young Basque soldier, Zabalvetia, that before the unstoppable advance of the Russian armored vehicles that were putting in serious danger the Spanish positions, threw himself with a mine in the chains of an

Joaquin Amaro Lasheras' Assault Engineer Diploma. (Archives Amaro)

enemy tank. Man and machine jumped in the air. With the irony of destiny, that 10 February he received notification from Madrid of his promotion to Captain Interventor.

It is better to let the documents speak for themselves; here is the completely reproduced report of Captain Jose Luis Aramburu Topete, with the OK given by the Battalion Chief Ezequiel Roman.

DON JOSE LUIS ARAMBURU TOPETE, ENGINEERS CAPTAIN, HEAD OF THE THIRD COMPANY OF THE COMBAT ENGINEERS BATTALION, 250th SPANISH DIVISION OF VOLUNTEERS, COMMANDED BY COMMANDER EZEQUIEL ROMAN GUTIÉRREZ.

I CERTIFY: That Lieutenant MAXIMILIANO AMARO LASHERAS got assigned to the Company under my control on July 17, 1942, in the position of Sapolje.

In the Wolchow front, he took part in several patrols and in placing minefields. He was distinguished in the position of "the nose," rendering services under intense enemy fire, to the point that they suffered 50% losses in a few days.

At the Saint Petersburg front, he remained in instruction from the first of September to 10 October, where he released the detachment of the company in the Sector of the Grenadiers Regiment 269. He placed two minefields and made six patrols between enemy lines. He was repeatedly congratulated by the Colonel of the Regiment several times.

On 30 December 30 he took part in scouting into deep enemy territory along several patrols of the Company, his Unit being the one that reached the enemy minefields, blowing away their barbed wires.

On January 30, 1943, he went again to the Sector of Krany-Vor, where he placed more than two thousand mines. On 10 February, during the violent Russian attacks, his values, courage, and skills were confirmed once again, managing yet again to maintain their line and placing a mine under several enemy tanks during the battle, one of which resulted in severe wounds to him.

Colonel Amaro's awards and medals.

Before entering the hospital, and although his wound was not light, he traveled several kilometers to notify the command of important enemy information, refusing to evacuate himself until he could render his report.

This officer, by his high spirit, and not very often imitated courage, has been one of the masts of the Combat Engineers Assault Battalion.

He was congratulated several times personally by Generals Muñoz Grandes and Esteban Infantes, and he is in possession of an Iron Cross, second class, as well as proposed for the Assault Plate, Pin of Close Combat Clasp, Spanish Military Cross, and the Red Cross.

To all the effects, and to witness this action, I certify this document at the Russian Front, today April 4, 1943.

Signed: Captain Aramburu Topete

OK by Commander Ezequiel Roman

To confirm this, we only need to read the article published by the best author following the Blue Division, and recently passed away Fernando Vadillo, who in his book *They fought in Krasny-Vor* mentions on several occasions Lieutenant Amaro Lasheras, and from which we recall:

".....At your orders my General. I am Lieutenant Amaro of the Third Combat Engineers Company.

Tell me.

He arrives wounded. He brings a bulky bandage in the rear of his trousers and, judging by the pale color in his face, he should have lost a lot of blood.

Captain Aramburu has ordered me to evacuate. My company is surrounded, but maintains the position....

It is 3:00 in the afternoon, and the general listens in silence to the report of Lieutenant Maximiliano Amaro Lasheras, and gives him thanks....

I asked the General to help Aramburu, who was being surrounded, to send support with aviation or artillery. I received a laconic answer:

We do not have it Amaro, we do not have it."

The rest is history. That 10th of February, after an impressive artillery preparation, 44,000 Russian soldiers, along with one hundred tanks, were sent to the lines being defended by 5,600 Spaniards. The numbers speak of the greatness of the Spanish victory. Eleven thousand Russians lost their lives that day, compared to the 3,645 losses of the Spaniards (approximately 2,500 died). The setback was so impressive that the Russian commissioners, when interrogating the captured Spanish prisoners, asked them for the secret weapon they were using. That was the only logical explanation.

Already a Captain, Amaro, shines with his medals and awards. There are many, but all were obtained in military actions. On his

Lieutenant Colonel Gomez Iñiguez, Commandant Alfredo Bellod Gomez (250 Assault Engineers battalion), Intendance Group Commander Jose Parra Mateos, and Lieutenant Interventors Ripoll and Amaro. (Archives Ripoll)

chest, the medal of Sufferings by the Mother country with the wounded vanes, three Red Crosses, the Military Spanish Cross, the Iron Cross second class, and the medal of the Campaign. He wears also the hard to achieve ones, like the *NAHKAMPF-SPANGE* (German emblem for the participants in close combat clasp); the *STURMABZEICHEN*, created for those who participated in several assaults, and the *VERWUNDETEN- ABZEICHEN*, a plate for those hurt in combat. On the sleeve of his single-breasted uniform jacket are two angles for wounded in combat actions.

After his recovering in diverse hospitals, including Mestelevo, Wilna, Konigsberg, Hof, and Berlin, in which he remained hospitalized until 26 March, he returned to the Front. When appearing in front of General Esteban Infantes to request command of a combatant unit again, the General's comments to him were:

"Amaro, you have already fulfilled with excess all your duties. I have decided to make you a gift," and extended to him an order to take a flight to Berlin.

He returned to Spain on 20 April.

Falange Española
Tradicionalista
y de las J. O. N. S.

Junta Central de Recompensas y Distinciones

En nombre de S. E. el Ministro Secretario General del Movimiento y a propuesta de la Junta Central de Recompensas y Distinciones, vengo en conceder el Aspa Roja con una barra roja al camarada MAXIMILIANO AMARO LASHERAS de acuerdo con lo establecido en el Decreto de 2 de Agosto de 1943.

Madrid, 26 de abril de 1944

El Presidente,

Alfredo Jiménez-Millas

Expediente núm. 869

F. E. T. y de las J. O. N. S. Junta Central de Recompensas — Secretaría General

Colonel Amaro award.

His return to Spain was due to the anxiety attack suffered by his mother upon receiving notice of his combat injuries while listening to the daily report given by National Radio. To that day, she thought her son was assigned to administrative functions only, very far away from any front.

In 1981 he passed to the Reserves with the rank of Colonel Inspector.

Captain Amaro and spouse Alicia Roldan, 1945. (Archives Amaro)

War Comissary, 2nd Class - D. Francisco Ponce González.

Born in Olot, Gerona, November 24, 1903.

Having passed the entrance exam, he started in the Infantry Academy on September 28, 1923, and swore allegiance to the flag on 11 November.

In July 1926 he received the grade of *Alférez*, and left the Toledo Academy with the grade of "Outstanding." His first assignment was with the Mountain Battalion of *Alba de Tormes nº 2*, with headquarters in Ronda.

He next moved to Tarifa until August 2, 1927, when he was assigned to the Tetuan Headquarters of the Hunters Battalion *África nº 6*, and received the order to take interim command of the 1st Cia. He remained until 4 December. In December he joined the *Mehala Jalifiana de Gamara nº6*, moving to Had-Land and assuming the command and administration of the *Mia de Caballería*.

On February 3, 1928, he was reassigned to the 11ª Mia with quarters in Anlerd.

In 1929 he rendered honors with his Unit to the S.A. the *Jalifa*, while he visited *Xauen*. He ended this year with the command of the 2º *Tabor de la Mehala*.

As a direct result of the advertised announcement in the R.O.C of July 3, 1930 (D.O. nº147), to fill twenty positions of Official 2º to the Corps of Intervention, and the R.O.C. of 5 September (D.O. nº 201) he received assignment of duties as *Disponible forzoso* from the Central Payroll Office with the intention of undergoing the necessary education and training.

By Order of July 29, 1931, he received the grade of *Oficial Segundo del Cuerpo De Intervención Militar*, and his first assignment to the *Intervention* of the Army Headquarters High Command.

He was declared *apto* to be elevated to the grade of *Oficial Primero* by Order of 23 August, and received the commission 16 September.

He married Dª María de la Consolación Rubio y de Benito in 1932.

In 1934, by Order Memorandum of the Finances Ministry of 4 May, he received the post of serving "El Protectorado," with duties and assignment to the *Inspección de Intervenciones y Fuerzas Jalifianas*, in the Tetuan quarters.

In 1936 he received the certificate from the *Academia Oficial de Árabe y Bereber* located in Tetuan after studying for three years with the grade of "Excellent."

At the beginning of the 18 July *Alzamiento,* he quickly enlisted with the Nationals. He received the grade of *Interventor Delegado del Servicio Económico Legal del Protectorado*.

At the end of the Civil War he was assigned duties as *Interventor Delegado en la Delegación de Fomento de la zona del Protectorado*.

Up to that time he received the following awards: *La Medalla del Homenaje rendido a S.S. M.M.*, *la Medalla de la Paz de Marruecos*, *Medalla conmemorativa de las Campañas de África*, *distintivo de Mehalas Jalifianas*, and *La Medalla de la Campaña con distintivo de vanguardia*.

He remained at this post until August 21, 1943, when by memorandum nº 2047 from the *Intervención General del Ministerio del Ejército* he was nominated to the position of Chief of *Servicios de Intervención de la División Española de Voluntarios*. He traveled on 6 September, crossing the French border with the lieutenant *Interventor* Luis Rosón Álvarez, arriving at Hof on the 9th, and to the Headquarters of the Unit in Pokroskaia by the 15th, where he remained, serving in the *Jefatura de Intervención en Campaña*.

On 11 September the position was moved from Pokroskaia to Nikolayevka.

On November 21, 1943, when the Official Order indicating the dissolution of the *La División Española de Voluntarios* was received, he was assigned the duty of receiving all archives,

Left: King Alfonso XII, Africa Medal at Tetuan. Right: Commandant Interventor Ponce and Captain Interventor Rosón with some soldiers of the Intervention Headquarters at Nikolayevka, September 1943. (Archives Rosón)

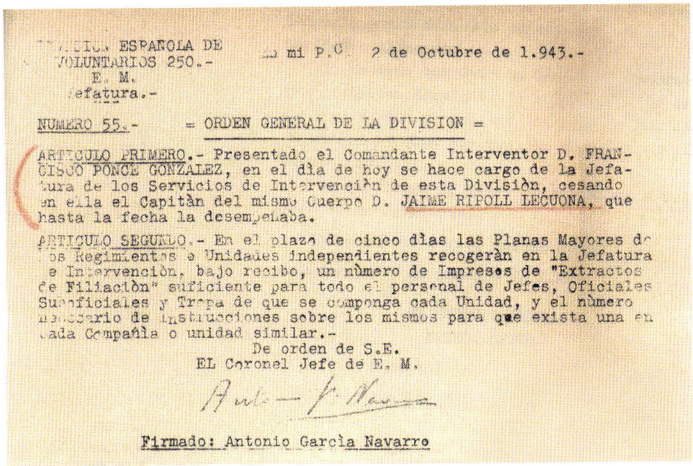

[illegible] ESPAÑOLA DE
VOLUNTARIOS 250.-
E. M.
Jefatura.-

[illegible] mi P.C. 2 de Octubre de 1.943.-

NUMERO 55.- = ORDEN GENERAL DE LA DIVISION =

ARTICULO PRIMERO.- Presentado el Comandante Interventor D. FRANCISCO PONCE GONZALEZ, en el dìa de hoy se hace cargo de la Jefatura de los Servicios de Intervenciòn de esta Divisiòn, cesando en ella el Capitàn del mismo Cuerpo D. JAIME RIPOLL LECUONA, que hasta la fecha la desempeñaba.

ARTICULO SEGUNDO.- En el plazo de cinco dìas las Planas Mayores de los Regimientos e Unidades independientes recogeràn en la Jefatura de Intervenciòn, bajo recibo, un nùmero de Impresos de "Extractos de Filiaciòn" suficiente para todo el personal de Jefes, Oficiales Suboficiales y Tropa de que se componga cada Unidad, y el nùmero necesario de instrucciones sobre los mismos para que exista una en cada Compañìa o unidad similar.-

De orden de S.E.
EL Coronel Jefe de E. M.

Firmado: Antonio Garcìa Navarro

All Ponce documents.

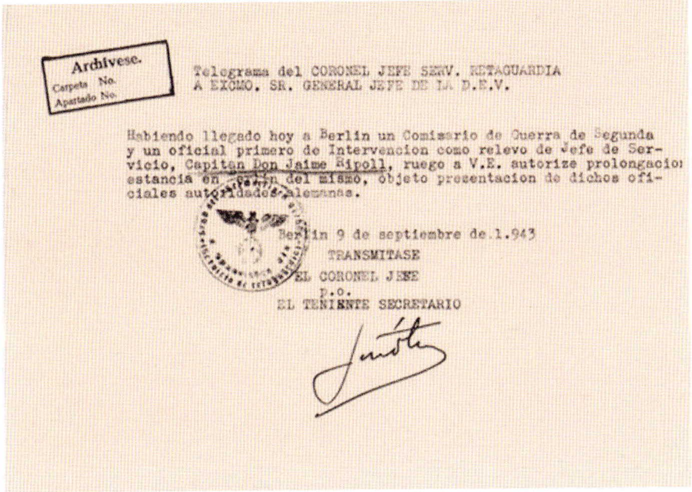

Archìvese.
Carpeta No.
Apartado No.

Telegrama del CORONEL JEFE SERV. RETAGUARDIA
A EXCMO. SR. GENERAL JEFE DE LA D.E.V.

Habiendo llegado hoy a Berlin un Comisario de Guerra de Segunda y un oficial primero de Intervencion como relevo de Jefe de Servicio, Capitan Don Jaime Ripoll, ruego a V.E. autorize prolongacion estancia en [illegible] del mismo, objeto presentacion de dichos oficiales autoridades alemanas.

Berlin 9 de septiembre de 1.943
TRANSMITASE
EL CORONEL JEFE
p.o.
EL TENIENTE SECRETARIO

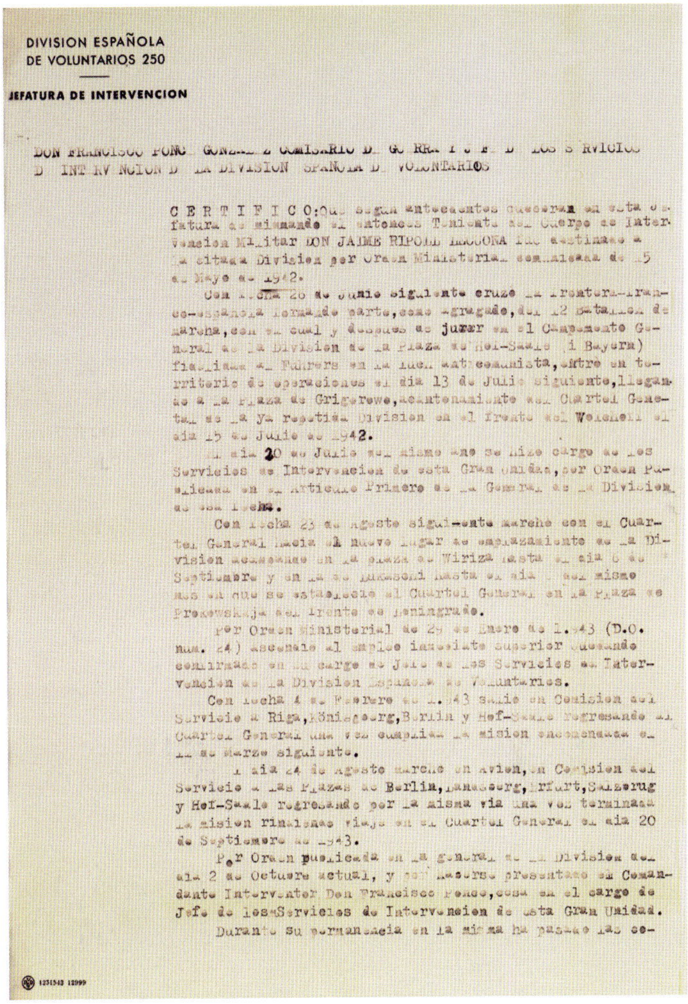

DIVISION ESPAÑOLA
DE VOLUNTARIOS 250

JEFATURA DE INTERVENCION

DON FRANCISCO PONCE GONZALEZ COMISARIO DE GUERRA [illegible] DE LOS SERVICIOS DE INTERVENCION DE LA DIVISION ESPAÑOLA DE VOLUNTARIOS

C E R T I F I C O: Que [illegible] esta Jefatura [illegible] Teniente del Cuerpo de Intervencion Militar DON JAIME RIPOLL LECUONA [illegible] la citada Division por Orden Ministerial [illegible] de Mayo de 1942.

Con fecha 26 de Junio siguiente cruzo la frontera franco-española formando parte, como agregado, del 12 Batallon de marcha, con el cual y despues de jurar en el Campamento General de la Division de la plaza de Hof-Saale (Baviera) fidelidad al Fuhrer en la lucha anticomunista, entro en territorio de operaciones el dia 13 de Julio siguiente, llegando a la plaza de Grigorowo, acantonamiento del Cuartel General de la ya repetida Division en el frente del Wolchow el dia 15 de Julio de 1942.

El dia 20 de Julio del mismo año se hizo cargo de los Servicios de Intervencion de esta Gran Unidad, por Orden [illegible] en el Articulo Primero de la General de la Division de esa fecha.

Con fecha 23 de Agosto siguiente marcho con el Cuartel General hacia el nuevo lugar de emplazamiento de la Division [illegible] en la plaza de Wiriza hasta el dia 6 de Septiembre y en la de [illegible] hasta el dia [illegible] del mismo [illegible] en que se establecio el Cuartel General en la plaza de Prokowskaja del frente de Leningrado.

Por Orden Ministerial de 29 de Enero de 1.943 (D.O. num. 24) ascendio al empleo inmediato superior quedando confirmado en el cargo de Jefe de los Servicios de Intervencion de la Division Española de Voluntarios.

Con fecha 4 de Febrero de 1.943 salio en Comision del Servicio a Riga, Königsberg, Berlin y Hof-Saale regresando al Cuartel General una vez cumplida la mision encomendada el [illegible] de Marzo siguiente.

El dia 24 de Agosto marcho en avion, en Comision del Servicio a las plazas de Berlin, [illegible], Erfurt, Salzburg y Hof-Saale regresando por la misma via una vez terminada la mision [illegible] en el Cuartel General el dia 20 de Septiembre de 1943.

Por Orden publicada en la General de la Division del dia 2 de Octubre actual, y por haberse presentado el Comandante Interventor Don Francisco Ponce, cesa en el cargo de Jefe de los Servicios de Intervencion de esta Gran Unidad.

Durante su permanencia en la misma ha pasado las co-

documentation, and official equipment to be transported back to the Spanish Army Headquarters in Madrid. When he sent the protocol and official documentation he received orders from the Madrid High Command to remain at this assignment. He kept the position and assignment until January 9, 1944, when he crossed the border, returning to Spain.

During his German Eastern Front tenure he was awarded the *Cruz de Guerra de 1ª clase*.

The Army promoted him to the grade of General Interventor. He passed away in June 1978.

Left: Colonel Francisco Ponce Gonzalez in the 60s. He finished his military career as the Spanish Army General Interventor. (Archives Dolado) Right: Commandant Interventor Ponce and Captain Interventor Rosón, who will take command of the headquarters at the Division dissolution when the Blue Legion was organized. Nikolayevka, September 1943. (Archives Rosón)

1st Officer - D. Luis Rosón Pérez.

Born in Becerreá, Lugo, on July 6, 1918. He was an active militant of *Falange Española de las J.O.N.S*, where he was the local Chief.

In July 1936, after the declaration of war, he presented himself in the San Fernando Quarters (*Cuartel de San Fernando*) of the Lugo command. The next day, armed appropriately and with the officer designated by the Military Authority, he intervened in the occupation of the town of Becerra, and the rural zone of the adjoining provinces of Lugo, Leon, and Asturias.

In 1937 he received a transfer to the Somiedo and Torrebarrio positions, where he remained until 14 March, at which time he abandoned the position on the *Centuria de Falange Española* to become a volunteer in the 30th Infantry Regiment. He served in the 3er Cia. of the 12th Battalion, returning to the Asturias front at the Tineo sector. He was part of the 20 April movement of troops to the denominated position of "*la Modestina*" area of very hard combats.

Once the Asturias general offensive commenced he participated in the conquest of Cubillas, Casares, Viadangos, the heights of Castro, mountains of Bermejas, and with special attention to the mountain of la Plaza, where both sides suffered a large number of casualties. For his participation he received congratulations in the daily report of operations: "**The Interim Corporal D. Luis Rosón Pérez, while commanding his *escuadra* that was covering and supporting the second group, arrived first at the objectives. He commanded his group with singular bravery and decision.**"

Captain Interventor Luis Rosón Perez, Chief Interventor and Administrator of the Blue Legion High Command.

During the early hours of 15 June he offered himself as volunteer for a surprise attack that was critical in conquering the position known as *Peña Muezca*. This action resulted in his again being congratulated in the daily report as follows:

"The Interim Corporal D. Luis Rosón Pérez, commanding five soldiers from his group, was the final one to reach la Peña and maintain the position. During all this time he was at the front line, encouraging his fellow soldiers, elevating their morale, and assisting the sergeant in the care of the wounded who could not be evacuated from the position."

He suffered a bullet wound to his head, but he did not get evacuated from the position.

On 9 November his Unit was assigned to duties to *Caderita* (*Navarra*) where they reorganized.

In 17 December, with the breakage of the Teruel Front by the Popular Army, they received orders to move to the front. They participated in battles at the positions of "*Los Molinazos*," "*Los Morrones*," and "*Las Ramblas*."

In February 20, 1938, they intervened in the assault to take the City, where his Unit received orders to cut the highway to Valencia.

During March he participated in advancing to the positions of the elevation 955, 965, 988, 992, *Vértice Galiana*, and *Puerto Escandón*, and the successive positions along the road to Sagunto.

On 4 June, and under the heavy offensive of the enemy at the elevation 1558, Puebla de Valverde Sector, he was again wounded. Once more he distinguished himself, because he remained in his position for two more counterattacks after having been inflicted wounds.

He was finally evacuated due to the nature of his wounds to the following Hospitals: Teruel, Mercantil de Zaragoza, Padernes (Bilbao), and finally Santander, where he had to undergo surgery for the removal of pieces of metal.

On 1 August he returned to and entered the Temporary Officials Academy of Avila, until his promotion to Alférez on 19 October.

He returned to the South Army at the 4th Cia. of the 5th Battalion of the Sicilia Regiment nº 8 in the 22 División with a new star.

In January 1939 he participated in the occupation operations of the province of Jaen, specifically those dealing with scouting, occupation, and disarmament of *La Sierra de Cazorla*.

At the end of the war he was assigned as Corps Judge to the Infantry Regiment No 30.

In 1941, after passing the required tests, he entered the *Academia de Intervention Militar* where he pursued the promotion to the position of Lieutenant Interventor. Once he received the same he was assigned to The General Intervention of the Army, where he received the promotion to Captain in February 1943.

On August 23, 1943, he received an assignment to the *División Española de Voluntaries*, and traveled in the same train as the Commissary 2ª Ponce, arriving at the *Hof Camp* on 9 September. Captain Ripoll received the duty of introducing Commissary Ponce and the Official Rosón to the German Authorities in Berlin.

He also traveled to the General Headquarters of the General Esteban Infantes at the Leningrad front, where he was assigned the duties of auxiliary official to the Intervention Chiefs.

On 21 November, after the dissolution of the Division, he returned to *Jambur* to the newly created Spanish Volunteer Legion, where he performed other duties in addition to the Intervention in the Chiefs of the High Command Administrative Staff.

On 16 December they left Jambur, in the Wolebow direction, to the Wesfalia sector, where he remained until the last days of January.

In February, due to the great Russian offensive, there commenced a general retreat from this front area. He was placed in charge of the Unit transport.

The situation was difficult, and in order to insure a safe and successful retreat he was forced to take command of the troops on several occasions (Kostowo, Ljibon, Skanoje, Waisco, Soponje...).

His actions were rewarded in the following certificate extended by García Navarro, the Colonel Chief of the Legion:

"During the retreat from the Mgá front on the way to Estonia, I had the occasion to observe how he directed and harangued the troops with intelligent, enthusiastic, and notorious and risky services...."

Fernando Vadillo, in his book *Balada Final de la División Azul, Los Legionarios*, told us the gravity of the situation :

"Twenty-one kilometers to the North of Lyuban, the Capitán Interventor Luis Rosón Pérez sees a Wehrmacht *car approaching. At the same time as the fire progresses in buildings illuminating with a sinister spirit the roads.*

-¡Halt! ¡Blau Legión!

The breaks sound while the cars stop.

-¡Ja, kameraden...!

The Captain exhales with relief. He has been waiting for the convoy that was promised by the Chief of Staff of the German side for long hours. It was an exhausting and nervous situation, since the Colonel Garcia Navarro gave him the order to recover the food, ordinances, and equipment that had been abandoned with the retreat. ...Roson, you must save as much as you can. Wait for

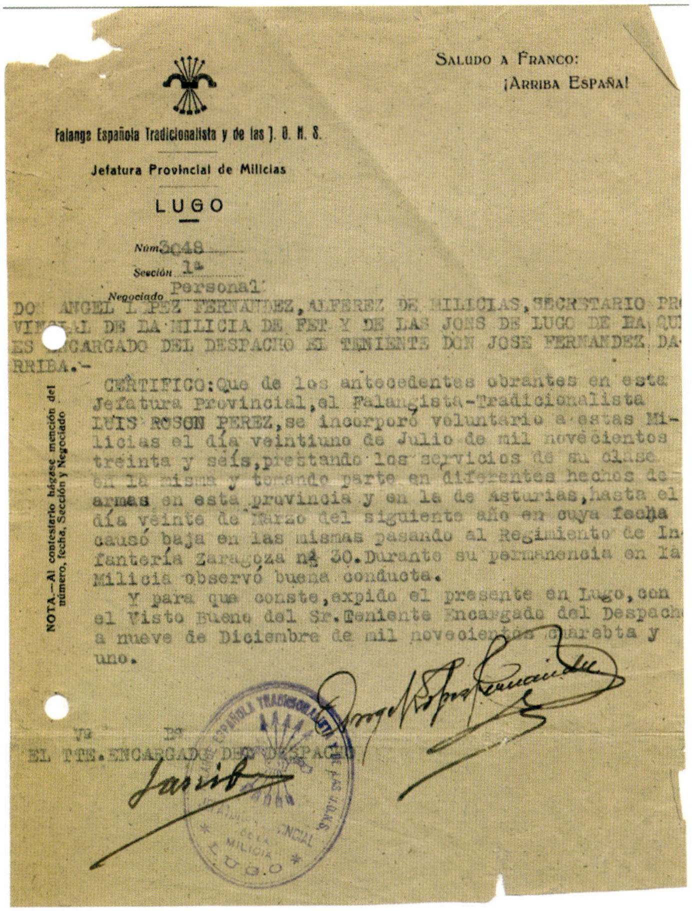

SALUDO A FRANCO:
¡ARRIBA ESPAÑA!

Falange Española Tradicionalista y de las J. O. N. S.

Jefatura Provincial de Milicias

LUGO

Núm. 3048

Sección 1ª

Negociado Personal

DON ANGEL LOPEZ FERNANDEZ, ALFEREZ DE MILICIAS, SECRETARIO PROVINCIAL DE LA MILICIA DE FET Y DE LAS JONS DE LUGO DE LA QUE ES ENCARGADO DEL DESPACHO EL TENIENTE DON JOSE FERNANDEZ DARRIBA.-

CERTIFICO: Que de los antecedentes obrantes en esta Jefatura Provincial, el Falangista-Tradicionalista LUIS ROSON PEREZ, se incorporó voluntario a estas Milicias el día veintiuno de Julio de mil novecientos treinta y seis, prestando los servicios de su clase en la misma y tomando parte en diferentes hechos de armas en esta provincia y en la de Asturias, hasta el día veinte de Marzo del siguiente año en cuya fecha causó baja en las mismas pasando al Regimiento de Infantería Zaragoza nº 30. Durante su permanencia en la Milicia observó buena conducta.

Y para que conste, expido el presente en Lugo, con el Visto Bueno del Sr. Teniente Encargado del Despacho a nueve de Diciembre de mil novecientos cuarebta y uno.

Vº Bº
EL TTE. ENCARGADO DEL DESPACHO

NOTA.—Al contestario hágase mención del número, fecha, Sección y Negociado

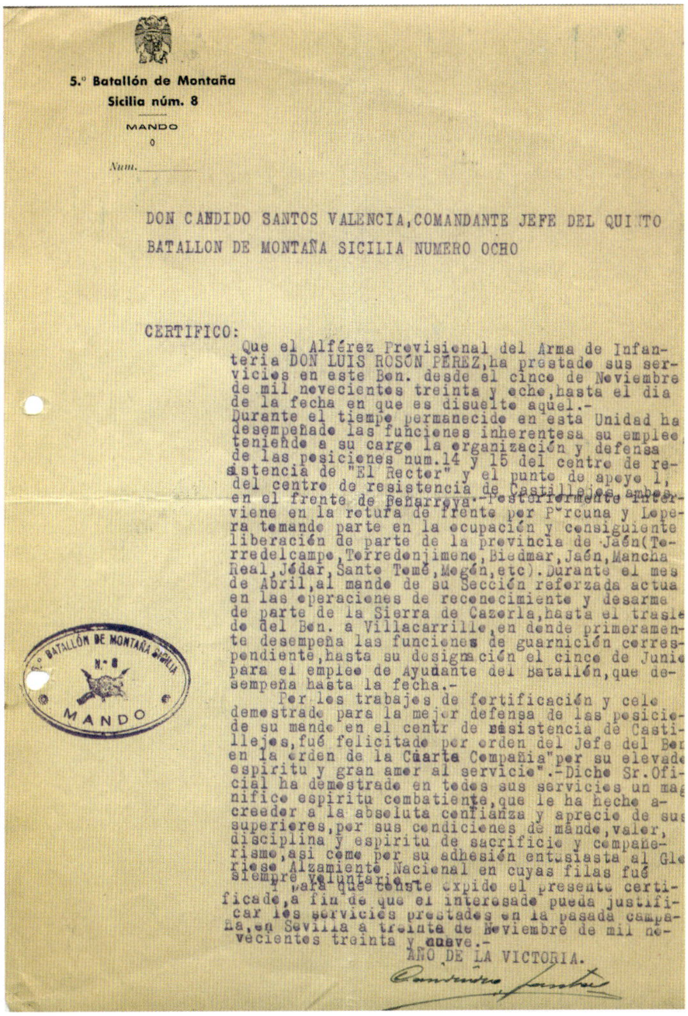

5.º Batallón de Montaña
Sicilia núm. 8
MANDO
Num.

DON CANDIDO SANTOS VALENCIA, COMANDANTE JEFE DEL QUINTO BATALLON DE MONTAÑA SICILIA NUMERO OCHO

CERTIFICO:

Que el Alférez Provisional del Arma de Infantería DON LUIS ROSON PEREZ, ha prestado sus servicios en este Bon. desde el cinco de Noviembre de mil novecientos treinta y ocho, hasta el dia de la fecha en que es disuelto aquel.-
Durante el tiempo permanecido en esta Unidad ha desempeñado las funciones inherentesa su empleo, teniendo a su cargo la organización y defensa de las posiciones num. 14 y 15 del centro de resistencia de "El Rector" y el punto de apoyo 1, del centro de resistencia de Castillejos, ambos en el frente de Peñarroya.- Posteriormente interviene en la rotura de frente por Porcuna y Lopera tomando parte en la ocupación y consiguiente liberación de parte de la provincia de Jaén (Torredelcampo, Torredonjimeno, Biedmar, Jaén, Mancha Real, Jódar, Santo Tomé, Mogón, etc). Durante el mes de Abril, al mando de su Sección reforzada actua en las operaciones de reconocimiento y desarme de parte de la Sierra de Cazorla, hasta el traslado del Bon. a Villacarrillo, en donde primeramente desempeña las funciones de guarnición correspondiente, hasta su designación el cinco de Junio para el empleo de Ayudante del Batallón, que desempeña hasta la fecha.-
Por los trabajos de fortificación y celo demostrado para la mejor defensa de las posiciones de su mando en el centr de resistencia de Castillejos, fué felicitado por orden del Jefe del Bon en la orden de la Cuarta Compañía "por su elevado espiritu y gran amor al servicio".- Dicho Sr. Oficial ha demostrado en todos sus servicios un magnifico espiritu combatiente, que le ha hecho acreedor a la absoluta confianza y aprecio de sus superiores, por sus condiciones de mando, valor, disciplina y espiritu de sacrificio y compañerismo, asi como por su adhesión entusiasta al Glorioso Alzamiento Nacional en cuyas filas fué siempre voluntario.-
Y para que conste expido el presente certificado, a fin de que el interesado pueda justificar los servicios prestados en la pasada campaña, en Sevilla a treinta de Noviembre de mil novecientos treinta y nueve.-
AÑO DE LA VICTORIA.

Rosón documents.

Radiotelegramas Vía Transradio Española para todo el mundo

BERLIN 657 37 12 1330 13 1100 DKJ JBM
ELT CORONEL ESTADA ESPAÑOLETO 13 MADRID
RUEGO COMUNIQUE A CAPITAN INTERVENCION LUIS ROSON PEREZ QUE POR
ORDEN JEFE E M C HA SIDO DESIGNADO FORMAR PARTE COMISION ARMAMENTO
DEPENDIENTE ESTA AGREGADURIA STOP DIGOLO EFECTOS INCORPORACION
STOP
AGREGADO MILITAR BERLIN

Radiogram from the Military Attaché to the Spanish embassy in Berlin.

Captain Rosón and Captain Auditor Santiago Pardo Canalis, The Legion War and Justice Auditor.

the truck convoy, follow my order, and follow us. You will catch up with us down the road...

...The last Spaniard to enter the dubious bunker of Lyuban were the Captain Interventor Roson, the Captain Payable De No, and a dozen sergeants and hundred "guripas" *that were picked up in their way. A few get down from two cars and a truck from Kosovo, while the others were packed like sardines in a couple of the* Wehrmacht vehicles, *whom Roson had convinced with a couple of bottles of liquor. The retreat was less expeditious and safe than was ever predicted. Captain Rosón will never forget the human sensations that were the product of the spectacle of a full and disorganized retreat. It was the fires, the abandoned towns, the explosions of the piles of ammunition and explosives, and the bridges—all hell broke loose, literally. The demolition units of the SS were the elite, and without a doubt due to their well trained methods and cold blooded ways the only ones putting up any fight at all. Their mission was to destroy anything that could be used by the Bolshevist army. If they could not disarm a piece of armament, they would blow it up. Bodies of animals and soldiers, cars, radios, kitchens, all went to the sides of the roads: -¡Schenell! ¡Wohlan! ¡Kehrt....!*

Behind then only a devastated scenario is left, almost like a maximum intensity earthquake will generate, while the sounds of the canons, projectiles, and explosives are mixed together and at once. Enormous fire embraces the last ones. Between these ones, the last forces of the La Legion Azul *finally arrived at Lyuban well into the night of the 23rd.*

-¡Rosón!

The Colonel García Navarro embraces his Captain, his PC.

- At your orders my Colonel.

- We were worried about your luck, Rosón. We were really worried, thinking you were not going to make it. Now I am rejoicing just to see you!

- Thank You.

But Lyuban was no peace oasis either...."

Finally, via Luga they arrived at the town of Pleskau, where the retreat ended.

At the same time, the diplomatic pressures continued to build up, and the dissolution of the Division was decided and the Unit was ordered to return home.

The Legion was regrouped and moved to Janeda, Reval, Riga, and Konigsberg (*Prusia Oriental*). Rosón was assigned to be the Interventor of the Liquidating Commission. In May 24, 1944, he finally crossed the border on his way back to Spain.

He was not back home for long. On May 16, 1944, the Spanish Embassy Military Attaché via Transradio communicated the following message:

Colonel Estada
Españoleto 13 Madrid.

Please inform Capitan of Intervention D. LUIS ROSÓN PEREZ, that the Chief of the High Command orders him to the position of Attaché.
To the incorporation effects.
The Embassy Military Attaché in Berlin.

In mid-June of 1944 he joined the Armament and Material Commission until February 15, 1945—the beginning of the Berlin battle. With Russian troops already at the suburbs of the city, he received orders to move all the Spanish Embassy personnel to Bern. They crossed the border position of St. Margarethen, at the German Swiss border, and reported to the Head of the Spanish Embassy. He moved his residence to Geneva.

At the end of the world conflict he received orders to organize an expedition to return Spanish refugees from Germany and other

Members of the Blue Legion Administrative High Command. Second from the left, a German officer " Beamten auf Kriegsdauer" (officers while at war).

European countries that had been concentrating in the neutral Swiss territory home.

The group train was assaulted in the French town of Chambery.

Rosón received the following awards during this conflict: Iron Cross 2nd Class for gallant attitude at the risk of life above and beyond the call of duty, *Cruz Roja al Merito Militar*, *Cruz de 2ª clase de Servicios de Guerra con espadas*, *Medalla conmemorativa de la Campaña de Rusia*, and a *Medalla conmemorativa de los Voluntarios españoles contra el Bolchevismo*.

He later held high positions in the political sector of the Spanish government. He was promoted to the General position, being named the Interventor General.

On November 21, 1984, he suffered a brutal terrorist attack by the vasque separatist group E.T.A., from which he miraculously saved himself, but the effects accompanied him to the end of his days physically and morally.

He passed away at Becerreá, Lugo, on September 28, 1995.

Captain Rosón and a German NCO at Danzig, Oriental Prussia, May 1944. Rosón will stay in Germany after the Legion repatriation, as a member of the liquidating commission.

Members of the Blue Legion Administrative High Command. Second and third from the left, German officers of the "Beamten auf Kriegsdauer" (officers while at war).

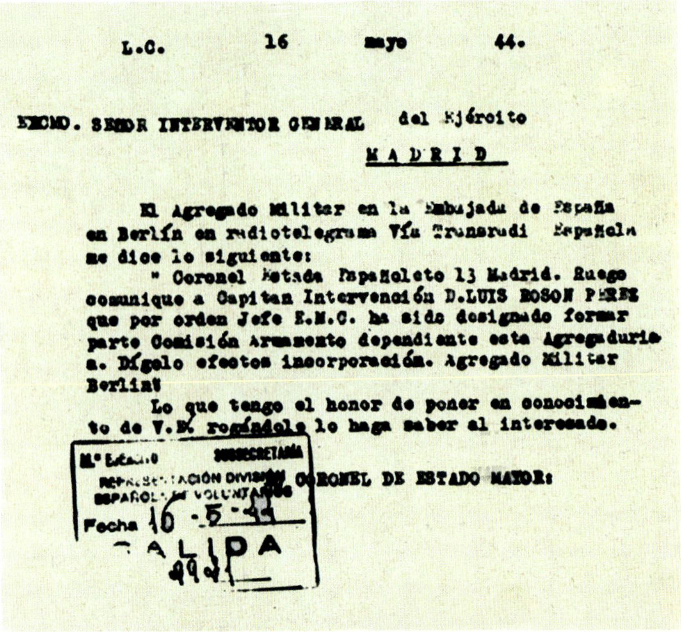

L.C. 16 mayo 44.

EXCMO. SEÑOR INTERVENTOR GENERAL del Ejército

MADRID

El Agregado Militar en la Embajada de España en Berlín en radiotelegrama Vía Transradio Española me dice lo siguiente:

" Coronel Estado Mayor Espalioleto 13 Madrid. Ruego comunique a Capitan Intervención D.LUIS ROSON PEREZ que por orden Jefe E.M.C. ha sido designado formar parte Comisión Armamento dependiente esta Agregaduría. Dígalo efectos incorporación. Agregado Militar Berlin"

Lo que tengo el honor de poner en conocimiento de V.E. rogándole lo haga saber al interesado.

EL CORONEL DE ESTADO MAYOR:

M° Estado SUBSECRETARIA REPRESENTACION DIVISION ESPAÑOLA DE VOLUNTARIOS Fecha 16-5-44 SALIDA 442

Above: Radiogram for Rosón. Below: The Blue Legion goodbye at Stablack-Süd, March 1944. Rosón still wearing the German Uniform. He remained two more months in the Reich territory.

The Infamy of Chambery

The almost unknown (for better words than a cover up) events in the French town of Chambery were a cowardly aggression, organized by the communist party and tolerated partially, if not instigated, by the French government.

Thanks to the personal archives of General Rosón, we made an exact description of what happened in this heroic "arms combat" practiced by the "*maquis*" and that, until now, was so little known. The inevitable fall of the Third Reich, and specially due to the brutal Soviet offensive, mobilized the Madrid government to repatriate all those Spaniards who desired it. Upon the transfer of the Berlin Embassy to Bern, they tried to concentrate all the compatriots in Switzerland, on the orders of the Spanish diplomatic delegation in Geneva.

The negotiations with the French Provisional Government began, and after several refusals, they approved a visa for transit through their territory. Four hundred seventy Spaniards obtained the permit with the condition that the Spanish authorities allow thirty thousand French refugees of the North Africa war to pass through Spanish territory who wished to return to their country.

Once the expedition was authorized, a French delegation was transferred to the Helvetic country where they extended, after an exhaustive investigation, a collective visa. The expedition was composed of civil employees, doctors, and Spanish scholarship holders, working Spaniards of the Thor organization, and refugees fled from Spain after our Civil War who, by their affability or by force, ended up working for the German industry of war.

The convoy left Bern in the direction of Montreux, where a French escort of twenty-eight members of the French Mobil Guard commanded by a lieutenant waited for them.

At two o'clock in the afternoon, as they were approaching the town of Chambery, the machinist sounded the train whistle three times, stopping the convoy. At the signal, a French multitude related to the "*maquis*" and accompanied by some exiled Spanish, in a well thought and planned military action, and with the absolute acquiescence of the official escort, assaulted the train.

During the aggression they struck without mercy and with extreme violence women, children, patients, and wounded; some were undressed, and all of them were robbed of the few belongings they possesed. All type of abuses and rape of the passengers were committed.

In the train traveled an ex-sergeant, Primitivo Benavente Perez. Boxer, volunteer of the Blue Division and Legion, that after the repatriation of the Legion decided not to abandon his comrades in arms and enlisted in the Wallon Division, to the orders of Leon Degrelle, with whom he participated in the Berlin defense. He escaped the city to finally fall prisoner to the U.S. troops, who sent him to a concentration camp from which he managed to escape and traveled up to Switzerland. Presented in the Spanish Legation, his falsified documentation passed the examination of the French Police delegation.

After several incidents with some exiled Spanish communists, and due to the fear caused by the information facilitated after the escape and passage to France of several of them, as well as the threats appearing in several articles published by the Swiss communist party, he decided to hide a pistol in the train that Captain Rosón had obtained. That decision would be miraculous.

During the heat of the assault he managed to recover the weapon and to infiltrate the locomotive, forcing the machinists to return to Switzerland under his gun. After their return to the Helvetic country, they were sent to the concentration camp Laplaine by the Swiss authorities, where they remained nine days. Practically all of the passengers had to be treated for contusions, and seventy-two in critical condition had to be hospitalized. At least two of the travelers passed away because of the wounds received. Seven women who traveled pregnant had miscarriages that night.

The Spanish Government immediately filed a formal complaint, to which the French Government answered, alleging that the attack was committed by uncontrolled people, and that the escort had not acted out of fear to hurt some other members of the expedition. The Spanish diplomats weakly accepted the explanation without answering in a more strong way, such as that it was an act of infamy.

Once freed on 21 June, Captain Rosón traveled to St. Gallen, where he was put in charge of the Spanish Legation in Bern of all matters related to personnel sheltered in Switzerland and pending repatriation to Spain. On 26 November he received the following order:

His Excellence, Mr. Luis Calderon and Martin, Spanish Minister at Bern:

CERTIFY: That the Commander Don Luis Rosón has been assigned to direct and escort the Spanish refugees train departing from Chiasso to a final destination in Genoa, the 28th of this month.

All personnel must obey this Commander's instructions related to the well being of the expedition.

Bern at 26 of November, 1945.

Finally, on 28 November the expedition left, and crossed the border with Italy by Chiasso to arrive at the port of Genoa. Here they boarded the "*Plus Ultra*," finalizing their journey to Barcelona on December 1, 1945.

Writing to the Spanish Ambassador in Switzerland, both of them thanked the extraordinary effort and treatment given to them by the Italians and the Allies. The Ambassador was reminded in the letter that there were still twenty refugees that were too scared to travel out of the Embassy.

Once in Spanish territory a request form was presented, along with a complaint signed by the totality of the refugees. They received, as answer, that the government was making all efforts to recover their belongings.

In 1948 *Commandant* Rosón sent the Chief General of the Joint Chief Staff the following communication:

YOUR EXCELLENCE:

DON LUIS ROSÓN PÉREZ, Commandant Interventor assigned to the Army Polytechnic School, to his Excellence reports and respectfully presents the following report:

I was assigned in the Commission of Material and Armament Purchases under the chain of command of the Military Attachment to the Spanish Embassy in Berlin, to which I belonged until I received orders to return to Spain via Switzerland having completing my mission due to the military situation of Germany in February 1945.

After residing several month in Switzerland, I started traveling back to Spain in the train transporting the Spanish workers and colony in Germany and suffered the attack and looting of the train in Chambery.

Upon returning to Switzerland, I cursed the elementary report describing my recollection of the mentioned acts that was transmitted to your Excellency by the Spanish Military Attaché in Bern.

That after returning to Spain December 1, 1945, I requested verbally of the Colonel Chief of the 2nd Section of the High Command the postponement of any resolution about my indemnification, to which I had merits until the Spanish Authorities were able to recover all the stolen property that was publicly known to be under the custody of the Chief of Police of Chambery.

Said petition was based and made with the intention of being paid by the Army Ministry, since the real loss was his personal belongings that counted with personal memorabilia of great sentimental value that he was informed was being transported back in a truck, saving it from the thieves unlike the rest of the passengers' belongings.

Since their arrival I have been able to salvage some of the articles in question, but I need to send to your Excellency a list of the articles that were stolen or lost with the intention of fulfilling all the elementary steps for achieving the official indemnification. I respectfully request to be paid.

God Bless Your Excellency Many Years,

In Madrid 18 of March, 1948.

The Official answer was devastating:

MINISTRY OF THE ARMY
Undersecretary

RESERVED

Your Excellence:

In relation to your request 2ª1º negotiated nº B-200, of the 30th of March ppdº, which documented the instance of the Commander Interventor D. LUIS ROSÓN PEREZ, with

destiny in the Army Institute of Technology, for payment for the losses suffered in the assault of the train suffered when traveling for repatriation to Spain, in Chambery (France) of June 15th, 1945.

I have the honor to inform V.E, that the case of the Colonel military attaché to the former Embassy of Spain in Germany, D. CARLOS MARÍN DE BERNARDO, and of the lieutenant colonel assistant military attaché D. IGNACIO MOYANO ARAIZTEGUI was raised before the proper authorities, and the government maintained the criterion of not granting indemnification in these cases to any one of the plaintiffs.

God will guard V.E. many years
Madrid, 3rd of May, 1948

GENERAL UNDERSECRETARY
P.O.
SECRETARY GENERAL

Excmo. Lieutenant General, Head of the Joint Chiefs Staffs of the Army
Casa

Due to the response, the affected ones decided to try again, for which they delegated all the actions to Commander Rosón, who on 29 September wrote to the Spanish authorities.

This unpublished document, directed to the Minister of Foreign Affairs, Mr. Alberto Martin Artajo, relates to us through one of the protagonists, in the name of all the others, what really happened:

Excmo. Sir:

Don LUIS ROSÓN PEREZ, attorney at law, of legal age, married, with residence in this capital, at the Marques of Urquijo street, No. 33, before V.E. appears, and exposes:

First. - That by order and in representation of the four hundred seventy Spaniards who approximately constituted the contingent of repatriated personnel coming back from Germany, which suffered the assault and sacking of the train in which they were returning to Spain on the 15th of June of 1945 in Chambery (France). Being the one exposing one of them, elevates to V.E. the present request.

Second. – Using as background the plea herein summarized later, the purpose of this writing, to point out the circumstances in which generically concur the victims of the vandalism and uncivil act, and those others actions that are related to the evacuation of the Spanish refugees coming from Switzerland.

A. - Groups that constituted the repatriated mission:

1º) – Public Officials: Chancellors of the Embassy of Spain in Berlin, Consulate of Prague, Commander and Captain of the Army, and civil employees of the Ministry of Work, who were both directing the convoy, and Spanish phalange members in Berlin.

2º) - Spanish Families with permanent residence in Germany.

3º) - Spanish Scholarship holders who were taking studies in Germany and contracted Doctors.

4º) - Workers controlled by the C.I.P.E.T.A.

5º) - Spanish Workers in Germany coming as refugees in France after our War of liberation.

All the personnel who traveled in the mentioned group had valid Spanish documentation, and their stay outside Spain and directly in Germany was properly legalized and authorized, even the ex-refugee cases which were not a direct consequence of the official and public functions assigned to them.

B. - Circumstances under which the trip was made:

The trip returning to Spain from Germany of the Spanish refugees in Switzerland had official character, and was conceived and projected under the direct responsibility of the corresponding state organisms.

The previous affirmation rests in a set of reasons that schematically are expressed:

1º) - It was organized by the C.I.P.E.T.A. in direct communication with the Ministry of Foreign Affairs, Paris Embassy, and legation in Bern.

2º) - It was directed by official order of a Delegate sent to Switzerland by the C.I.P.E.T.A (Mr. Catalá, and in agreement with our Government instructions).

3º) - It was mandated, although in many cases it was not wanted by the affected personnel. The mandatory nature of the trip is reflected in the directive note of the Spanish Legation in Bern issued with the clear intention that the person, or people, who did not make the trip would not enjoy any subsidy or protection. Which, in fact, translated also to the Swiss police not extending the leave of permanence in territories of the Confederation.

4º) - The trip was made under the protection of an escort of the French Mobil Guard, who would not be provided if the referred train did not have the character of official transport.

5º) - The trip was preceded by a detailed examination of the documentation of each one of the then presumed travelers made by the French Police, in territory of the Helvetic Confederation and with the approval of the Spanish representation.

C. - Determining Reasons for the incident of Chambery:

The sacking and aggression suffered by the components of the mentioned train were not evidently a casual act. The circumstances surrounding the act clearly indicated with exactitude their precedence.

The offensive against the Spanish refugees in Switzerland, coming from Germany, was initiated by one active campaign written in the different numbers of the newspaper "*the Voix Ouvriére*" of Geneva (organ of the communist party), and that was echoed by the French press.

With impunity a thesis was developed regarding non-Spanish people traveling between the refugees. Also there was the climate of an active participant of those just defeated, that aside from low, was more in line with the campaign at those moments developed against our Government and our country.

The origin of the sacking and the aggression was due more for the personality of the refugees, than due to certain fact that they returned to Spain and for that reason they were no longer "reds." In their special language, the attackers expressed their hatred of us for being "Franco supporters." The eagerness of aggression was not towards the concrete people who traveled in the train, but rather the aggression, the depredation, and the insult was towards Spaniards whose greater crime was that they were returning to their Mother country, considered a "fascist" country at the time.

The aggression was, on the other hand, inconceivable if we take in consideration that all the components of the train "had been examined and judged" by a Court of the French Police, which could and in fact did exclude all those they considered should not travel from amongst the Spanish refugees then in Switzerland.

There were in the organization of the transport evident failures. One that was conveniently ignored was that the Government of Paris did not control, at those moments, all the Departments by which the convoy was to pass, and it is not unjust to maintain the position that in such conditions the collective trip was inconceivable.

The aggression was a preconceived plan with which the Committees of Resistance were familiar. The Committees at that time dominated the zones of passage of the mentioned train.

D. - Reach and consequences of the aggression and the sacking:

From the 470 people who traveled in the train, approximately 200 were injured of greater or smaller gravity. As a result of the injuries, there were some members who later died in Switzerland. Other injuries were also irreparable.

As far as the looting, it can only be said that nothing was left, absolutely nothing, in the train, and that many travelers were even deprived of their clothes and shoes.

The reach of the suffered losses varied. Many lost all their means of life (families with permanent residence in Germany, some civil employees, etc...), while others lost the results of years of effort, since their income had translated into "things of value" as a result of the lack of value of the money in the country. Others lost their scientific or technical works, summaries of many years of effort. All lost everything they had.

To that it is necessary to add, the moral damages and prejudice suffered by the loss of the additional five months of all the professional or labor activities.

Also, the Spanish State would have to pay a great invoice of expenses that constituted the support of the refugees, in better or worse conditions, during the five months after the incident, while they stayed in Switzerland.

E. - Recovery of objects:

The rest of the looted luggage had arrived in Spain, and except for a few articles everything was a rotten pile of things. Everything was unacceptable, and nothing arrived completely. Dirty remainders that only to a few could have some sentimental value.

F. - Present Situation:

All the people present in the mentioned train believe that, in justice, we have the right to indemnification for the damages, dangers, and injuries suffered.

Individual complete declarations must be a part of the archives of that Ministry, and also in the Ministry of the Interior (General Directory of Charity and Social Works), in which was cursed a file of information to later credit the losses as well as the limited recoveries.

In this file were only reported and filed claims of the material damages, not of the morals, nor by of injuries or death, etc. At the moment, the normalization of economic relations with France has shown signs surely of the improvement of the political approach between the governments. For that reason, it seems it has arrived reframed and in due terms, the hour once again, that the victims of the incident of Chambery elevate before the State the plea for our demand.

In doing so, we think that the organ upon whom it is incumbent to reach a suitable resolution is the Ministry of Foreign Affairs, and it is for these reasons that I respectfully request and present:

a). - The facts occurred outside Spain, and we were the direct and unique victims, the Spaniards traveling in the assaulted train.

b). - The attackers, plunderers, and aggressors were citizens of a third country: France.

c). - The determining cause of the incident was a general political reason that affected, in its intention and aims, our Mother country as a whole, more than the people who were the direct victims.

d). - The offense was so direct against Spain that its existence and meaning were gathered in the Official Note of

offenses that our Government issued with the closing of the Spanish-French border in 1946.

By all the issues exposed, to V.E. we PLEA,

You must consider the receipt of the present writing and consider the different points exposed, to decide:

That the Ministry of Foreign Affairs, for pertinent resolution concluded in its file that on the losses in the assault of the train of Spanish refugees was recorded on the 15th of June, 1945 in Chambery (France), and was followed by the Ministry of the Interior (General Directory of Charity and Social Works).

Agree or replace in the Government's name such file, should be completed and finished with a justice indemnification, and to that effect be reclaimed of the French state such indemnification.

Which I plea to V.E. in my own name and in representation of the victims of Chambery, I consider it just for the previously exposed reasons.

God will guard V.E. many years
Madrid, 29th of September of 1949

The request was never addressed. The delicate diplomatic situation by which Spain crossed began to alleviate itself with the approach of the U.S. The creation of the G.D.R., and every time more influential Soviet policy, finished with the Potsdam agreements, and later with the evacuation of the ambassadors.

In 1950 Spain was admitted into the United Nations. It was not the moment for international claims. The Infamy of Chambery only remains in the memory of the people who suffered it…

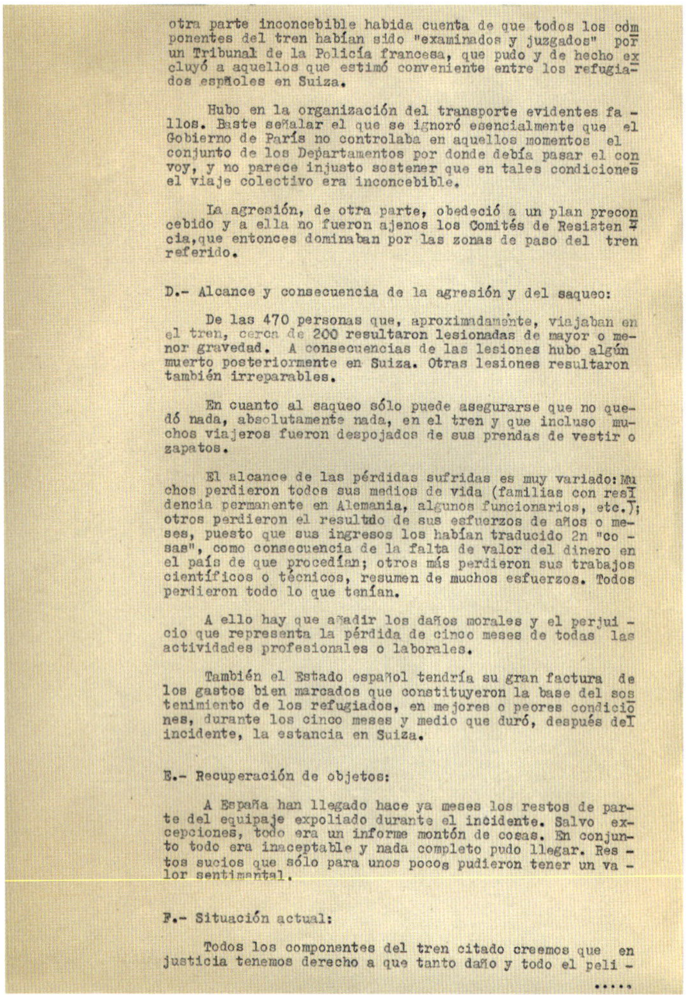

otra parte inconcebible habida cuenta de que todos los componentes del tren habían sido "examinados y juzgados" por un Tribunal de la Policía francesa, que pudo y de hecho excluyó a aquellos que estimó conveniente entre los refugiados españoles en Suiza.

Hubo en la organización del transporte evidentes fallos. Baste señalar el que se ignoró esencialmente que el Gobierno de París no controlaba en aquellos momentos el conjunto de los Departamentos por donde debía pasar el convoy, y no parece injusto sostener que en tales condiciones el viaje colectivo era inconcebible.

La agresión, de otra parte, obedeció a un plan preconcebido y a ella no fueron ajenos los Comités de Resistencia, que entonces dominaban por las zonas de paso del tren referido.

D.- Alcance y consecuencia de la agresión y del saqueo:

De las 470 personas que, aproximadamente, viajaban en el tren, cerca de 200 resultaron lesionadas de mayor o menor gravedad. A consecuencias de las lesiones hubo algún muerto posteriormente en Suiza. Otras lesiones resultaron también irreparables.

En cuanto al saqueo sólo puede asegurarse que no quedó nada, absolutamente nada, en el tren y que incluso muchos viajeros fueron despojados de sus prendas de vestir o zapatos.

El alcance de las pérdidas sufridas es muy variado: Muchos perdieron todos sus medios de vida (familias con residencia permanente en Alemania, algunos funcionarios, etc.); otros perdieron el resultado de sus esfuerzos de años o meses, puesto que sus ingresos los habían traducido 2n "cosas", como consecuencia de la falta de valor del dinero en el país de que procedían; otros más perdieron sus trabajos científicos o técnicos, resumen de muchos esfuerzos. Todos perdieron todo lo que tenían.

A ello hay que añadir los daños morales y el perjuicio que representa la pérdida de cinco meses de todas las actividades profesionales o laborales.

También el Estado español tendría su gran factura de los gastos bien marcados que constituyeron la base del sostenimiento de los refugiados, en mejores o peores condiciones, durante los cinco meses y medio que duró, después del incidente, la estancia en Suiza.

E.- Recuperación de objetos:

A España han llegado hace ya meses los restos de parte del equipaje expoliado durante el incidente. Salvo excepciones, todo era un informe montón de cosas. En conjunto todo era inaceptable y nada completo pudo llegar. Restos sucios que sólo para unos pocos pudieron tener un valor sentimental.

F.- Situación actual:

Todos los componentes del tren citado creemos que en justicia tenemos derecho a que tanto daño y todo el peli -

.....

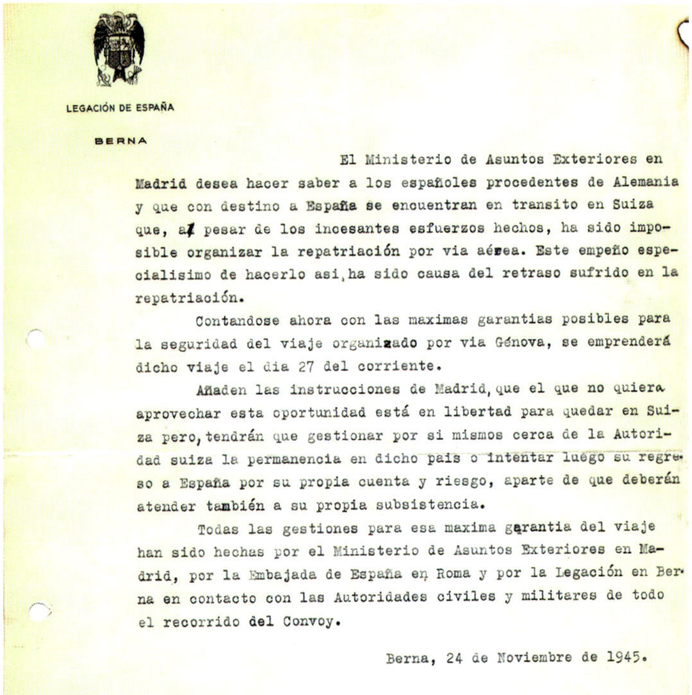

LEGACIÓN DE ESPAÑA

BERNA

El Ministerio de Asuntos Exteriores en Madrid desea hacer saber a los españoles procedentes de Alemania y que con destino a España se encuentran en transito en Suiza que, a pesar de los incesantes esfuerzos hechos, ha sido imposible organizar la repatriación por via aérea. Este empeño especialisimo de hacerlo asi, ha sido causa del retraso sufrido en la repatriación.

Contandose ahora con las maximas garantias posibles para la seguridad del viaje organizado por via Génova, se emprenderá dicho viaje el dia 27 del corriente.

Añaden las instrucciones de Madrid, que el que no quiera aprovechar esta oportunidad está en libertad para quedar en Suiza pero, tendrán que gestionar por si mismos cerca de la Autoridad suiza la permanencia en dicho pais o intentar luego su regreso a España por su propia cuenta y riesgo, aparte de que deberán atender también a su propia subsistencia.

Todas las gestiones para esa maxima garantia del viaje han sido hechas por el Ministerio de Asuntos Exteriores en Madrid, por la Embajada de España en Roma y por la Legación en Berna en contacto con las Autoridades civiles y militares de todo el recorrido del Convoy.

Berna, 24 de Noviembre de 1945.

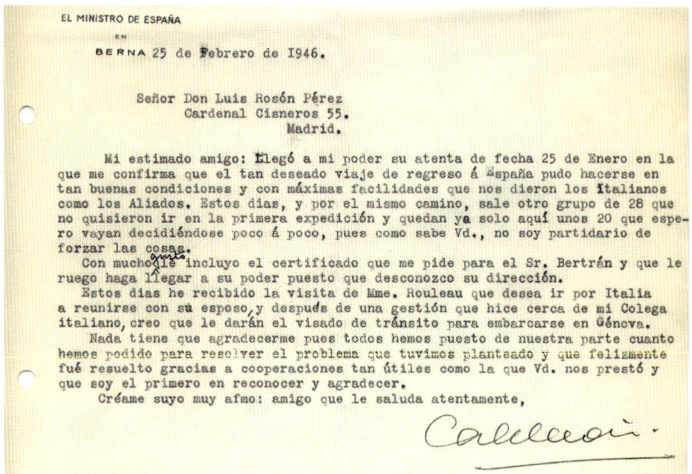

EL MINISTRO DE ESPAÑA
EN
BERNA 25 de Febrero de 1946.

Señor Don Luis Rosón Pérez
Cardenal Cisneros 55.
Madrid.

Mi estimado amigo: Llegó a mi poder su atenta de fecha 25 de Enero en la que me confirma que el tan deseado viaje de regreso á España pudo hacerse en tan buenas condiciones y con máximas facilidades que nos dieron los Italianos como los Aliados. Estos dias, y por el mismo camino, sale otro grupo de 28 que no quisieron ir en la primera expedición y quedan ya solo aquí unos 20 que espero vayan decidiéndose poco á poco, pues como sabe Vd., no soy partidario de forzar las cosas.

Con mucho gusto le incluyo el certificado que me pide para el Sr. Bertrán y que le ruego haga llegar a su poder puesto que desconozco su dirección.

Estos dias he recibido la visita de Mme. Rouleau que desea ir por Italia a reunirse con su esposo, y después de una gestión que hice cerca de mi Colega italiano, creo que le darán el visado de tránsito para embarcarse en Génova.

Nada tiene que agradecerme pues todos hemos puesto de nuestra parte cuanto hemos podido para resolver el problema que tuvimos planteado y que felizmente fué resuelto gracias a cooperaciones tan útiles como la que Vd. nos prestó y que soy el primero en reconocer y agradecer.

Créame suyo muy afmo: amigo que le saluda atentamente,

Calderón

Excmo. Señor:

Don LUIS ROSÓN PÉREZ, Licenciado en Derecho, mayor de edad, casado, con domicilio en esta capital, calle de Marqués de Urquijo, número 33, ante V.E. comparece y como mejor proceda expone:

Primero.- Que por encargo y en representación de los cuatrocientos setenta españoles que, aproximadamente, constituían el contingente de repatriados procedentes de Alemania, que sufrieron el asalto y saqueo del tren en que realizaban el viaje de regreso a España, acaecido el 15 de Junio de 1945 en Chambery (Francia), entre los cuales figuraba el propio exponente, eleva a V.E. el presente escrito.

Segundo.- Como antecedentes de la súplica que resume, posteriormente, la finalidad de este escrito, estima indispensable hacer constar las circunstancias que concurren genéricamente en las víctimas del vandálico e incivil hecho y aquellas otras en que se realizó la evacuación de los refugiados españoles desde Suiza.

A.- Grupos que constituían el conjunto de los repatriados:

1º) - Funcionarios públicos: Cancilleres de la Embajada de España en Berlín, Consulado de Praga, Comandante y Capitán del Ejército y funcionarios del Ministerio de Trabajo, entre los cuales estaban los dos que mandaban el convoy, y funcionarios de Falange Española en Berlín.

2º) - Familias españolas con residencia permanente en Alemania.

3º) - Becarios españoles que estaban ampliando estudios en Alemania y Médicos contratados.

4º) - Trabajadores controlados por C.I.P.E.T.A.

5º) - Trabajadores españoles en Alemania procedentes de refugiados en Francia después de nuestra Guerra de Liberación.

Todo el personal que viajaba en el expresado tren tenía su documentación española en regla y su estancia fuera de España y más concretamente en Alemania, estaba debidamente legalizada y autorizada, aun en el caso del pequeño número de ex-refugiados, cuando no era consecuencia directa del desempeño de funciones oficiales y públicas.

B.- Circunstancias en que se realizó el viaje:

El viaje de regreso a España de los refugiados españoles en Suiza, procedentes de Alemania, tuvo carácter ofi

.....

cial y fué concebido y proyectado bajo la responsabilidad directa de los organismos estatales correspondientes.

La afirmación anterior descansa en un conjunto de razones que esquemáticamente se expresan:

1º) - Fué organizado por C.I.P.E.T.A. en relación con el Ministerio de Asuntos Exteriores, Embajada en París y Legación en Berna.

2º) - Fué dirigido por encargo oficial por un Delegado enviado a Suiza por C.I.P.E.T.A. (el Sr. Catalá) y de acuerdo con instrucciones de nuestro Gobierno.

3º) - Fué obligatorio, pese a que en mucho casos no fué querido por los interesados. La obligatoriedad del viaje queda reflejada en la nota conminatoria de la Legación de España en Berna concebida en el sentido de que la persona o personas que no efectuasen el viaje no gozarían de subsidio ni de protección, con lo que la Policía suiza no prorrogaba los permisos de permanencia en territorio de la Confederación.

4º) - Se realizó el viaje bajo la protección de una escolta de la Guardia Móvil francesa, que no se concedería si el tren referido no tuviese el carácter de transporte oficial.

5º) - El viaje fué precedido de un examen detenido de la documentación de cada uno de los entonces presuntos viajeros realizado por la Policía francesa, en territorio de la Confederación Helvética y con la tolerancia expresa de la representación española.

C.- Motivos determinantes del incidente de Chambery:

El saqueo y la agresión de que fueron víctimas los componentes del tren mencionado, no fué evidentemente un incidente casual. Las circunstancias en que ocurrió ponen de relieve la exactitud de tal certidumbre.

La ofensiva contra los refugiados españoles en Suiza, procedentes de Alemania, fué iniciada por una activa campaña en contra de los mismos que quedó para siempre escrita en distintos números del periódico "La Voix Ouvriere" de Ginebra (órgano del partido comunista) y que fué recogida por la prensa francesa.

Impunemente se desarrolló la tesis de que existían personas no españolas entre nuestros refugiados, así como el clima de un colaboracionismo activo de aquéllos con los pueblos entonces recién derrotados, que aparte de mendaz, era interesado en la campaña que en aquellos momentos se desarrollaba contra nuestro Gobierno y nuestro país.

El saqueo y la agresión, tuvieron por origen, más que la personalidad de los refugiados, el hecho cierto de que regresaban a España y por ello no eran aquéllos rojos. En su lenguage especial expresaban los asaltantes su odio a nosotros por "franquistas". No fué un afán de agresión hacia las personas concretas que viajaban en el tren, sino la agresión, la depredación y el insulto hacia unos españoles cuyo mayor delito era que regresaban a su Patria, entonces, al menos, considerada país "fascista". La agresión personal era de

.....

gro o las lesiones sufridas sean objeto de una adecuada indemnización.

Sendas declaraciones juradas deben figurar en los archivos de ese Ministerio y también en el de la Gobernación (Dirección General de Beneficencia y Obras Sociales) en el que fué seguido un expediente o información para acreditar las pérdidas como también posteriormente las limitadas recuperaciones.

En dicho expediente se trató de los daños materiales, no de los morales; tampoco de los derivados de lesiones o muerte, etc.

En estos momentos se ha iniciado la normalización de relaciones económicas con Francia, signo seguramente del mejoramiento de las políticas, y por ello parece llegada la hora de que, una vez más, y replanteado en sus debidos términos el incidente de Chambery, los damnificados en aquél elevemos ante el Estado nuestra súplica y también nuestra demanda.

Al hacerlo creemos que el órgano a quien compete la resolución adecuada, es el Ministerio de Asuntos Exteriores, y ello por razones que me honro en exponer:

a) - Los hechos acaecieron fuera de España y de ellos fuimos víctimas directas y únicas los españoles que veníamos en el tren asaltado.

b) - Los asaltantes, saqueadores y agresores eran ciudadanos de un tercer país: Francia.

c) - La causa determinante del incidente fué un motivo político general que afecta, en la intención y en los fines, a nuestra Patria como unidad total, más que a las personas concretas que resultamos víctimas directas.

d) - El agravio fué tan directo contra España que su existencia y significación fué recogida en la Nota Oficial de agravios que publicó nuestro Gobierno en ocasión del cierre de la frontera hispano-francesa en el año 1946.

Por todo lo expuesto, a V.E.

S U P L I C A tenga a bien considerar como recibido el presente escrito y estimando sus distintos extremos acordar.

Que el Ministerio de Asuntos Exteriores reivindique para la resolución pertinente el expediente que sobre las pérdidas sufridas en el asalto del tren de refugiados españoles acaecido el 15 de Junio de 1945 en Chambery (Francia) fué seguido en el Ministerio de la Gobernación (Dirección General de Beneficencia y Obras Sociales).

Acordar o proponer que por parte de nuestro Gobierno se resuelva tal expediente con la indemnización que sea procedente en justicia o, alternativamente, se reclame del Estado francés tal indemnización.

Todo lo cual suplica a V.E. en nombre propio y representación de los damnificados de Chambery, por estimarlo de justicia por las razones expuestas anteriormente.

Dios guarde a V.E. muchos años.

Madrid, 29 de Septiembre de 1.949.

EXCMO. SEÑOR

DON LUIS ROSON PEREZ, Comandante-Interventor con destino en la Escuela Politécnica del Ejército, ante V.E. comparece y respetuosamente, expone:

Que estuvo destinado en la Comisión de Compras de Armamento y Material dependiente de la Agregaduria Militar de España en Berlin a la que perteneció hasta el momento en que por la Superioridad se ordenó su salida para España, via Suiza, como consecuencia de la terminación de la misión de aquélla a causa de la situación militar de Alemania en el mes de Febrero de 1.945.

Que después de varios meses de estancia en Suiza inició su viaje a España en el tren que transportaba a la Colonia y trabajadores españoles en Alemania, habiendo sufrido el asalto y pillaje de dicho tren en la estación francesa de Chambery.

Con tal motivo, y a su regreso forzado a Suiza, formuló el correspondiente parte relatando sus vicisitudes desde la salida de Alemania y relacionando las pérdidas sufridas en el asalto y pillaje mencionados, que fué transmitido a V.E. por el entonces Agregado Militar de España en Berna.

Que a su regreso a España el 1 de Diciembre de 1.945 solicitó verbalmente del Sr. Coronel-Jefe de la 2- Sección de ese Estado Mayor se aplazase cualquier resolución sobre la indemnización que pudiera corresponderle por las pérdidas sufridas hasta que nuestras Autoridades Diplomáticas consiguiesen la recuperación del resto de los equipajes sustraidos que se sabia custodiaba el Prefecto de Policia de Chambery.-

Tal petición estaba fundada en el deseo del que suscribe de evitar al Ministerio del Ejército el pago de la indemnización, con el consiguiente ahorro para aquél, a la vez que en la preferencia de recuperar su equipaje en el que figuraban objetos y recuerdos de un valor de afección superior al que pudieran tener

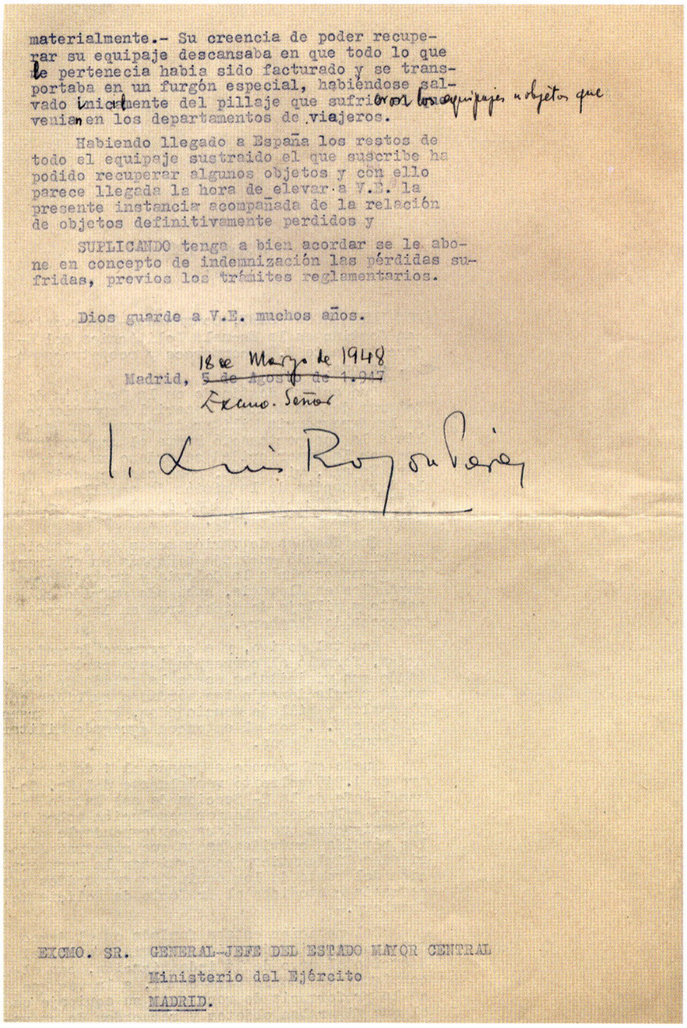

materialmente.- Su creencia de poder recuperar su equipaje descansaba en que todo lo que le pertenecia habia sido facturado y se transportaba en un furgón especial, habiéndose salvado únicamente del pillaje que sufrieron los equipajes u objetos que venian en los departamentos de viajeros.

Habiendo llegado a España los restos de todo el equipaje sustraido el que suscribe ha podido recuperar algunos objetos y con ello parece llegada la hora de elevar a V.E. la presente instancia acompañada de la relación de objetos definitivamente perdidos y

SUPLICANDO tenga a bien acordar se le abone en concepto de indemnización las pérdidas sufridas, previos los trámites reglamentarios.

Dios guarde a V.E. muchos años.

Madrid, 18 de Marzo de 1948 ~~5 de Agosto de 1.947~~

Excmo. Señor

EXCMO. SR. GENERAL-JEFE DEL ESTADO MAYOR CENTRAL
Ministerio del Ejército
MADRID.

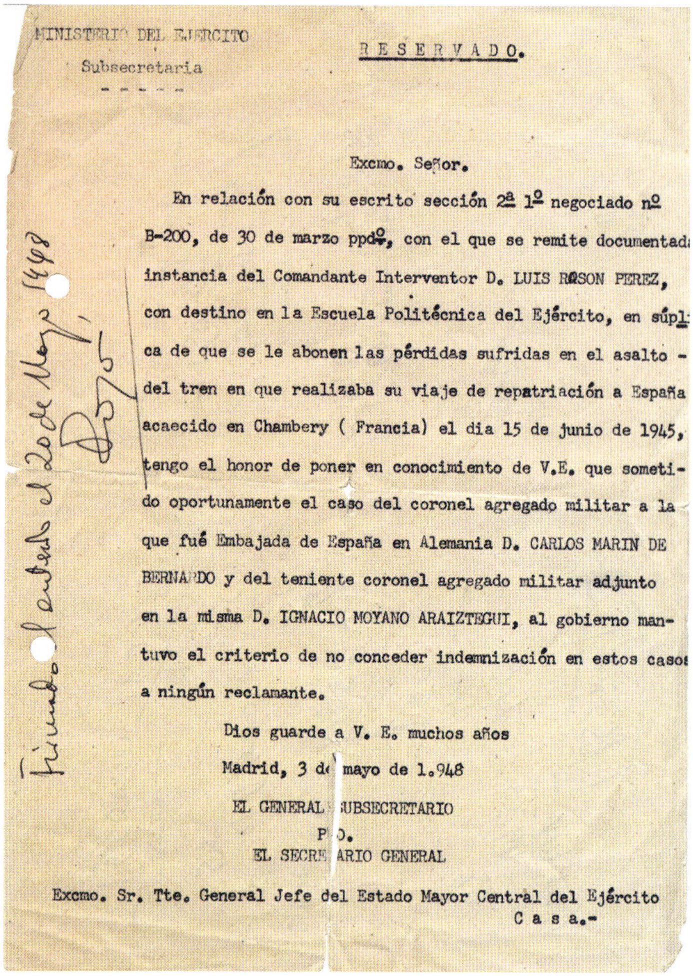

MINISTERIO DEL EJERCITO
Subsecretaria

RESERVADO.

Excmo. Señor.

En relación con su escrito sección 2ª 1º negociado nº B-200, de 30 de marzo ppdº, con el que se remite documentada instancia del Comandante Interventor D. LUIS ROSON PEREZ, con destino en la Escuela Politécnica del Ejército, en súplica de que se le abonen las pérdidas sufridas en el asalto del tren en que realizaba su viaje de repatriación a España acaecido en Chambery (Francia) el dia 15 de junio de 1945, tengo el honor de poner en conocimiento de V.E. que sometido oportunamente el caso del coronel agregado militar a la que fué Embajada de España en Alemania D. CARLOS MARIN DE BERNARDO y del teniente coronel agregado militar adjunto en la misma D. IGNACIO MOYANO ARAIZTEGUI, al gobierno mantuvo el criterio de no conceder indemnización en estos casos a ningún reclamante.

Dios guarde a V. E. muchos años

Madrid, 3 de mayo de 1.948

EL GENERAL SUBSECRETARIO
P. O.
EL SECRETARIO GENERAL

Excmo. Sr. Tte. General Jefe del Estado Mayor Central del Ejército
Casa.-

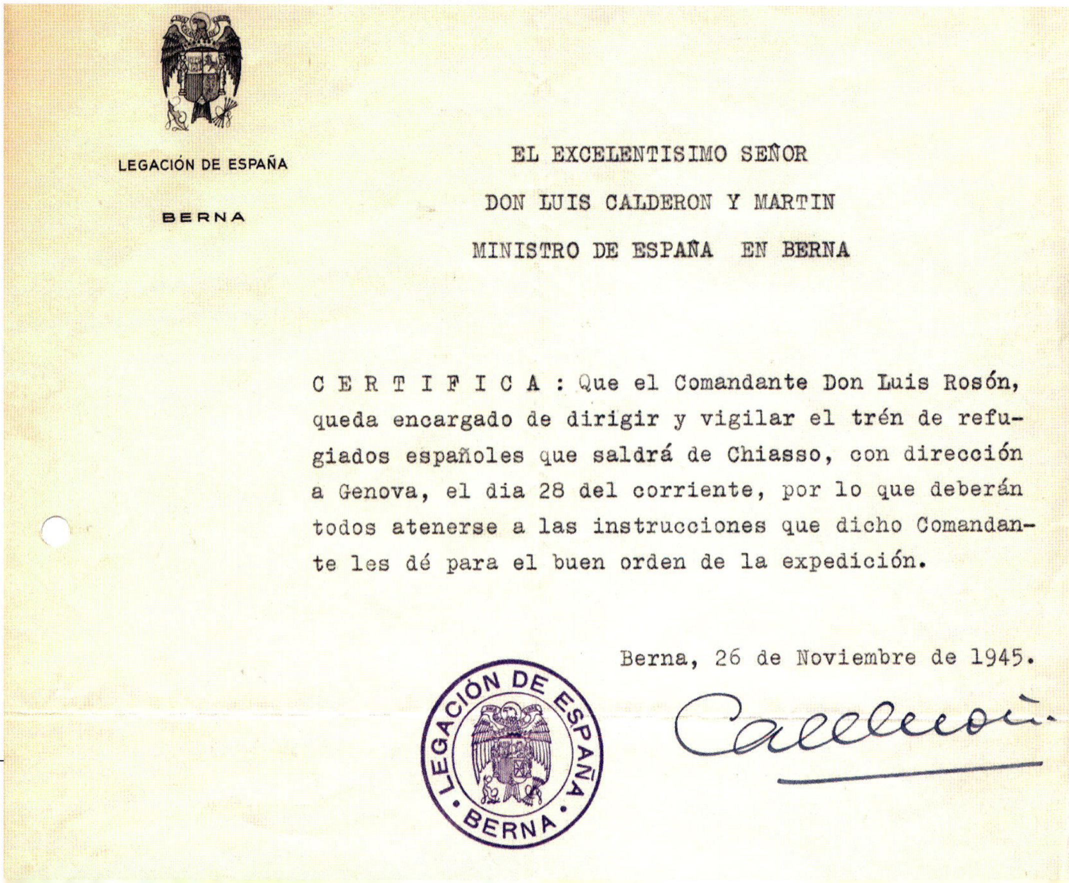

LEGACIÓN DE ESPAÑA
BERNA

EL EXCELENTISIMO SEÑOR
DON LUIS CALDERON Y MARTIN
MINISTRO DE ESPAÑA EN BERNA

C E R T I F I C A : Que el Comandante Don Luis Rosón, queda encargado de dirigir y vigilar el trén de refugiados españoles que saldrá de Chiasso, con dirección a Genova, el dia 28 del corriente, por lo que deberán todos atenerse a las instrucciones que dicho Comandante les dé para el buen orden de la expedición.

Berna, 26 de Noviembre de 1945.

The Volunteers in Russia

We cannot neglect the opportunity to speak of three other volunteers who at their return from Russia would enter the Intervention Corps.

Lieutenant of Artillery, Manuel Nieto Rioboo.

Manuel Nieto Rioboo, Artillery Complement Lieutenant, 1941. (Archives Nieto)

Navy soldier Nieto Rioboo (second from the right) on board the Cruise Canarias, where he participated in numerous combats. (Archives Nieto)

The Canarias cruise, September 1936. (Archives Nieto)

He was a mercantile Professor. At the beginning of the uprising of July 18, 1936, he enlisted as a volunteer on 22 July in the Infantry Regiment Zamora No. 29, which later formed part of the Knights Militia of *La Coruña*, where he served until 22 September. He embarked on board the Canary Islands cruise as a volunteer sailor, where he participated in numerous actions of arms.

On May 21, 1937, he was admitted, as a cadet, to the Academy of Provisional Alfereces of Artillery in Alcala de Guadaira (Seville), arriving on 25 May. On 30 June he was promoted, being destined to the 16th Artillery Regiment in the 8th Corps of the Army, where he incorporated on 1 August.

On 1 October, under the command of colonel Muñoz Grandes, he moved to the front of *Asturias*, at the *Riaño* sector, being incorporated to a Mountain Artillery Battalion.

On 25 October he was hospitalized with a serious disease in the Oviedo hospital, later being transferred to the Red Cross in Lugo hospital. He was discharged on January 1, 1938, returning to the High Command of the Regiment.

Alferez (then) Nieto during the Spanish Civil War. (Archives Nieto)

Above and Below: Germany, August 1941.(Archives Nieto)

By Order of 21 January he received a commission to the First Gun Battalion of 75/27 cm in Artillery Regiment No. 15, which at that time was at the front of Teruel, a sector of Torrecilla del Rebollar, then participating in operations to stabilize the Teruel Front.

On 1 March he was transferred to the Galicia Army, to participate in the offensive towards the east. On March 11, 1939, while in the temporary command of his battery, he was promoted to Provisional Lieutenant of Artillery, being destined to the Reconnaissance Battery of the 43rd Regiment, with quarters in Paterna.

On January 4, 1940, he was destined as a professor to the Academy of Sergeants, in which he served until 24 April, when he returned to Artillery Regiment No. 48, taking control of the 3rd Battery.

Volchof Front, November 1941. (Archives Nieto)

By the Order of March 5, 1941, he was sent to cover a vacancy as a Cadet at the Military Academy of Artillery. However, he did not appear in the Segovia center because he applied for the position of Cadet to the Military Intervention Academy.

On 16 July he embarked to Germany as an officer in the Spanish Division of Volunteers. After the period of training in the Camp of Grafenwöhr he marched towards the Eastern Front, as liaison officer of the High Command of the 3rd Group.

On 19 August, and without the authorization of the Lieutenant, the Division in the *Españoleto* street received the following memorandum signed by his Exc. Manuel Vicente Nieto and Nieto, father of the officer and man of great prestige and influences in La Coruña.

His Excellence General-Undersecretary of the Ministry of the Army

Excellence Sir:

***MANUEL VICENTE NIETO Y NIETO*, 54 years old, married, with residence in *La Coruña*, domiciled in Betanzos street, No. 1-2nd left, to V.E., respectfully exposes:**

That he is the father of the Artillery Officer MANUEL NIETO RIOBOO, member of Regiment No. 48, with quarters in La Coruña, whom had opportunely requested by the chain of command to be able to present his application to the vacancies at the Military Intervention Corps.

That at the moment, the mentioned Officer is incorporated in the Blue Division, created to fight communism; but informed whom subscribes, by his good faith, of the most vivid desire that his mentioned son has to be considered for the advertised vacancies, for being a Corps with a greater relation to his professional field of Mercantile Intendant.

He pleas to V.E that to avoid damages and prejudice that could result from Lieutenant of Artillery Manuel Nieto Rioboo, to order a reclamation to the Unit to which he belongs, in order to be able to assist in the procedures to fill the advertised vacancies.

Grace he hopes will be granted by V. E., and asking God guards you for many years.

In Madrid, 19th of August of 1941.

Riga, December 1941. (Archives Nieto)

Nieto's marriage.

The protests of the Officer were not accepted, and he was ordered to leave the Front. On 4 December he crossed the border, returning to Spain. During this tenure he received the Medal of the first winter.

Above: 3rd Military Intervention Corps promotion. In the middle, kneeling, is Lieutenant Interventor Manuel Nieto wearing the Campaign medal, and with the German style band of the first winter. (Archives family Dolado) Right: Nieto being congratulated by General Franco.

Incorporated to the Military Intervention Academy, he was not able to finish the academic year. On July 27, 1942, the Colonel Director of the Center, by memorandum No. 826, and in fulfillment of the requisition made by the Chief General of Military Education and Training, ordered him to drop from the rolls, since he exceeded the permitted leave of attendance by missing classes on a third of the lecture days.

Again he returned to his Unit in La Coruña, where he was destined to the Headquarters of the Regional Intervention of the 8th Military Region. On September 1, 1943, he was accepted as an Intervention Cadet to the General Military Academy, in which he obtained his first star. On 11 January he went to the Corps Academy in Madrid, from which he left as a Lieutenant Interventor on 27 December, being destined to the Intervention Headquarters of the 8th Military Region.

Left: Volunteer Manuel Guijarro Agero. Right: Old Guard of Phalange medal with the First Line band. (Archives Guijarro Family)

Volunteer, Manuel Guijarro Agero.

During the Spanish Civil War he was enlisted at 15 years old, with a Century of Spanish Phalange. He actively participated in the bloody operations of the Alcubierre mountain range.

When the Military Command discovered his age he was ordered to leave. He refused to leave until his Unit was released from duty, an act for which he received a commendation in Order of the Army Corps.

On July 2, 1941, he enlisted as a volunteer and crossed the Hispanic-French border.

After his preparation and fidelity oath at the camp of Grafenwörh, he marched thousands of kilometers on foot with his unit to the Russian front. He was destined to the machine guns Section of the 4th Company, 3rd Battalion of Regiment 262.

On 15 November he crossed the Voljov in the direction of Possad, participating in one of the most terrible battles that ever surrounded this Unit. On 28 December, and after several refusals, he was evacuated, because he was suffering first degree freezing wounds in both feet. In February 1942 he returned, destined position known as "The finger," where they received the hardest Russian attacks, especially those that took place on 3 April.

He returned to Spain in the month of July and entered the Corps in March 1946.

For his performance at the front he received the Medal of the First Winter, the Military Merit Red Cross, and a War Cross.

Group of volunteers: first on the right, Manuel Guijarro Agero, Grafenwörh, 1941. (Archives family Guijarro)

Guijarro being congratulated by General Franco.

Volunteer Jaime Dolado Gonzalo.

Volunteer, D. Jaime Dolado Gonzalo.

On October 25, 1935, at twelve years of age, he decided to join the Phalange's Spanish Students Union (SEU), militating in the squads of "*Balillas*" at the Institute *Cardinal Cisneros* (achieving, in spite of his young age, the assistant representative position). He participated actively in the anxious days of the prewar in Madrid.

After the arrest of all the Political Group of the Spanish Phalange, and its dissolution after being declared an illicit association (both police actions were declared illegal and null by the Supreme Court), the "*Balillas*" assumed an important role as the ones in charge of transmitting the orders given from the prison by the Phalange command, guardians of compromising documentation, and of the transport and concealment of weapons. They were the targets of continuous aggression on behalf of the Marxist militias.

The uprising of 18 July surprised him in the Spanish province of Soria, where he was recovering from a fractured leg in the house of a priest named Eliseo Gonzalo. The priest, along with Colonel Muga, prepared the uprise movement in that Spanish province.

Given his physical incapacity at the moment, all his attempts to escape to fight at the front were frustrated by his family. Finally resigned to his destiny, he accepted to teach the "*Cara al Sol*" (Spanish Phalange Hymn) to the local militias. He also collaborated in the Provincial Hospital, reading and writing with the wounded.

He returned to Navarre in August 1936, having been named the head of the phalange's O.J (Youth Organization) of Pamplona. There he would make several attempts to escape to the front.

In 1937, and with the absence of combatant military groups at the time in the city of Pamplona, he participated, being fourteen years old, in the confrontations and capture of the fugitive prisoners of San Cristóbal Fort.

Upon the conclusion of the War he returned to Madrid to continue his studies in the Institute Cardinal Cisneros.

In the summer of 1941, as soon as the inscription pennants opened for the roster of volunteers to the Blue Division, he used his personal condition as founder of the *SEU* and falsified the documentation relative to his age (making it appear that he was older than he really was), getting enlisted in the Spanish Division of Volunteers. But as soon as he entered the Quarter, given his

With the cape, volunteer Jaime Dolado Gonzalo, Volchof Front, March 1942. (Archives Dolado)

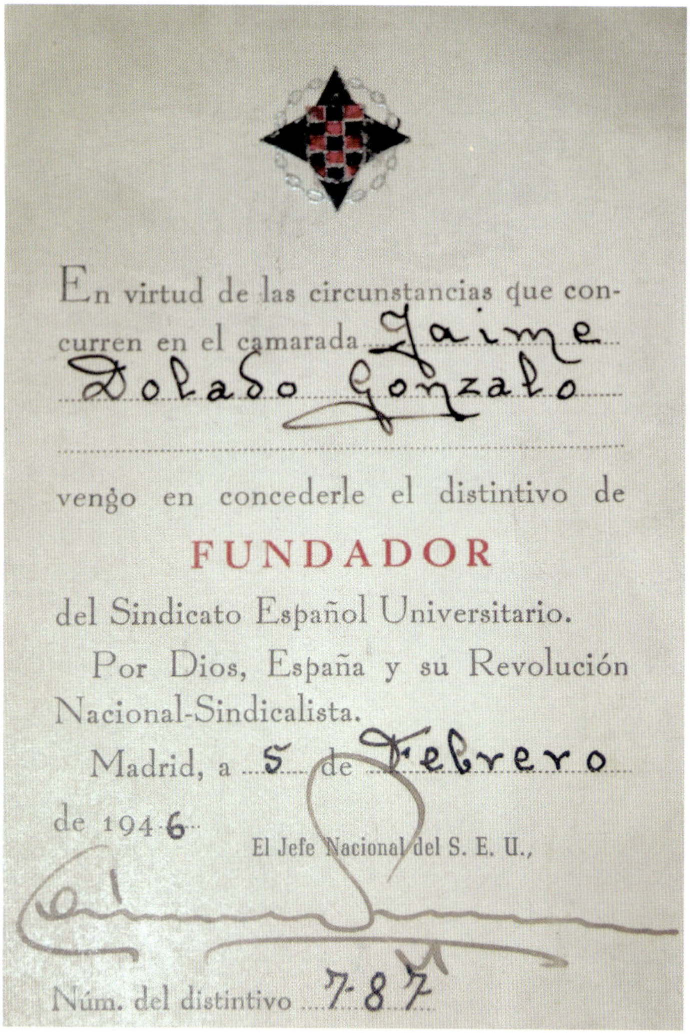

En virtud de las circunstancias que concurren en el camarada Jaime Dolado Gonzalo

vengo en concederle el distintivo de

FUNDADOR

del Sindicato Español Universitario.

Por Dios, España y su Revolución Nacional-Sindicalista.

Madrid, a 5 de Febrero de 1946

El Jefe Nacional del S. E. U.,

Núm. del distintivo 787

SEU founder diploma.

young appearance, his deceit was quickly discovered, and he was immediately rejected.

Not being satisfied with this action, he decided with three other "*Balillas*" to try again. This time they planned better. After selling their clothes and books at the famous flea market in Madrid, and with the money thus obtained they purchased military articles that helped them to disguise their youth.

On January 3, 1942, with no money in their pockets to make the trip, they embarked like stowaways on a train going to San Sebastian. Upon arriving at the *Burgos* station, one of them was arrested because his family had made a plea for his capture. The others made it and continued their trip.

Upon their arrival at the Basque capital they discovered the absence of an Enlistment Pennant, because the prepared expedition of volunteers had been fitted with military units.

They returned to Madrid, and had to promise not to try again. He returned to his studies until the middle of January when, passing by an Office of Recruitment, he decided to get ready and enlist again. He departed on 8 February towards the Quarter of Loyola in San Sebastian, crossing the border on the 24th. He arrived in Germany at Camp Hof - Saale on the 28th.

After the period of preparation and the Oath of Fidelity, he left for the Russian Front on 15 March, arriving at Novgorod on 25 March, where he remained in a period of training until 23 April, and was incorporated, as a rifleman, to the 3rd Section of the 5th Company 2nd Infantry Battalion of Regiment 263 at the front at the Voljov.

In the month of May he was transferred to the first Section, having rendered services of connection.

On 23 June the Lieutenant Colonel, Chief of the 2nd Section, received the following request from Spain:

His Excellence, Minister General Secretary of the Party

Don Jose Dolado Bicondo, of 51 years of age. National teacher of Ororbia (Navarre) and accidentally addressed in Madrid, street of the River No. 20, father of the phalangist Jaime Dolado Gonzalo of 18 years of age, volunteer in the glorious "Blue Division" and at the moment destined in the 2nd Battalion of Esparza, with quarters in Nowgorod (North Sector), to V.E. respectfully exposes:

That due to the delicate state of health of my wife, and mother of the volunteer mentioned above, condition that has been worsening since the march, that he made guided by a strong phalangist's ideal, without my consent and taking advantage of having been studying in Madrid, reason why I did not have the news of his leave; I direct this request to you V.E., in order to request a favor for the good, and if you think it may be convenient, to issue the necessary orders for him to return to Spain from his voluntary assignment.

A grace that we hope to attain of your excellence's kind heart, and whose life God will keep for many years, for the good and welfare of our loved Spain.

Madrid, May 10, 1942

Volunteer Dolado Gonzalo driving a car.

During one of the habitual visits to the Units of General Muñoz Grandes he was interested in this case, calling the volunteer to his presence.

Ironically, the General affirmed:

• *So poorly are we now, that we must bring the children to War?*

The answer, full of firing ardor could not be more direct:

• *The fields of Spain are full of youngsters' tombs, and many of them, much younger than I, who gave their life for the Mother country.*

After a congratulation from the General the request was denied.

During his stay at the front lines he volunteered on a multitude of occasions. Mentionable was the night raid of the enemy positions located at Chutiny on 30 July, for which he was congratulated by his superiors.

SEU emblem.

On 26 August, while on active guard duties, he was rescued from a state of unconsciousness because of palúdic fevers, and evacuated from the front to the field hospitals Luga and Plescao (Russia). He was moved later to Allesteine and Konigsberg (Germany).

When he was discharged from the hospital, in spite of the request for return to his Unit at the front, a direct order of the Director of the Hospital Fernando Garcia Santandreu left him with the sanitary detachment, whereby his behavior with his wounded comrades earned him 10 days permission to Spain in July 1943.

During his tenure in this detachment he participated in several expeditions for evacuation of wounded volunteers. In August 1943 he was given the *loss* condition from the Unit due to being repatriated, although he did not leave Germany until the end of September 1943. Commander Garcia Santandreu named him as his assistant during a medical commission ordered by the Spanish Government. Finally, after traveling via Czechoslovakia, Austria, and Germany, he returned to Berlin, initiating a trip to return to Spain. He crossed the French-Hispanic border on 1 October.

He was awarded the Medal of the First Winter, and on January 26, 1945, was given the right to use the symbol of Founder Member of the SEU on his uniform.

On June 26, 1944, he received notice of being granted a scholarship from the *Deussches Studienwerk für Ausländerpor* (German student work for foreigners) from the Institute of German Culture. He had to return to Germany to study Sound Engineering in the Superior Technical School of Dressden.

The definitive change in the course of the war, along with the indiscriminate bombings of allied aviation on civil targets and objectives, did not permit this trip to be realized. Returning to

Military and German civilian personnel at the Cathedral of Prague. On the right, with the Spanish uniform, are Medical Commandant Fernando Garcia Santandreu and volunteer Jaime Dolado Gonzalo. (Archives Dolado)

Knight Alferez Cadet Interventor Jaime Dolado with his future wife, Elena Esteban Ureta. (Archives Dolado)

study in Spain, he received a degree in Economic Sciences from the Central University of Madrid, entering the Intervention Corps in 1950.

MINISTERIO DEL EJERCITO
DIRECCION GENERAL DE RECLUTAMIENTO Y PERSONAL
NUM. 10
Reclutamiento

Se autoriza a JAIME DOLADO GONZALO, perteneciente al reemplazo de 1.944, actualemnte con permiso de 3 años, 2 meses y 10 días, para que pueda trasladarse a Alemania al objeto de que pueda seguir los estudios de Ingeniero de Sonidos en la Escuela Supeiror de Dresde, para la que le ha sido concedida una beca.

Madrid, 28 de Julio de 1.944.

De Orden de S.E.
EL TENIENTE CORONEL DEL S.E.M. JEFE ACCIDENTAL DE LA SECRETARIA.

MINISTERIO DEL EJERCITO — DIRECCION GRAL. DE RECLUTAMIENTO Y PERSONAL

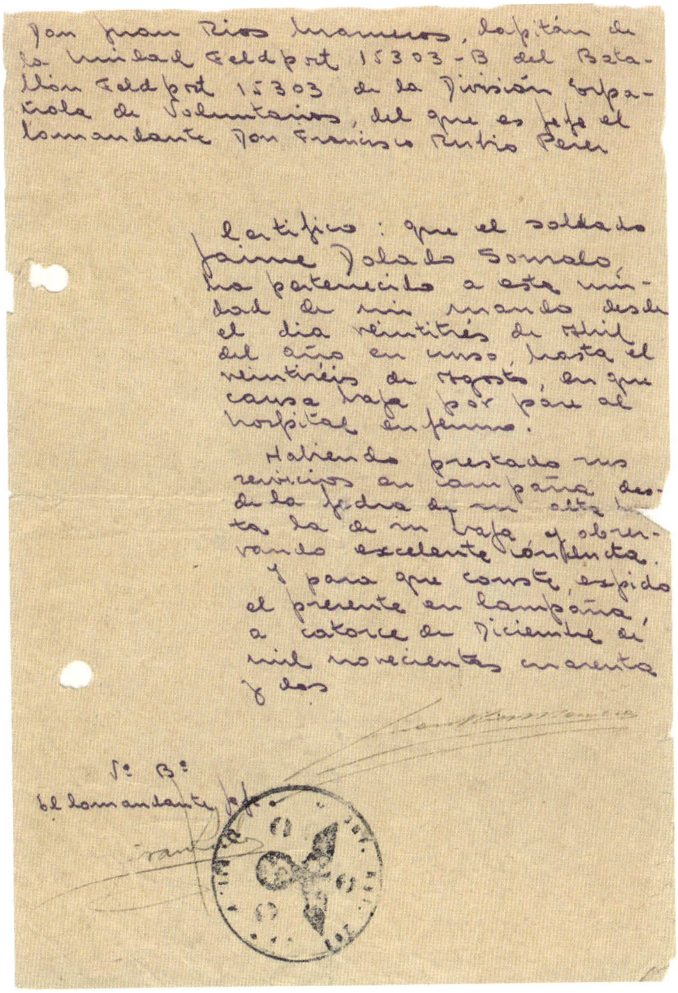

Don Juan Ríos Moreno, Capitán de la Unidad Feldpost 15303-B del Batallón Feldpost 15303 de la División Española de Voluntarios, del que es Jefe el Comandante Don Francisco Rubio Pérez

Certifico: que el soldado Jaime Dolado Gonzalo, ha pertenecido a esta unidad de mi mando desde el día veintitrés de Abril del año en curso, hasta el veintiséis de Agosto, en que causa baja por pase al hospital enfermo.

Habiendo prestado sus servicios en campaña desde la fecha de su alta hasta la de su baja y observando excelente conducta.

Y para que conste, expido el presente en Campaña, a catorce de Diciembre de mil novecientos cuarenta y dos

Vº Bº
El Comandante Jefe

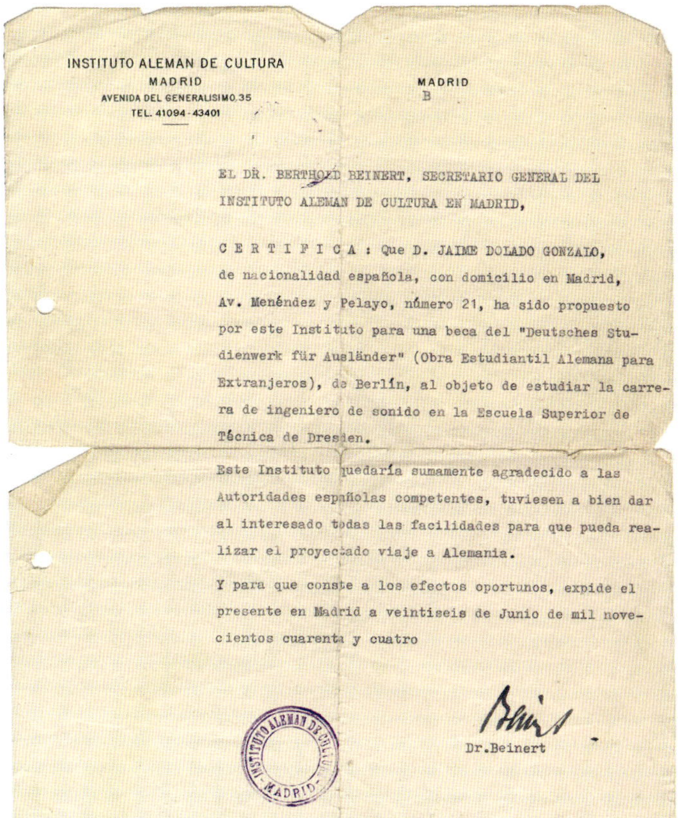

INSTITUTO ALEMAN DE CULTURA
MADRID
AVENIDA DEL GENERALISIMO, 35
TEL. 41094 - 43401

MADRID
B

EL DR. BERTHOLD REINERT, SECRETARIO GENERAL DEL INSTITUTO ALEMAN DE CULTURA EN MADRID,

C E R T I F I C A : Que D. JAIME DOLADO GONZALO, de nacionalidad española, con domicilio en Madrid, Av. Menéndez y Pelayo, número 21, ha sido propuesto por este Instituto para una beca del "Deutsches Studienwerk für Ausländer" (Obra Estudiantil Alemana para Extranjeros), de Berlín, al objeto de estudiar la carrera de ingeniero de sonido en la Escuela Superior de Técnica de Dresden.

Este Instituto quedaría sumamente agradecido a las Autoridades españolas competentes, tuviesen a bien dar al interesado todas las facilidades para que pueda realizar el proyectado viaje a Alemania.

Y para que conste a los efectos oportunos, expide el presente en Madrid a veintiseis de Junio de mil novecientos cuarenta y cuatro

Dr. Beinert

INSTITUTO ALEMAN DE CULTURA — MADRID

The Uniforms

It has already been discussed in the uniform chapter regarding the civil employees' uniforms of the German Military Administration. We did not try to do an exhaustive study on uniforms, as we are attempting to present the different uniforms used by the components of the Intervention Corps during its permanence in the Blue Division.

When speaking of the uniforms used by the voluntary interventors, we will distinguish between the Spanish and the German models.

The first one was used for the departure and return to Spain, as well as—in those cases in which, in Service Commission or to enjoy a permission—when it was necessary to return temporarily to Spain. On those occasions they deposited the German uniform, returning to dress in it after their return from Spain.

The second one was given by the Germans and used during their permanence in Germany, regardless of whether located on the front lines or in the rear positions.

The interventors, due to their classification as Chiefs and Officers, made use of the prescribed Army uniform, although we will distinguish between those obtained in the Division before and after the publication of the Uniforms Regulation of 1943.

The interventors incorporated between 1941 and 1942 started off with the 1926 uniform model. In this year, the obligatory nature of the use of a unique uniform was reached. The uniform, of khaki color, was used for all the Corps and Units, as well as for all the ranks or classes in the Spanish Army.

The Regulation established that the new single-breasted uniform jackets must have a turtle neck, with four pockets, and

Second Class War Commissary (assimilated to Commandant). Uniform model 1926 with officer cap. (Assoc. Retogenes)

Above: Intervention Corps Emblem (Sun with oak leaves) detail. Below: Intervention Corps Emblem (Sun with oak leaves) lapel detail.

D. Second Class War Commissary (assimilated to Commandant). Uniform model 1926 with officer beret and Phalange emblem. (Assoc. Retogenes)

E. Second Class War Commissary (assimilated to Commandant). Uniform model 1926 with officer beret and Phalange emblem. Detail. (Assoc. Retogenes). The Spanish government wanted to make clear that the Unit was composed of Volunteers. All the members had to wear two distinctive objects of National Movement Militia: the blue shirt of the Phalange and the red beret of the Traditionalists.

buttoned with five wood or paste buttons. In the collar of the single-breasted uniform jacket there was, embroidered or in metal, the emblem of the Weapon or Corps to which it belonged.

The mounting trousers had to be made of the same fabric as the single-breasted uniform jacket, although generally, and in spite of the direct prohibition, the denominated "golden purl" model was used, characteristic of Spain's corps and cavalry and frequently used by the officer class.

Without a doubt, the Phalange had the biggest influence in the creation of the Unit. So important, to the point that the "*mahon*" blue color of its uniform (the Phalange chose the blue color mahón for being "Serious, whole, and Proletarian"), the one that would give the name to the Unit by which it would be best known: The Blue Division.

The Spanish government had great interest in making clear that the new Unit was formed of volunteers, and not comprised of members of the Regular army. For this reason, it was decided that all their members would have on their uniform two articles characteristic of the militia of the National Movement: the blue shirt of Phalange, and the red beret of the traditionalist groups.

This decision did not have a great acceptance with either of the two "unified" groups by the Order of April 1937. Perhaps it was the Old Guard of the Phalange (almost all the prewar Phalange had been assassinated or killed in combat during the Civil War, and the few survivors did not doubt to enlist in this Unit).

Lieutenant Interventor Amaro and Pulido at their arrival at Hof. Both are wearing the officer uniform model 1926. (Archives Ripoll)

The "tomato," a contemptuous name given by the phalangists to the red beret, represented for them the hard line and nostalgic *carlismo*, dreamers of the monarchic restoration. The reader must realize that, in the words of the founder of the Phalange, Jose Antonio Primo de Rivera, that in theory it was a "gloriously dead" cause.

Regarding future interventors who were enlisted as troops, although for the first expedition all the privates and corporals were equipped with a uniform made up of single-breasted uniform jacket and trousers of a "chick-pea" color, of the model known as the "Norwegian." This clothing material came (according to Jose Mª Bueno in his work *The Division and the Blue Squadron*, edited by Aldaba Militaria) from captured warehouses of the republican Army.

The reality was the division members used a great variety of uniform articles when leaving Spain that had little or nothing to do with the described model.

In January 1943, and before the evident necessity to summarize in a single disposition concerns as to clothes and fighting equipment, D.O No. 24 was published, and by virtue of its approval the regulation was created as: Regulations of Uniformity, Dress and Equipment for the Spanish Army.

Lieutenant Interventor Amaro, Captain Cano, and Alferez Auslander with the new German uniform after swearing in ceremonies, Hof 1942. (Archives Ripoll)

Left: Members of the "Balillas" youth group on their way to Germany. Second from the left is the phalangist Jaime Dolado. (Archives Dolado) Right: The extremely young legionary Gregorio del Pozo, who came from the Youth Front organization to serve in the Blue Division and Legion. (Archives Del Pozo)

F. New Intervention Corps Emblem (Sun with oak leaves and the spade with the wheat shaft) detail.

The new Regulation, with clear German influence, is without a doubt the most complete of all the published regulations up to that time.

In its first chapter was defined what new emblems would be used for all the components of the Spanish Army: the Imperial Eagle, the Cross Sword of the Apostle Santiago, and the Imperial Crown.

In Chapter VII the branch insignias are regulated for the different Corps, Arms, and Services.

The traditional emblem of the Intervention Corps, a sun trimmed between oak leaves, was modified, adding the Sword and the Pen, and enclosing it all in a rhombus emblem.

The volunteers incorporated in the Battalions of March 1943, especially the officers, began to use it; even in the German uniform some of these new articles were used.

As to the uniformity and equipment effects, the volunteers had the same treatment as the rest of the German soldiers.

Upon their arrival to Grafenwörh or Hof, the Division members would change the Spanish uniform for the German.

Since this study is centered on the officers of the Interventors Corps, we will center our interest, mainly, in articles of uniform used by these officers, making a brief reference to those used by the sergeant majors and soldiers.

G. In January 1943, D.O. No. 24 published the new regulations for the Spanish Army. With a clear German influence, it was the most complete ever published. (Assoc. Retogenes)

Typical military closet drawing.

H. Typical military uniform worn by the Volunteers.

I. Typical military uniform jacket worn by the Volunteers. (Assoc. Retogenes)

Before we begin, we must recall that like the rest of the *Heer*, the uniforms of the troops and sergeant majors were distributed for free between the components of the Division (giving them the possibility of acquiring or improving certain articles on their own). This did not happen between the officers, who had the obligation to acquire their articles at the cost of their salaries.

Like the German legislation, the Spanish prohibited the exit of any amounts of money in cash from its national territory. Evidently, this norm denied the possibility of having sufficient monetary resources for the acquisition of articles that composed the new uniform.

In order to correct this problem, and with the purpose of being able to face the first expenses for their acquisition, the amount of 250 marks for each official was deposited in the Finance offices of each Unit. In addition to this economic contribution, and to avoid delay of the preparation and tailoring of the new uniforms, a basic uniform made up of regulation articles was distributed to them.

VII.= DIVISAS.

Las divisas que deberán usar los Jefes y Oficiales de Intendencia serán:

Para los procedentes de academia: en el cuello y hombreras y los de "Intendantur" poniéndose además en las hombreras una "I".

Los demás Oficiales o sea los Pagadores las del Cuerpo donde presten sus servicios con una "I" en las hombreras y los destinados en los Servicios de Intendencia las del Cuerpo de "Zahlmeister" con una "I" en las hombreras.

Spanish regulation of emblem use on the uniforms.

Captain Interventor Rosón wearing the typical Infantry jacket model 1941, September 1943. (Archives Rosón)

Typical German Infantry jacket worn by Volunteers.

Typical belt buckles of the German uniforms.

Captain Amigo of the 2nd Section Bis (Information regarding our troops) wearing the cords of the Patrol Services, Heerestreifendienst. (Archives Ripoll)

In order to take care of the maintenance and repair of uniform articles, the officers received an economic compensation denominated as "Clothing Bonus."

There were no specific norms as to the uniforms of the interventors of the Division, so in order to make this chapter, we based it on the transmitted information given to us by then Lieutenant Interventor Maximiliano Amaro Lasheras, destined then, via the orders of Captain Aramburu Topete, to the 3rd

Typical Spanish Arm patch.

Typical German *Kolbenstikerei* of the Superior Services Officers.

Typical German Infantry *Kolbenstikerei*.

Typical Officer Jacket with the Spanish Arm patch. (Militaria: Assoc. Retogenes)

Typical Spanish Catholic Sacred Heart patch. (Assoc. Retogenes)

Cap with the phalange silver symbol. Assoc. Retogenes)

Cap. (Assoc. Retogenes)

Above: Russian Cap. Right: Officer Cap. (both Assoc. Retogenes)

Officer with uniform next to a Junker airplane.

Typical cap without emblem, Model 42.

Left: Typical White colored emblem of Infantry cap. Right: Typical White colored emblem of Infantry cap, Model 38.

Above: Alferez Auslander with the Model 38 cap. Below left and right: Officer with typical cap without emblem, Model 42.

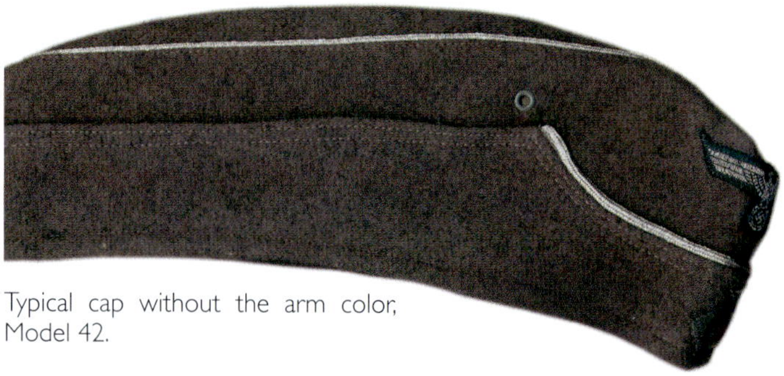

Typical cap without the arm color, Model 42.

From left to right: JAG Captain Serafin Pardo, Captain Villasevil, and Lieutenant Interventor Ripoll.

Above: Intendance Commandant Parra Mateo. (Archive Ripoll)

Typical cap with the silver treated edge ribbon, Model 42.

Officers group of the Blue Legion Headquarters. Second from the right, Captain Interventor Rosón. (Archive Rosón)

Above: Typical field cap, Model 43, detail. Below: Volunteer Gregorio del Pozo in the recently created Blue Legion. (Archive Del Pozo)

Extremely young volunteers in Krottingen, Lithuania, 1944. (Archive Del Pozo)

Company of Combat Engineers. In addition we used the personal and photographic archives of Captain Interventors Ripoll Lecuona and Rosón Perez, of the Division and Blue Legion, respectively.

The uniform of the Spanish officials has few variations from the ones used by their German comrades, whish is why, in order not to repeat the information already given in the chapter dedicated to the uniforms of the *Beamten*, we will limit ourselves to comment on the peculiarities of those articles used by the Officers of the Blue Division.

The Steel Helmet (*Stahlhelm*)

Denominated as model 1935, the helmet was made of a stamped steel plate. This article was used by the three branches in the armed forces, and did not suffer practically any variation throughout the war.

Typical Stahlhelm, Model 35, used by the Spanish and German soldiers, detail. (N & T Militaria)

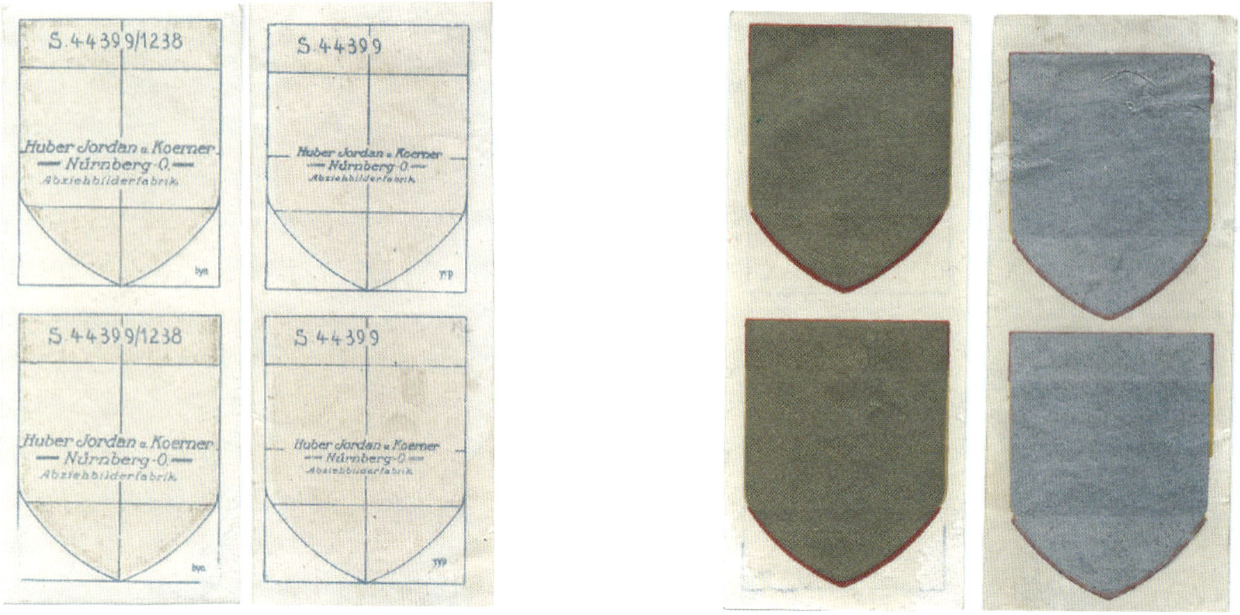

Front and back of the stickers with the national Spanish colors.

The first model was characterized by the use and wear along the left side of a glued shield of the *Heer*, and on the right side another with the colors of the Spanish flag (the Germans had one with the tricolor emblem of the Reich).

In March and August 1943 were published dispositions which deleted the flag colored transfer of the helmets and the eagle, although both had little repercussion.

As is demonstrated in a multitude of photographs, the interventors used generally the same uniform as the infantry officers. Even though the order of the uniforms and symbols given to the members of the Intendant Corps also extended to the interventors, neither one of the groups followed this order literally, especially between the lieutenants and captains.

All the interventors had the ranks of Superior duty officers, but only on a few occasions did they use the symbols or names specified in the German hierarchy that they were entitled to use.

As an example, Commissioner Gomez Garcia dressed as the regulated uniform of *beamten*. Trigo Cabrerizo only used it for down time and strolls, while at the front they wore the required troops uniform with the white colors of the Infantry.

The rest of the interventors did not use administrative badges, with the exception of Captain Ripoll, who used them while he was in charge of Service Interventor of the rear positions.

It was, without a doubt, the single-breasted uniform jacket of the campaign (the *FELDBLUSE*) where the Spanish origin of the volunteers was most noticeable. Regulated since 1933, with a first

Lieutenant Interventor Ripoll wearing a privately purchased jacket, model 1935, in Hof, 1942. (Archive Ripoll)

Returning Battalion members, July 1942. In the center is Manuel Guajardo Aguero; note the German National Emblem taken from the returned uniforms.

variation in 1935, Spanish officers used styles of troop and others of particular acquisition, made in cloth or fabric of the raincoat *feldgrau* color.

As we have already seen, it suffered, throughout the war, several modifications in its design, which is why it is not strange

Corporal Jose Mª Pellicer, son of Lieutenant Colonel Francisco Pellicer Taboada, first assistant to General Esteban Infantes. (Archives Ripoll)

Above: JAG Lieutenant Pedro Cuyas Ortiz returning from the Russian front where he served as an Infantry Sergeant. Below: Legionaries' hopeful goodbye to the German territories. (Archives Del Pozo)

Legionaries on their goodbye from the German territories. (Archives Del Pozo)

to find photographs of volunteers with all the styles that were made (years 1935, 1940, 1941, 1942, and 1943).

The single-breasted uniform jackets showed on the collar the *kragenpatten* (collar tabs). For the interventors the pads were the *Kolbenstikerei*, characteristic of the Superior Service officers, although, as already seen, they were practically never used, using instead the Infantry ones.

The *FELDBLUSE* had over the right pocket a German national emblem, in metallic thread silver-plated for the officers, and machine woven for the sergeant majors and troops.

Like the rest of the foreign volunteers who served in the *Wehrmacht*, the Spaniards used, on the right sleeve of their single-breasted uniform jackets, a fabric shield (in BeVo) with the national flags.

The use of the blue shirt or Spanish symbols was also very common with this single-breasted uniform jacket. They used the yoke and the arrows, the chess table monogram, the geese of the SEU or the Front of Youths, and the "bullet-stop."

Like in the single-breasted uniform jackets, the interventors of the Division generally used the service infantry caps, on which the soutache wore the colors of the weapon, instead of the dark green of the *beamten*.

All the officers used the campaign cap model 38, which unlike those of the troops contained a vivid silver-plated aluminum thread in which the cap badge was located within a circle of the colors of the *waffenfarbe*.

In 1942 it was ordered that the new caps be made without the circle of the colors of the arm, retiring all of those already made. Also in this year a new cap was created that was to be regulated for privates and corporals and sergeant majors, but became very popular between the officials, so they added the silver-plated cord.

In 1943 the campaign cap, model 1943, was introduced for all the army. Like its predecessors, those worn by officers were distinguished by the silver soutache placed at the superior edge of the cap.

When the volunteers returned to Spain, concentrated in the camp of Hof, they had to return the German uniforms and dress in their Spanish ones. The volunteers were forced to give up all articles, whatever their acquisition method, and they received an indemnification for the amount of the purchase.

Back in Spain, the Division members wore on their uniforms not only the decorations received in the German Army, but also all types of effects not returned to the German warehouses.

Several modifications of the Spanish Symbol Arm patch.

Colonel Interventor Amaro Lasheras' uniform, with two wounded bands, and the symbols of the Regulares and the Division. (Assoc. Retogenes via Colonel Amaro)

Most of the volunteers wore on their uniforms the shield with the national flags on their sleeves, and on the chest the German national emblem, the eagle.

Due to the great proliferation of German emblems in the Spanish uniforms of the divisioneers, regardless of whether a military professional or plain civililian, on November 11, 1942, the Ministry of the Army communicated to the military Commissioner Alfredo Guedea Millans-Astray, Head of the Camp of Hof, the prohibition of lacking prescribed symbols on the Spanish uniform, authorizing in this same communication the use of the shield of nationality carried on the sleeve.

Ricardo Recio, in his work "the Service of Intendance of the Blue Division," transcribes for us, without a doubt, the order mentioned before.

In the daily orders of November 12, 1942, the Mixed Regiment of Machines of Support, No. 81, was published:

"It has been observed that many Chiefs, Officers, Sergeant majors, and soldiers who have served in the Spanish Division of Volunteers, wear on the uniform emblems and distinctive symbols of the German Army. Although they have to be used on the uniforms of the Armed Forces of the German Reich, we must avoid any claims that may arise by that government.

For that reason, the Minister decided that these emblems shall not be worn on our uniform, unless the personnel served in the mentioned Division and worn on the right arm the National Badge, distinguishing their forces but with no strange article added to them."

This Order was still in effect, although one may be able to find a multitude of graphical testimonies in which are found military personalities of our but recent history showing the diverse existing models shining on their uniform.

As it is easy to understand, in the camps of Grafenwörh or Hof all the volunteers received, next to the corresponding German uniform the application to the roster, which basically consisted of the Record of Identity and dog tag.

When finalizing their stay in the Division, the volunteers had to complete a credential document of the delivery of the equipment and material received by the German government, and simultaneously the corresponding passport that allowed their return to Spanish territory.

Medals and Awards of the 250th Infantry Division

There are two instruments used by the Army High Commands around the World to recognize the actions or merits of individual members or units: Awards and Insignias.

Award badges recognize individual acts of bravery, war actions, or even merits during periods of peace. The Insignia is normally used to recognize actions and special training or education of their members.

The designation as a German Unit of the Spanish Division by order of the German High Command made possible that any component of the 250th Infantry Division would be able to receive badges and insignias from both nations. In addition, an official Spanish national shield was authorized to be worn on the uniform on 9 July 1941. A pre-approval from the Unit commander was required before it could be used as part of the Spanish regular uniform after the war.

It is the *author's* interest to center the medal and awards study on the ones received by the *Interventors* and other members of the Blue Division. Before their members were in the Division, the

Left: Military Merit Red Cross Medal.
Right: Military Merit Red Cross Medal with additional band.

interventors were wearing, as part of their uniform, medals and badges obtained during their Civil War and Morocco Campaigns. Along with the Red Cross (*Cruz Roja*), one of the most common medals worn on the Division uniforms was the "*Medalla de Sufrimientos por la Patria*."

EN NOMBRE DEL GENERALÍSIMO
Y POR LOS
NOTABLES HECHOS REALIZADOS
EN LA CAMPAÑA DE RUSIA
CONCEDO AL
Capitan del Cuerpo de Intervención
DON JAIME RIPOLL LECUONA.
LA
CRUZ ROJA DEL MÉRITO MILITAR
EN RUSIA A 20 DE octubre DE 1943.
GENERAL JEFE
DE LA
DIVISIÓN ESPAÑOLA DE VOLUNTARIOS

Red Cross Diploma.

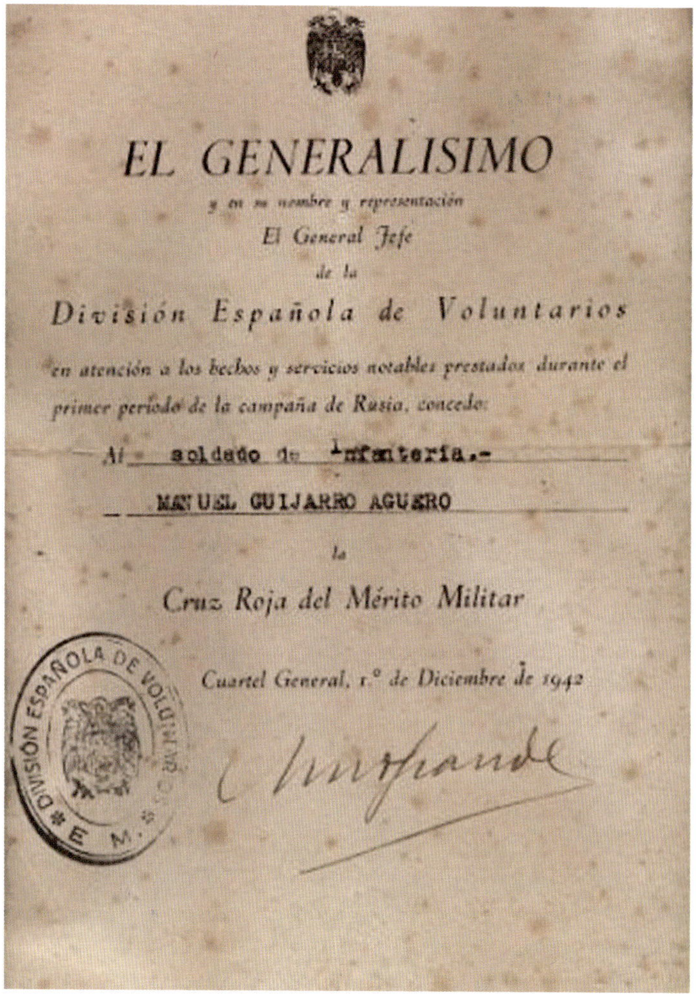

EL GENERALISIMO
y en su nombre y representación
El General Jefe
de la
División Española de Voluntarios
en atención a los hechos y servicios notables prestados durante el primer período de la campaña de Rusia, concede:
Al soldado de Infantería.-
MANUEL GUIJARRO AGUERO
la
Cruz Roja del Mérito Militar
Cuartel General, 1.º de Diciembre de 1942
DIVISIÓN ESPAÑOLA DE VOLUNTARIOS E. M.

Military Merit Red Cross Diploma.

The Third Section General Order establishing norms for the issuance of badges and rewards was published on May 27, 1942. The Division adopted the Rule that established the merits and goals to obtain a reward or badge as delineated in the March 14, 1942, law (C.L. 49).

Article 12 of the Rule identified as a necessary requirement for obtaining advance or promotion on the Scale Grade, and to obtain any badge or rewards, a minimum tenure of six (6) months of active duty at the front.

It established as the First period July 14, 1941, to February 28, 1942. Qualifying service was further defined as time at the front, or time spent in any Unit or Service of the Division, allowing as time the that used in the hospitals in the rear, if sickness was a consequence of combat injury or frostbite, but with non-qualifying time being for duties in the rear lines, common sickness, or vacation.

Article 30 of the regulation dictates the conditions necessary for receipt of the Red Cross to the Military Merit Award (*Cruz Roja al Mérito Militar*), stipulating that under no circumstances would the award carry any monetary compensation or pension, and allowing for the following categories:

- Silver: For the Troops
- Enamel and Gold: For the NCOs and COs.
- Plaque: For the Chiefs
- Grand Cross: For the Generals

Those acts of exceptional combat or services, with proven efficiency, were rewarded with the Red Cross (*La Cruz Roja*). It was understood that, in order to be defined as exceptional war actions, the individual or unit would have to demonstrate in front of the enemy exceptional acts of bravery, serenity, or intelligent initiative. In addition, those services and military duties had to be carried out with positive use of equipment, and with the personnel achieving successful enemy military objectives. In the two cases, it was imperative and a prerequisite that the action be carried out under extreme enemy induced circumstances.

This medal could only be received once per period of compensation. If it was received more than once, the rule established that only one badge could be worn on the uniform, with additional bars.

To recognize acts and services by the High Commands as "distinguished" because of their relevance and efficiency in the battle and combat the Grand War Cross (*La Cruz de Guerra*) was created. It was instituted with four classes:

- Troops: with a light blue and white band.
- NCOs and COs: with a plaque in Bronze.
- Chiefs: with a plaque in silver.
- Generals: Grand Cross in Gold, Band and Venera.

The use of metal bands was accepted for repetitive recipients. For those members that were nominated to receive it but did not fulfill the necessary requirements the Grand Cross with Palms (*La Cruz de Guerra con Palmas*) was instituted.

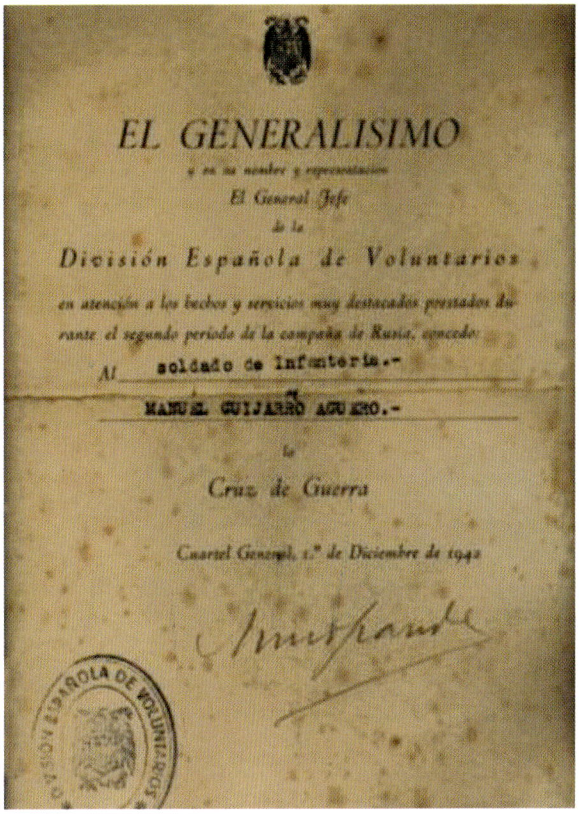
EL GENERALISIMO

El General Jefe

División Española de Voluntarios

en atención a los hechos y servicios muy destacados prestados durante el segundo período de la campaña de Rusia, concede:

Al soldado de Infantería.-

MANUEL GUIJARRO AGUERO.-

la

Cruz de Guerra

Cuartel General, 1.° de Diciembre de 1942

The War Cross Diploma.

The design varied with the award class. For troops they added two superimposed gold crossed palms. For NCOs, COs, Officers, Chiefs, and generals it included a dark red enamel emblem with the legend *To the campaign merit* (*Al Mérito en la campaña*) with two superimposed gold crossed palms.

The Spanish Government presented the Division and its members with a commemorative medal of their own. This award was surmounted by a Spanish Crown, with the main feature being a Spanish Eagle with an enamel Iron Cross in the center, representative of the collaboration between the two nations. The

The War Cross.

The DEV Russian Campaign medal.

Captain Amaro, returning from Germany, wears the 2nd Class Iron Cross, Close Combat Clasp emblem, and two wounded angle bands. (Archives Amaro)

reverse shows the Kremlin and the inscription "*Russia 1941*." The Ministerial Order of November 9, 1943, published its creation.

Instituted by Prussia's King Friedrich Wilhelm III on March 10, 1813, the Iron Cross was intended to be a temporary award for efforts against the Napoleon Army. It was considered that a general and a private both affected the outcome of a battle, differing only by their individual realms of responsibility. This rare logic of the time dictated that the Iron Cross would be awarded with all ranks being eligible for the same class. Without any doubt it was the most prestigious German Army decoration.

In 1939 the Iron Cross again was renewed as an order of the German Reich. The ribbon got the Reich's colors: black, white, and red. In contrast to the old Imperial orders, the Iron Cross grades or classes could be awarded regardless of military rank. The Iron Cross also became, for the first time, a real German decoration. Before that is was only awarded to the Prussian military.

The original symbolic Iron Cross remained unchanged, but the old Imperial and Royal symbols were replaced by the new Reich swastika. The year was changed to 1939 as the new date of institution. Four grades were instituted: 2nd Class, 1st Class, Knights Cross, and the Grand Cross.

- Knights Cross with Oak Leaves and Swords
- Knights Cross with Oak Leaves
- Knights Cross
- Knights Cross First Class
- Knights Cross Second Class

Captain Rosón at the Minister of the Army doors, with the Liquidating commission of the Blue Legion, May 1944. In June he would return to Germany as a member of the Material and Ammunition Commission.In the German style he wears the band of the 2nd Class Iron Cross and the first class War Cross. (Archives Rosón)

Left: The Knights Iron Cross. Center: The 1st Class Iron Cross. Right: The 2nd Class Iron Cross.

The *Wehrmacht* created for all the participants in the Eastern Front Campaign between November15 , 1941, and April 15, 1942, the medal of the First Winter (*La Medalla del Primer Invierno*, or *Wintreschalcht Im Osten 1941-42*), which came to be known by Spanish troops as the medal for the "frozen meat" due to the extremely low temperatures they suffered during that period of the campaign.

It was the most recognized German medal for the Interventors.

The *Kriegsverdienstkreuz* (*La Cruz al Mérito de Guerra*), or Cross of War, was created to reward Campaign Merits for bravery and service. It was awarded in six different classes:

The *Wehrmacht* First Winter Medal.

- The Knight's Cross of the Gold War Merit.
- War Merit Cross First Class.
- War Merit Cross First Class with Swords.
- War Merit Cross Second Class.
- War Merit Cross Second Class with Swords.

After the Blue Division (*La División Azul*) was dissolved in 1944, the German High command decided to create a commemorative medal to award the Spaniards that were members

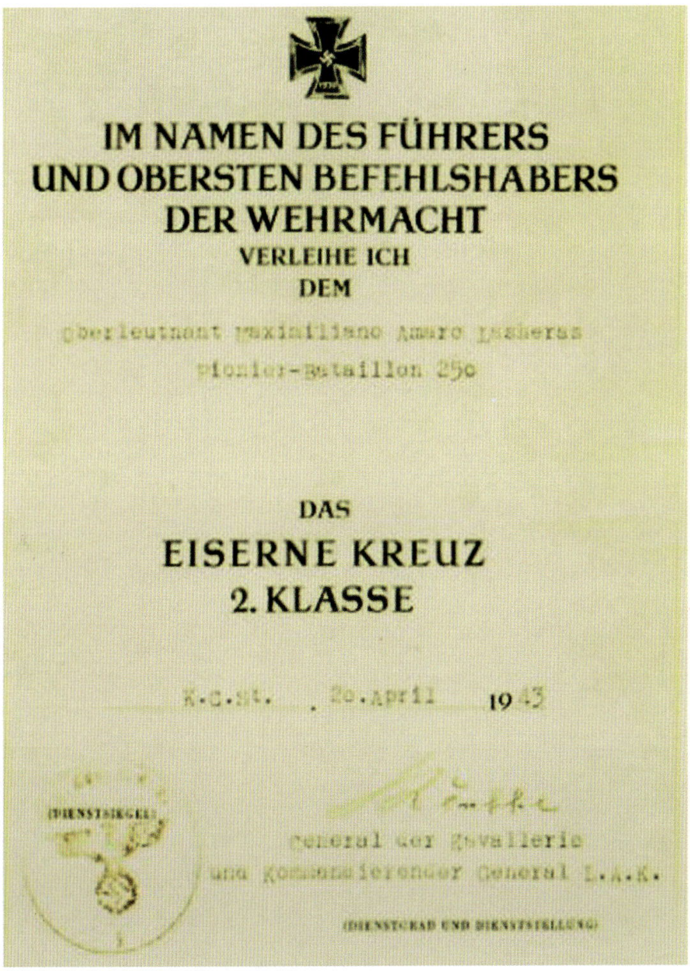

IM NAMEN DES FÜHRERS
UND OBERSTEN BEFEHLSHABERS
DER WEHRMACHT
VERLEIHE ICH
DEM

Oberleutnant Maximiliano Amaro Lasheras
Pionier-Bataillon 250

DAS
EISERNE KREUZ
2. KLASSE

K.G.St. , 20.April 1943

(DIENSTSIEGEL)

General der Kavallerie
und Kommandierender General I.A.K.

(DIENSTGRAD UND DIENSTSTELLUNG)

The 2nd Class Iron Cross Diploma.

IM NAMEN DES FÜHRERS
UND
OBERSTEN BEFEHLSHABERS
DER WEHRMACHT
IST DEM
Soldat
Jaime Dolado Gonzalo
Inf. Regt. 263
AM 27. September 1944

DIE MEDAILLE
WINTERSCHLACHT IM OSTEN
1941/42
(OSTMEDAILLE)
VERLIEHEN WORDEN.

FÜR DIE RICHTIGKEIT:
(DOEHR)
Generalmajor u.Militärattaché

The 1st Class Iron Cross Diploma.

Clockwise from above left: The Merit of War 1st Class Medal. The Merit of War 1st Class with swords Medal. The Merit of War 2nd Class Medal. The Merit of War 2nd Class with swords Medal.

of the 250th Infantry Division for their efforts against Bolshevism. The *Erinnerungsmedaille fur die Spanischen Freiwilligen im Kampf gegen den Bolschewismus* (Commemorative Medal for Spanish Volunteers in the Struggle against Bolshevism) is also referred to as the Spanish Blue Division Eastern Front medal.

Some of the important German awards obtained by Lieutenant Amaro Lasheras were:

STURMABZEICHEN, Infantry Assault Badge
VERWUNDETEN-ABZEICHEN, Gold Wounded Badge
NAHKAMPFSPANGE, Silver Close Combat Bar

Captain Interventor Jaime Ripoll (first from the right) after receiving the Merit of War 2nd Class Medal at the General headquarters, April 20, 1943. (Archives Ripoll)

Left: The Merit of War 2nd Class with swords Medal

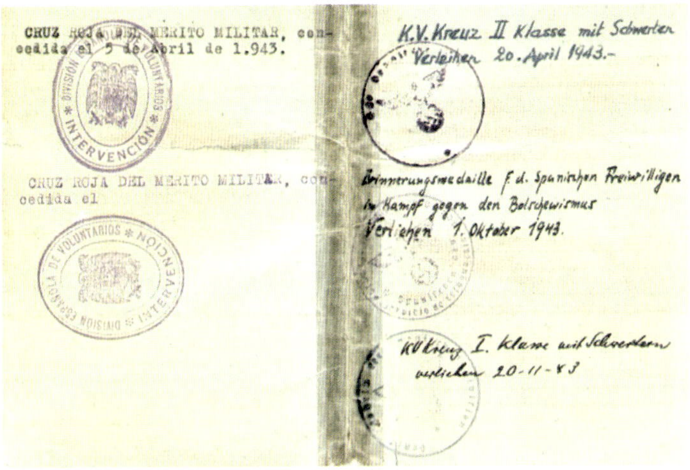

CRUZ ROJA DEL MERITO MILITAR, concedida el 5 de Abril de 1.943.

K.V. Kreuz II Klasse mit Schwertern Verleihen 20. April 1943.-

CRUZ ROJA DEL MERITO MILITAR, concedida el

Erinnerungsmedaille f. d. Spanischen Freiwilligen im Kampf gegen den Bolschewismus Verliehen 1. Oktober 1943.

KV Kreuz I. Klasse mit Schwertern verliehen 20-11-43

The Merit of War Notification. Below:

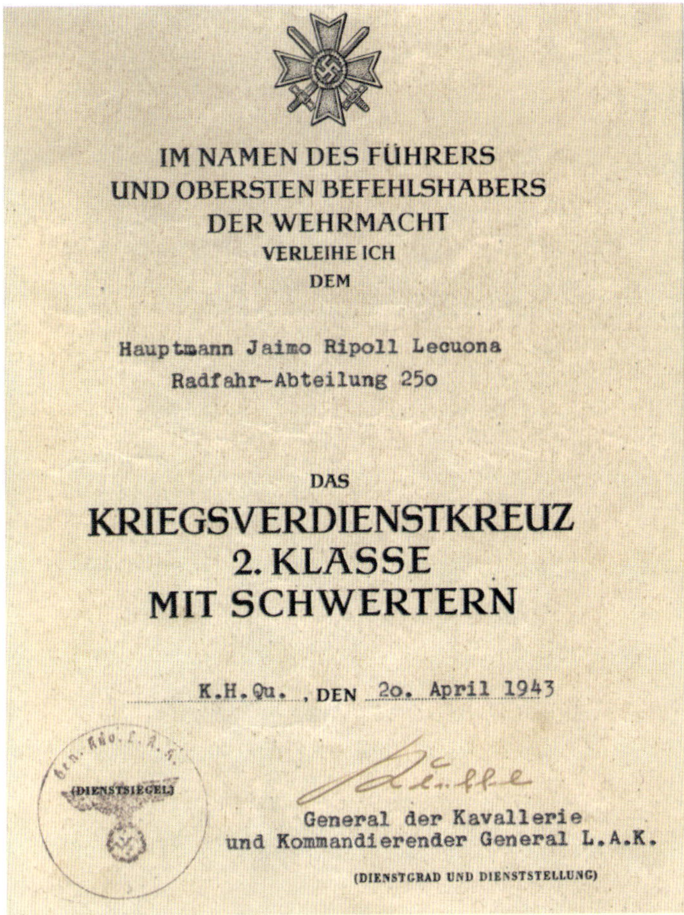

IM NAMEN DES FÜHRERS
UND OBERSTEN BEFEHLSHABERS
DER WEHRMACHT
VERLEIHE ICH
DEM

Hauptmann Jaimo Ripoll Lecuona
Radfahr-Abteilung 250

DAS
KRIEGSVERDIENSTKREUZ
2. KLASSE
MIT SCHWERTERN

K.H.Qu., DEN 20. April 1943

(DIENSTSIEGEL)

General der Kavallerie
und Kommandierender General L.A.K.

(DIENSTGRAD UND DIENSTSTELLUNG)

Above and below left: The Merit of War 2nd Class with swords Medal Diploma. Below right: The Merit of War 2nd Class Medal Diploma.

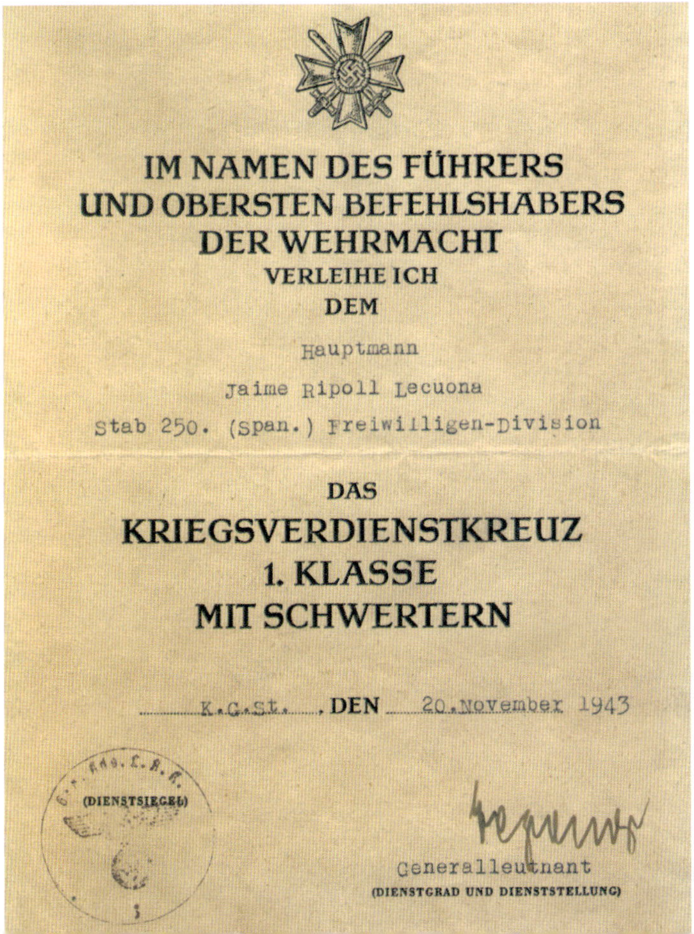

IM NAMEN DES FÜHRERS
UND OBERSTEN BEFEHLSHABERS
DER WEHRMACHT
VERLEIHE ICH
DEM

Hauptmann
Jaime Ripoll Lecuona
Stab 250. (Span.) Freiwilligen-Division

DAS
KRIEGSVERDIENSTKREUZ
1. KLASSE
MIT SCHWERTERN

K.G.St., DEN 20.November 1943

(DIENSTSIEGEL)

Generalleutnant
(DIENSTGRAD UND DIENSTSTELLUNG)

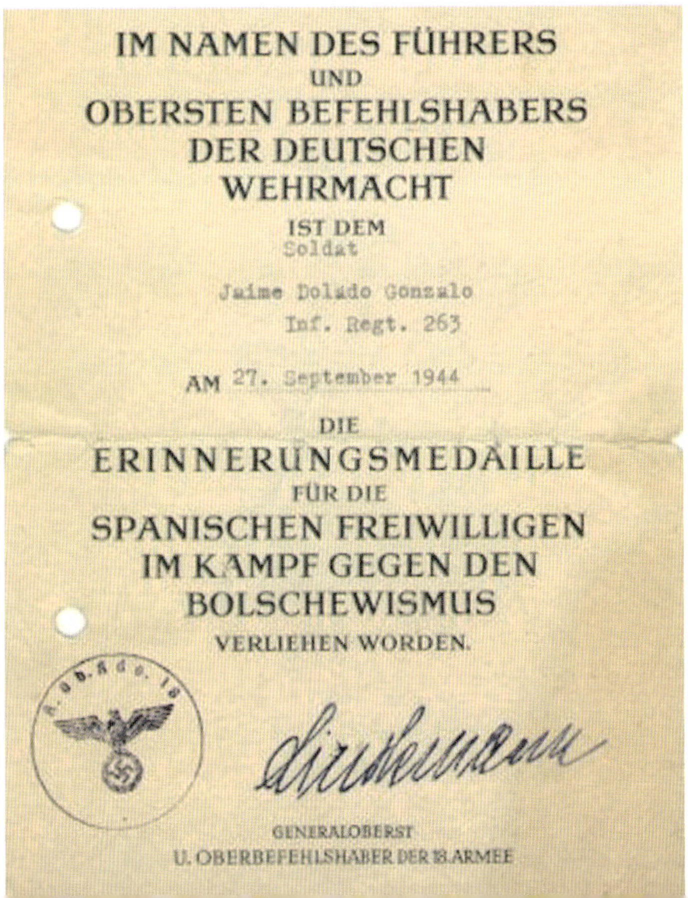

IM NAMEN DES FÜHRERS
UND
OBERSTEN BEFEHLSHABERS
DER DEUTSCHEN
WEHRMACHT
IST DEM
Soldat

Jaime Dolado Gonzalo
Inf. Regt. 263

AM 27. September 1944

DIE
ERINNERUNGSMEDAILLE
FÜR DIE
SPANISCHEN FREIWILLIGEN
IM KAMPF GEGEN DEN
BOLSCHEWISMUS
VERLIEHEN WORDEN.

GENERALOBERST
U. OBERBEFEHLSHABER DER 18.ARMEE

The Bronze Close Combat Clasp.

Left: Several assaults (*Sturmabzeichen*) Medal. Right: Wounded in Combat (*Verwundeten-abzeichen*) Medal.

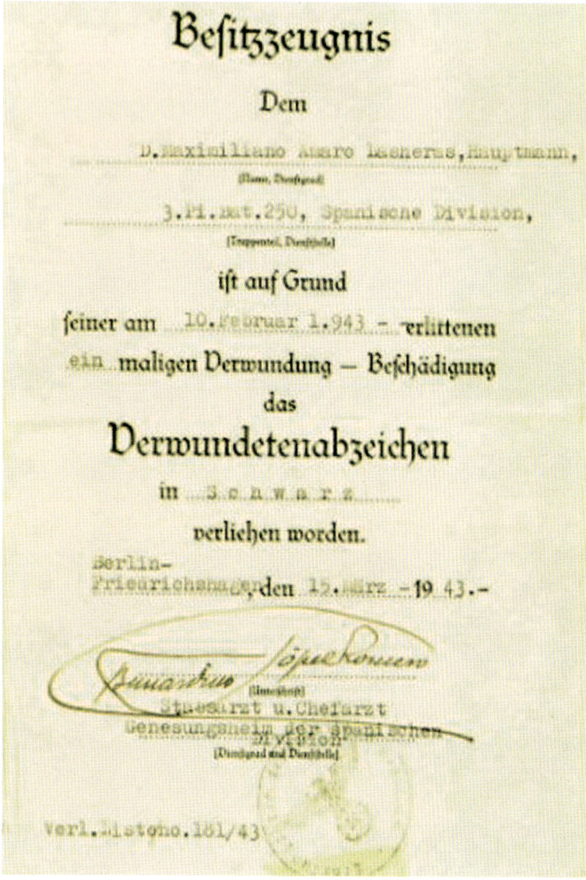

Besitzzeugnis

Dem

D. Maximiliano Amaro Lasheras, Hauptmann,

(Name, Dienstgrad)

3. Pi. Bat. 250, Spanische Division,

(Truppenteil, Dienststelle)

ist auf Grund

seiner am 10. Februar 1.943 - erlittenen

ein maligen Verwundung — Beschädigung

das

Verwundetenabzeichen

in Schwarz

verliehen worden.

Berlin-Friedrichshagen, den 15. März - 19 43.-

(Unterschrift)

Stabsarzt u. Chefarzt

Genesungsheim der spanischen Division

(Dienstgrad und Dienststelle)

Verl. Liste no. 161/43

The Wounded in Combat Medal Diploma.

The awards ceremony with the Division Head General Esteban Infantes. Next to him is his assistant, Commander Reinlein.

Daily Routine in the Division

Left: Standing is commandant José Alemany Vich, Chief of the 2nd Section, while working with Lieutenant Colonel Díaz de Villegas, High Command Chief of the Division. Right: Members of the 1st Section, from the left: Sergeant Moreno, Captain Martinez Ron, and commandant Tena. (Archives Ripoll)

The whole 1st Section: with the pelted hat is Captain Martinez Ron, and to his left Commandant Tena. (Archives Ripoll)

When the Spanish Division of Volunteers was formed the Intervention Headquarters got immersed, like all the other Services, within its General Headquarters.

Unlike the rest of the Division that adopted the German model, the General Joint Chiefs of Staff did not vary from the basic Spanish organizational system of French inspiration, which was made up of four dependent Sections of Headquarters. General Diaz de Villegas, who was Head of the Division General Staff, defines the conditions that had to reunite the Head of each Section:

"... A Head of the General Staff was needed with methodical order to command the First Section. Another one, with imagination, to be the head of the Second. In addition, we needed one with fulfilled technical abilities to direct the Third, leaving to the Fourth a foresighted commander."

The First Section in the Spanish model was the one in charge of personnel, its organization, instruction, and the administration of Justice (this was always governed according to the Code of Military Justice, having their own jails and disciplinary unit, and the sentences for crimes being carried out in Spanish military prisons).

Below left: Commandant Tena. Below right: The High command Headquarters. Next to the tree, left to right: soldier Jose Maria Pellicer, Lieutenant colonel Pellicer, and Lieutenant Navarro. (both Archives Ripoll)

Captain Fernandez Amigo in front of the palace of Prokovskaia. (Archives Ripoll)

Novgorod millenary monument, and in the background the Kremlin.

The Second Section took care of all things referring to Information. For its operation it was divided in two, the Second Section and the Second Section bis. The assignment of the first was to facilitate all the possible information on the enemy: its activities, material, and morale situation (it dealt with all the prisoners, deserters, civilians...to facilitate some useful data for the General Staff of the Unit). To the Second bis corresponded all the duties referring to information on the state of Spanish troops, and their morale and discipline.

A dependent service was the Awards Section, responsible for the recognition of the merits of the volunteers, and therefore with crediting them. Decisions were made by means of a Regulation of Awards. A general description and study of their function is in another chapter.

Another service in this Second Section was Publicity. That section was responsible for the projection of films, documentaries (from 1943 the famous Spanish NODO), and the organization of all those acts that in addition to being entertainment for the Spanish

Above: Detail of the Kremlin of Novgorod. Below: Commandant Jose Alemay Vich and Lieutenant Lizaur. (both Archives Ripoll)

Group of the 2nd Section: seating to the Chief's left is Commandant Alemany, with Captain Fernandez Amigo. (Archives Ripoll)

Palace of Prokovskaia, Headquarters of the Blue Division at the Leningrad Front. (Archives Ripoll)

troops supposed an approach to the Russian general population. Without a doubt, some of the most remarkable work of the Section of Publicity was the publication of the Leaf of Campaign, the division newspaper that in spite of being published in Riga, counted on continuous collaboration from combatant personnel.

The Third Section was without a doubt, in the Spanish organizational chart, the most important. All the other Sections worked for it, and on this depended all the operations of the Unit. From it emanated all the planning, dispositions, and instructions that would materialize in orders to be executed.

This Section was in charge of maintaining a historical record, and the daily report was to be sent to the Division Headquarters with details on combats, the low operativeness of the units, and all necessary information required for making opportune decisions.

This section was also responsible for the training of the reserve battalions and the tactical reorganization of the units.

The Fourth Section, whose main task consisted of facilitating the precise means for the Unit to be 100% operational; that is, the troops enter into combat with all the necessary materials, as well as the tasks of evacuation of the personnel, repair or substitution of the materiel, etc. The good operation of this Section required constant relations with the Heads of each Service.

Commandant Saiz, Lieutenant Colonel Palomares, and Lieutenant Mendel Trigo. (Archives Ripoll)

In addition to the tasks required by the Interventor function, many other functions were assigned to the officers of the Corps.

The knowledge, affection, and confidence that General Muñoz Grandes (in his Africanist stage, he collaborated closely with the Corps. His nephew, lieutenant Trigo Cabrerizo, entered the Corps under the advice of his uncle. Being Minister of the Army in the middle of the '50s, he was directly involved with the reforms of the Corps of Intervention and Intendance) had in the Corps of Intervention took him to use it and its components in the most different duties and services, which will be analyzed in the present chapter.

The deposited confidence in the heads and official interventors cannot be understood without studying the personal trajectory of each one of them. As to the interventors, we will distinguish

Group of the 4th Section, December 1942. (Archives Ripoll)

Left to right: Captain Sancho, Commandant Garcia Cortazar, Commandant Luis Borrero Roldan, Chief of the 4th Section, Captain Palomino, and Lieutenant Mendel Trigo. (Archives Ripoll)

Above left: Entrance to the Military Hospital of Konigsberg. (Archives Dolado) Above center: Alferez Auslander and a German Red Cross Officer. (Archives Ripoll) Above right: Lieutenant Auditor Pedro Cuyas Ortiz. (Archives De La Vega)

between those who entered before 1931 and after 1939 (from 1931 to 1939 the Body was declared extinct). The first group that entered the Corps, after approving the corresponding entrance exam and practice, came from the Infantry. The second would enter after the corresponding position advertisement and pass by the Corps Academy. It came to be that all the volunteers were from the first promotion, which in addition were the Lieutenants of Complement: Trigo, Amaro, and Rosón of Infantry, and Ripoll of the Legal Corps.

As we have seen in their respective personnel records, all accounted for an ample experience in combat, either in the Campaigns of Africa or in the Spanish Civil War. This condition was demonstrated during their stay in the Unit, the Gomez Garcia and Guedea, directing troop establishments. Amaro and Rosón were immersed in the rage of the combats, exerting both control over the troops and obtaining, through their behavior, individual Iron Crosses.

The multitude of services and locations that supported the Division, and which were distributed from the Spanish border to the front, required constant displacements. This reality was partially solved with the creation in 1942 of a Headquarters for the Services on the rear, and the establishment of a camp in Hof. The new volunteers would go to the camp in Hof, and from this camp they would take leave to return to Spain. The headquarters of the camping was entrusted to Gomez Garcia, being replaced, on his return to Spain, by commander Guedea.

The functions, in addition to the administrative ones, that were assigned to them, are those related to the organization of the Units, their instruction, plan of adaptation, uniformity, and oath to the *Führer*, while also serving simultaneously as connections and representation of the General with the German control. For the fulfillment of this work they maintained constant communication with the Third Section of the German General Staff.

On October 7, 1943, Captain Interventor Ripoll was sent to Hof as Interventor of the rear Services. In addition, he assumed the position of the Office of Censorship.

During the exercise of this position he worked in continuous contact with the Postal Services (4th Section) and the *Gendarmerie* of the Division, employees of 2nd Section bis of the High Command.

Lieutenants Pulido and Ripoll during a travel stop towards Hof. (Archives Ripoll)

Spanish doctors in the Military Hospital of Konigsberg. (Archives Dolado)

The Mother Land sketch. (Archives Dolado)

He was in charge of ensuring the fulfillment of instructions and normative on the military mail censorship, a task entrusted to the Military Police (served in the Unit by the Civil Guard).

According to the Instruction of April 3, 1943, of the Office of Censorship, sent to the units by the Head of the rear Services, the volunteers were strictly prohibited from stating the following in their letter correspondence:

1. It is prohibited to mention the names of towns or positions where the volunteers or Units are.
2. It is prohibited to send postcards with photographs of populations or military arms, like tanks, airplanes, speedboats, etc.
3. Drawings are prohibited in letters, whatever the reason, if they represent, speak of operations, or are written in Morse. Photographs need to be taken in such a way that they do not disclose your placement or location. Do not send matches, cigarettes, or caramels within your envelopes because they will be destroyed during the transport.

In August 1942, and with the intention of participating in operation "Light of the North," the Division was transferred

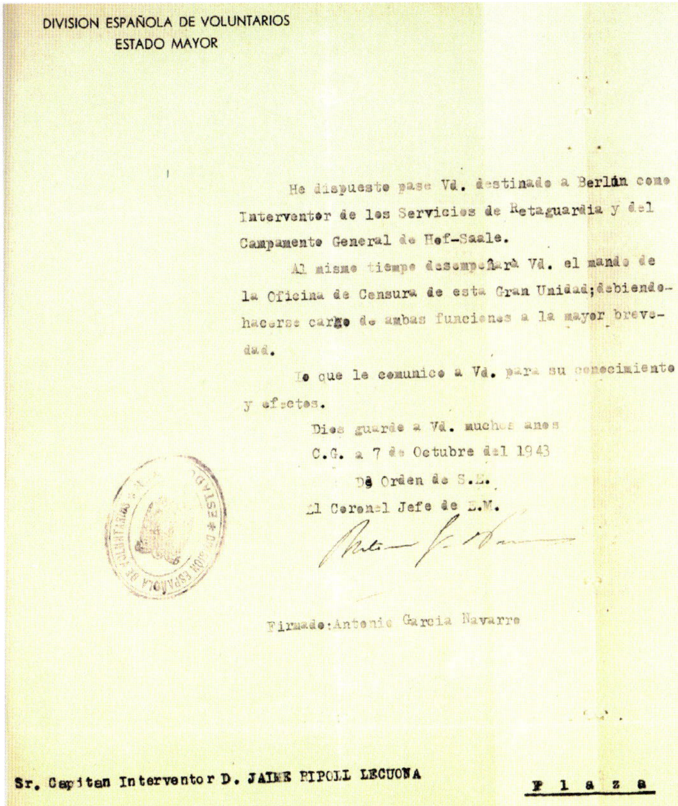

DIVISION ESPAÑOLA DE VOLUNTARIOS
ESTADO MAYOR

He dispuesto pase Vd. destinado a Berlín como Interventor de los Servicios de Retaguardia y del Campamento General de Hof-Saale.

Al mismo tiempo desempeñará Vd. el mando de la Oficina de Censura de esta Gran Unidad; debiendo hacerse cargo de ambas funciones a la mayor brevedad.

Lo que le comunico a Vd. para su conocimiento y efectos.

Dios guarde a Vd. muchos anos
C.G. a 7 de Octubre del 1943
De Orden de S.E.
El Coronel Jefe de E.M.

Firmado: Antonio Garcia Navarro

Sr. Capitan Interventor D. JAIME RIPOLL LECUONA — Plaza

Document on marching.

towards the suburbs of Leningrad. The Third Section of the Division General Staff planned the displacement meticulously, giving opportune instructions.

The complex transfer of the units and services of the Division was made on a staggered basis by railroad, settling down at a collection point in the town of Wyriza. Once concentrated, the Division was moved to the Puschkin-Kolpino sector, as close as 20 kilometers from the old Saint Petersburg, where they relieved German Division 121.

On August 19, 1942, once the new location was established, Lieutenant Jaime Ripio Lecuona, Interventor of the Division, received the following Headquarters order:

SPANISH DIVISION OF VOLUNTEERS No.250
E.M.
3rd SECTION

In the boardings of the Units of this Division to your new zone of establishment you will have my representation, and will attend on them, giving to the Heads of the Expeditions the instructions that were verbally transmitted to you for the best use and advantage of the railway material.

God will guard you many years,
In Campaign, August 19, 1942

By Order of S.E.

The Lieutenant. Colonel High Command Chief

Signed: Antonio Gomez Goya

The new Headquarters was installed in an old palace in Prokovskaia. Muñoz Grandes issued the order to fortify the sector. Lieutenant Interventor Trigo Cabrerizo participated in this task.

This would not be the only occurrence when an Interventor was to command an expeditionary transport of the Division. In February 1944 Captain Interventor Rosón received the order of Colonel Garcia Navarro to facilitate the transport of the Unit during the retreat from the front of *Mgá*.

One of the main problems that volunteers had during their stay in the Eastern front was the search for suitable lodging. The daily life complicated the election of a place of shelter that would be comfortable. The rigors of the climate, and the stations of the year, would determine the type of establishment that the Unit would look for, depending on the different fronts at which the Division unfolded.

With their arrival to the Volchof front, the Spaniards found eminently rural surroundings, unlike the suburbs of Leningrad, where the development of an important industry had modified it considerably during the czars to an idyllic place.

Nevertheless, on both fronts a common element existed: the absence of stone buildings. Its deficiency, almost endemic, was materialized in a type of construction where wood, brick, and adobe reached maximum importance. Even the most symbolic buildings lacked this material, making them tremendously fragile to the rigors of war.

Division marching toward the Leningrad Front, August 1942. (Archives Dolado)

On November 3, 1941, not a month since the Division's baptism of fire, the General Staff published General training No. 4,036, having as a subject the construction of lodging and the protection against cold, fires, and air defense. Based on the "Page of Instructions for the construction of winter lodgings in the Army sector," published September 29, 1941, by the Army Command 16 (A.O.K. 16).

In the Page (in which the hand of the translator was clearly expressed) three types of shelter were described:

a) Lodgings of Campaign.
b) Provisional lodgings.
c) Permanent lodgings.

Respect to subparagraph a), all the measures to construct campaign lodgings are to be carried out by the troops themselves, according to the following prescriptions.

Respect to subparagraph b), these lodgings have to be constructed with the means which are available to the troops, using the already existing lodgings and of those in the surrounding populations. Also, it is important to consider in the construction horses and automobiles.

Warehouses.- It is necessary to pay attention not to disregard and waste existing lodging, mainly in the populations. The provisional lodgings have to serve as a base for the definitive lodgings, adding to the first ones small supplementary constructions.

The lodgings have to be made with the intention to be used in the future by units of the same arm, i.e. Company of Infantry, company of Machine guns, Batteries, etc.

Respect to sub paragraph c), they have to distinguish between three construction groups:

1).- Construction of permanent lodgings (for example, the construction would be used as a complement for the troops in uninhabited and completely destroyed regions.)

Instruction page of November 29, 1941, making it mandatory to camouflage all trucks while not traveling. (Archives Dolado)

2).- Additional Constructions for the lodgings and major repairs (3/4 of which are in good condition, and the remaining 1/4 has to be repaired)
3).- Additional light Constructions for permanent lodgings' small repairs.

With respect to subparagraph 1), the A.O.K would issue an order in writing to the Unit in charge of the construction. This one would choose the land in agreement with the tenants that would occupy the lodgings, and with the collaboration of the experts of hygiene, and the military Geologists who, after examining all the details, would issue the definitive order. The execution would be done with the help of the prisoners and inhabitants of the area, helped, if possible, by detachments of the Unit.
The Units for the protection of forests would cut and prepare the wood, helped by the Combat engineers. The remaining necessary materials would be provided by the O.T.

The office of construction of the Army was in charge of the implementation of the received orders.

Respect to subparagraph 2):

a) When built by the O.T.; execution as it indicates on paragraph 1. The A.O.K. will decide.
b) If it would not be constructed by the troops with the technical assistance of the Office of Construction of the Army and its sections, and with the manual labor provided by the troops or in the contrary then the material would be provided by the Office of construction of the Army.

With respect to subparagraph 3). – The measures that do not need technical collaboration are those not needing more than 10 cubic meters of cut wood; 100 square meters of cardboard for roofing, 30 kg of nails, 10 bags of cement or lime, and 10 kg of painting.

Execution by the troops. Technical advice by the Office of Construction of the Army.

Material requisition, by proceeding, if there is none in the Region.

B. - Measure of protection against fire, cold, and air defense.

I.- Defense against fires: (see special orders No. 82 of 20.9.1941)

Fire Signal, fix the warning system.
To mount guard against fires.
Guard for the deposits, mainly of explosive material (ammunition, fuels). Monitoring in wood houses if the heating is working at night.
To place sections to extinguish the fires, with clouds, etc (provision of water, sand, and wood sticks).
Guard constantly ignited fires, such as stoves, heating, etc.
Constant guard in the lodgings of troops. (It is prohibited to dry the clothes of any class in the stoves).
Forecasting against fires. Additional lodgings for troops and cattle must be located (in case of necessity more people would be placed in the ordinary lodgings of smaller capacity) in a safe location.

Inside the Isba used as their house are the pilots of the JU 52 used for connection between the Blue Air Squad and the Division headquarters. (Archives Ripoll)

Detail of the housing of Captain Interventor Ripoll and other Headquarter officers in the Leningrad Sector. (Archives Ripoll)

Interior of the Nazi Navaleno refuge.

Not to make large concentrations of arms and materials. In the camps located in forests, it is necessary to mount a "small hat" on the chimneys. The chimneys and tubes of stoves must stand out of the roofs and wood wall a minimum of 0.75 cm.

II.- Protection against the cold.

Accumulate large quantities of wood and peat moss, if possible.
These wood provisions must be placed outside, and brought closer to the walls of the lodgings, because besides protecting against the cold, they also protect against the shrapnel of the projectiles, but a small space must be left between the wall and the firewood.
The hollows left by placing the table against the walls, and the logs of the lodgings, must be re-nailed with light wood strips.
It is necessary to be aware that, when constructing with wood, that if it is not perfectly dry, while constructing, it will shrink, leaving spaces between the boards.
In the lodgings that during the night keep ignited stoves, it is necessary to leave monitoring personnel, because of the eminent danger to its occupants. The preparation of Denmark blankets is strongly advised, for which you only need to place newspapers between the sheets. It may be necessary to work them with your hands if they are too rigid. They are a good solution to the cold temperatures.
All pipes and pumps should be covered with hay. If frozen, use hot water to defrost. In these cases do not use the pump handle since it can be broken.
Cover all piping at least 1.50 or 2 m underground.

III.- Anti-aircraft protection

Construct closed trenches for anti-aircraft protection, located near to the lodging to be able to arrive at them when it snows heavily.
The firewood accumulated next to the walls is better than the use of earth, because it does not allow the humidity to pass to the interior, whereas the second does not provide these advantages.
Covering of the lights - It is necessary with the doors and windows, but without using blankets, as this is prohibited.

IV.- General Subjects. –

All the garbage or residues of any class, it is necessary to bury them or burn them daily.

V.- Equipment of lodging.

As far as equipping the lodging with material and means of consumption, see annex No. 28 special orders of 20.9.41.

Relieving German Comrades, October 1941: at the right is Sergeant Pedro Cuyas Ortiz. (Archives CUYAS)

Russian snow and a Russian farm.

First accommodation of Lieutenant Ripoll at Prokovskaia, September 1943.

The suburbs of Prokovskaia, 1942.

Russian farm house and the pond.

Lieutenant Mendez Trigo, Alferez Lakers, and Lieutenant Haxel, Grigorovo, July 1942.

Soldier Pedro Fernandez, typist of the intervention Service, and lieutenant Lizaur kidding with a Russian boy, January 1943.

Above: Lieutenant Rose, September 1943. Below: Lieutenant Ripoll in his bed at Grigorovo, July 1942.

Above: Church of Grigorovo, July 1942. Below: Grigorovo, July 1942.

Headquarters moving operations, September 1943.

The first unfolding of the Division was made on the western margin of the Volchof river, having occupied one half of a hundred half-destroyed villages, with little population, immersed in a typically rural landscape.

In the landscape, the only important urban nucleus was the deserted Novgorod, a city that in the beginning of the war had nearly 70,000 inhabitants. The population when the Spaniards arrived was already reduced to less than a third. The few buildings that still remained were disputed by the High Command staff of some Units. The Headquarters of Intervention settled next to the Headquarters in the nearby village of Grigorovo.

Captain Romaguera, Lieutenant Macrino, and Lieutenant Méndez Trigo. (Archives Ripoll)

Right: Lieutenant Interventor Ripoll Lecuona at the Leningrad Front, 1943. (Archives Ripoll)

Unlike the rest of the interventors from the Unit, first class Commissioner Manuel Gomez had his own house, which served as vanguard next to Headquarters. The rest of the members of the Corps, like the other officers of the services, resided in shared lodgings with comrades headed for the Division Services of similar graduation in wood houses typical of the Russian villages called "Isbas."

Thus, for example, Lieutenant Ripoll shared lodging with the Intendance Lieutenant Méndez Trigos, as well as Lieutenant Haxel and Alferez Lamers, both of the German High Command connection.

The *isbas* were of rough construction, made with tree trunks separated by packing material and adobe, that caught fire easily. They were generally single story cabins for a family, although in some cases they were shared by more than one. Like in most of the rural constructions of any part of the world cattle, stables, fences, etc. were leaned to the house.

For the official inspectors they not only served as a resting place, but also often served as unexpected offices used to prepare the daily task, and especially, far from the pressure of the Headquarters, to study the numerous causes in which they participated like defenders.

The obsession of General Muñoz Grandes for Justice in the Unit to be controlled was applied with rigor, but with all the guarantees for the accused. The auditors of the Division, by Order of the General and the defense of the accused, was always performed by officers and, if possible, with a law background.

In 1942, during several months the Lieutenants Interventor Ripoll Lecuona and Amaro Lasheras were destined, per their own request, as Combat engineers, and Cabrerizo Trigo in the function of officer assignments by the General. All of them were from the First Promotion of the newly created Army Intervention attorneys at law.

At the end of 1943 Captain Rosón would join them. He was also a lawyer and of the same military promotion. All had acquired legal experience at the end of the Spanish Civil War. Being lawyers, they were continuously assigned to the court martials.

In the first line of battle, the combatant Arms made their own assignments for this situation: combats, services of monitoring, listen, recognition, night raids, tasks of fortification, firewood, etc. The units would hardly live in the bunkers constructed by them or left by the enemy, whom *guripas* baptized as "*chabolas*." These were holes in the ground, with walls covered with trunks, and the ceiling with trunks and earth. Its approximate capacity was for a section, such as Lieutenant Interventor Amaro's, with command of a Section of 3rd Company of Combat engineers.

As is easy to imagine, the closer to the front the worse the lodging. The artillerymen and the members of the services were the most famous for obtaining the best places of shelter.

The volunteers, whenever the situation at the front allowed it, would retire toward the rear to use lodgings that were much more comfortable than the trenches, and better prepared to fight

Spanish Captain. (Archives Ripoll)

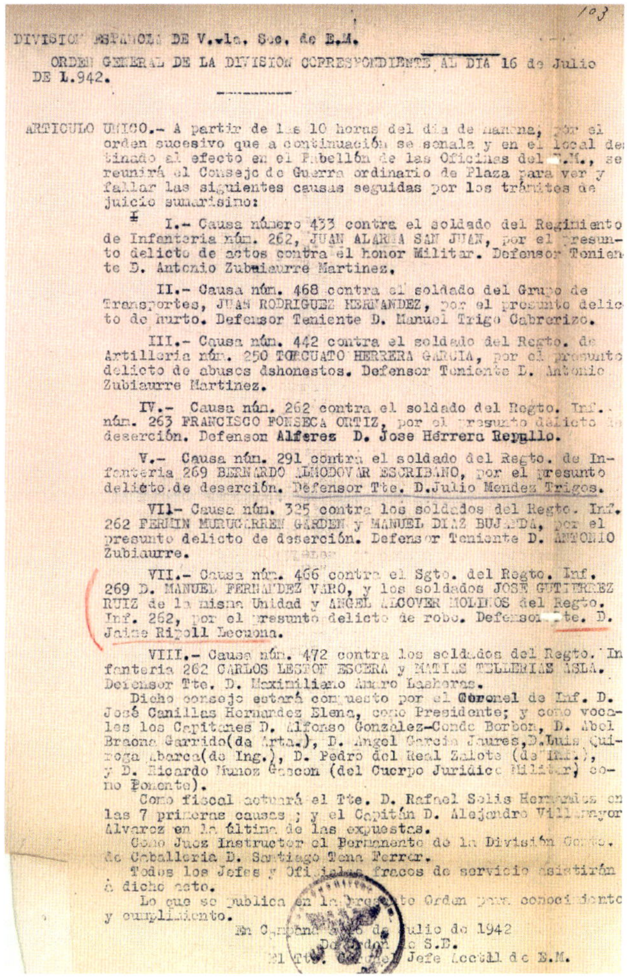

103

DIVISION ESPAÑOLA DE V.vla. Sec. de E.M.

ORDEN GENERAL DE LA DIVISION CORRESPONDIENTE AL DIA 16 de Julio DE 1.942.

ARTICULO UNICO.- A partir de las 10 horas del día de mañana, por el orden sucesivo que a continuación se señala y en el local destinado al efecto en el Pabellón de las Oficinas del E.M., se reunirá el Consejo de Guerra ordinario de Plaza para ver y fallar las siguientes causas seguidas por los trámites de juicio sumarísimo:

I.- Causa número 433 contra el soldado del Regimiento de Infanteria núm. 262, JUAN ALARCIA SAN JUAN, por el presunto delicto de actos contra el honor Militar. Defensor Teniente D. Antonio Zubaiaurre Martinez.

II.- Causa núm. 468 contra el soldado del Grupo de Transportes, JUAN RODRIGUEZ HERNANDEZ, por el presunto delicto de hurto. Defensor Teniente D. Manuel Trigo Cabrerizo.

III.- Causa núm. 442 contra el soldado del Regto. de Artilleria núm. 250 TORCUATO HERRERA GARCIA, por el presunto delicto de abusos dshonestos. Defensor Teniente D. Antonio Zubiaurre Martinez.

IV.- Causa núm. 262 contra el soldado del Regto. Inf. núm. 263 FRANCISCO FONSECA ORTIZ, por el presunto delicto de deserción. Defensor Alferez D. Jose Herrera Repullo.

V.- Causa núm. 291 contra el soldado del Regto. de Infanteria 269 BERNARDO ALMODOVAR ESCRIBANO, por el presunto delicto de deserción. Defensor Tte. D. Julio Mendez Trigos.

VI.- Causa núm. 325 contra los soldados del Regto. Inf. 262 FERMIN MURUGARREN GARDEN y MANUEL DIAZ BUJANDA, por el presunto delicto de deserción. Defensor Teniente D. ANTONIO Zubiaurre.

VII.- Causa núm. 466 contra el Sgto. del Regto. Inf. 269 D. MANUEL FERNANDEZ VARO, y los soldados JOSE GUTIERREZ RUIZ de la misma Unidad y ANGEL ALCOVER MOLINOS del Regto. Inf. 262, por el presunto delicto de robo. Defensor Tte. D. Jaime Ripoll Lecuona.

VIII.- Causa núm. 472 contra los soldados del Regto. Infanteria 262 CARLOS LESTON ESCERA y MATIAS TELLERIAS ISLA. Defensor Tte. D. Maximiliano Amaro Lasheras.

Dicho consejo estará compuesto por el Coronel de Inf. D. José Canillas Hernandez Elena, como Presidente; y como vocales los Capitanes D. Alfonso Gonzalez-Conde Borbon, D. Abel Braone Garrido (de Arta.), D. Angel Garcia Jaures, D. Luis Quiroga Abarca (de Ing.), D. Pedro del Real Zalote (de Inf.), y D. Ricardo Muñoz Gascon (del Cuerpo Juridico Militar, como Ponente).

Como fiscal actuará el Tte. D. Rafael Solis Hernandez en las 7 primeras causas; y el Capitán D. Alejandro Villamayor Alvarez en la última de las expuestas.

Como Juez Instructor el Permanente de la División Comte. de Caballeria D. Santiago Tena Ferrer.

Todos los Jefes y Oficiales francos de servicio asistirán a dicho acto.

Lo que se publica en la presente Orden para conocimiento y cumplimiento.

En Campaña 16 de Julio de 1942
De Orden de S.E.
El Tte. Coronel Jefe Acctal de E.M.

Court Martial minutes (above) and assignment notification (below).

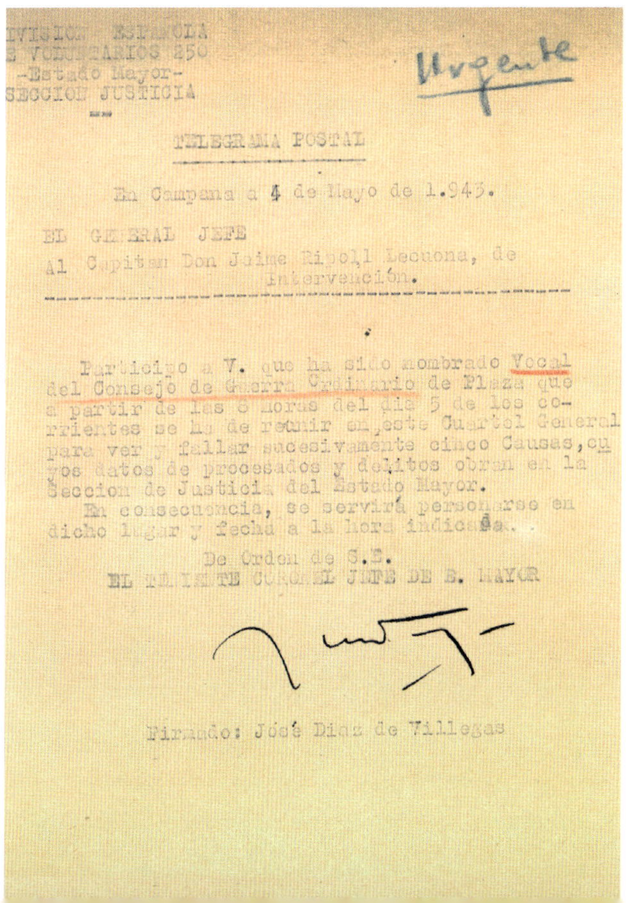

DIVISION ESPAÑOLA
DE VOLUNTARIOS 250
-Estado Mayor-
SECCION JUSTICIA

Urgente

TELEGRAMA POSTAL

En Campaña a 4 de Mayo de 1.943.

EL GENERAL JEFE

Al Capitan Don Jaime Ripoll Lecuona, de Intervención.

Participo a V. que ha sido nombrado Vocal del Consejo de Guerra Ordinario de Plaza que a partir de las 8 horas del día 5 de los corrientes se ha de reunir en este Cuartel General para ver y fallar sucesivamente cinco Causas, cuyos datos de procesados y delitos obran en la Sección de Justicia del Estado Mayor.

En consecuencia, se servirá personarse en dicho lugar y fecha a la hora indicada.

De Orden de S.E.
EL TENIENTE CORONEL JEFE DE E. MAYOR

Firmado: José Diaz de Villegas

On the porch, Chutyni, 1942. (Archives Dolado)

Chutyni, May 1942. (Archives Dolado)

the harshness of the Russian climate. The place chosen for rest by the *guripas* varied depending on the location of the front.

It was already mentioned that during the stay of the Division on the Voljov front there were few towns and constructions, with the exception of Novgorod—in which they stayed in the building of the Kremlin, as well as some palaces and villas where the Headquarters and Services were located—which is why lodging was made in isbas, in many occasions with their owners inside, or in the shacks.

In the front of Leningrad, where the suburbs had all the characteristics of the suburbs of a great city, their existed a multitude of towns and villages with old palaces or summer residences. There lodging was generally far better.

But even in the more advanced positions not everything was a fight, and there were moments for leisure and rest, as well as the festivities of each Weapon or Corps: *Perpetual Socorro* (Patron of the Health Corps); Santa Teresa de Jesus, Patron of Intendance; Santa Barbara of the Artillery; San Fernando of Engineers and Youth National-Unionist; Santiago, of Spain and the Weapon of Cavalry; The Pillar, of Spain and the Civil Guard; without a doubt 8 December, the date that the Catholic Church dedicates to the Immaculate Conception; and the Weapon of Infantry, Intervention, and Veterinary medicine. Plus the political holidays, such as: 18 July, anniversary of the uprising; 1 October, birthday of the Caudillo; or 1 April, the conclusion of the Civil War. They all became authentic social acts, as much between the members of the different Arms and Corps as with their German allies.

In its preparation it was implied to all the Units, and corresponding invitations were issued; with the greatest possible solemnity the banquet began with the celebration of Mass, and after the anticipated acts, a holiday menu was offered in agreement with the importance of the festivity.

On some occasions the participation of some company in varieties of *tournée* at the front was obtained. One tragic memory was the 7th Anniversary of the National Uprising celebration of the July 18, 1943. On that occasion, General Esteban Infantes wanted to celebrate the anniversary with greater solemnity. As was the custom, the acts began with the celebration of Mass, which was attended by all the Division General Staff, as well as all the heads

Dance Invitation for Russian women. Note the place of the event: Highway to Madrid, No. 25. August 1943.

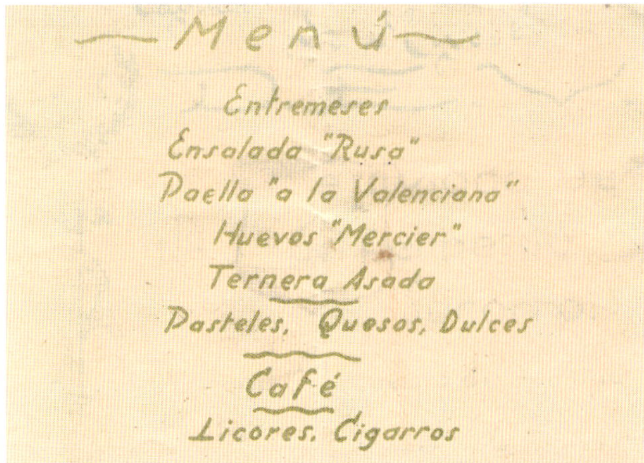

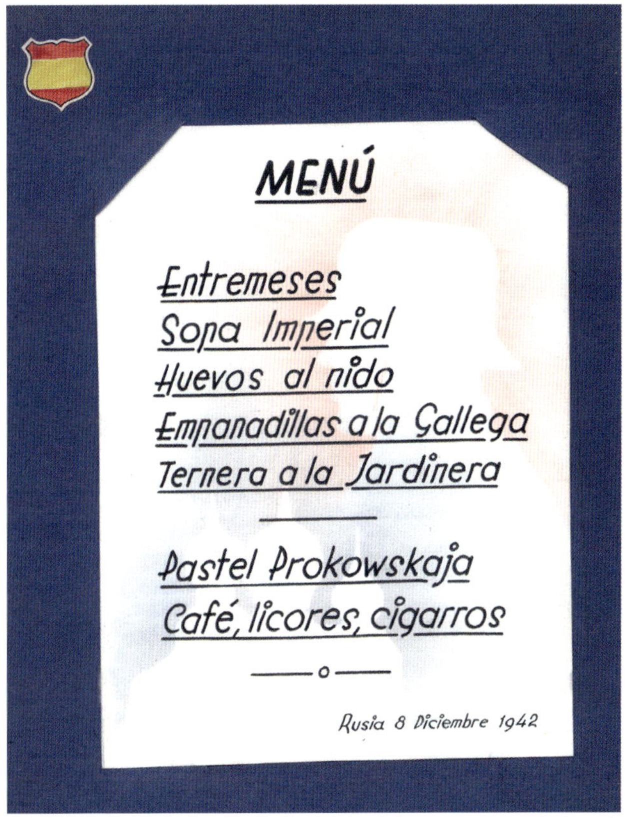

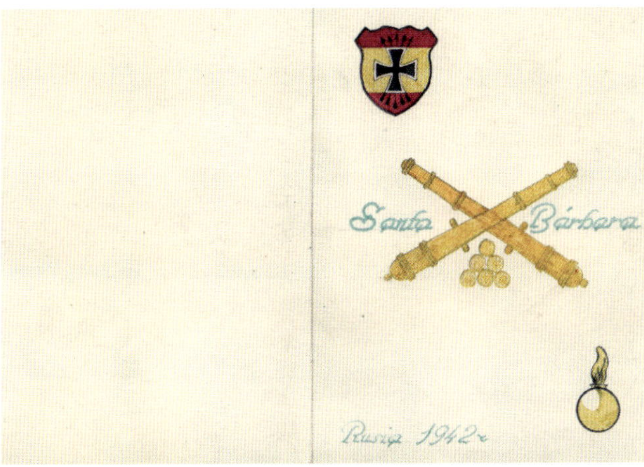

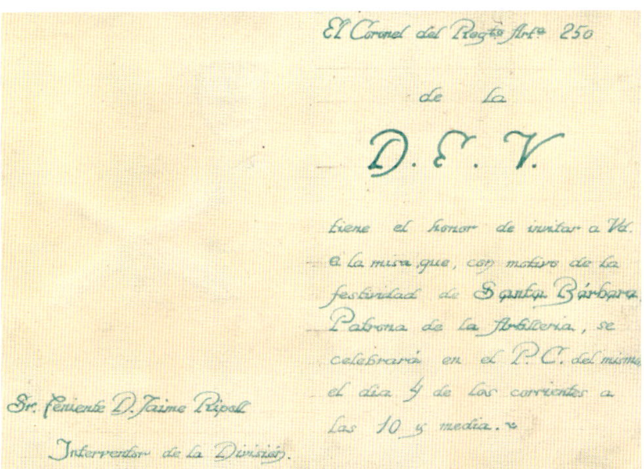

of the Units and the Services. Captain Ripoll Lecuona was among the guests.

Later the General arranged to personally receive all his guests: the German Generals Lindemann, Kleffel, Kinzel, Speth, Krause, and Köchling. All the authorities went to the palace of Prokovskaia and received military honors, rendered on the part of an antitank company, an act which followed the imposition of decorations: War Crosses for the Generals, and Red Crosses for the rest of the German committee.

Everything was going according to plan and cordially. Around two in the afternoon they began a very carefully prepared feast with wines just arrived from Spain. When hardly finishing serving the

Invitations and menu, as well as the great and tragic anniversary of July 18, 1943.

This page and following: General Esteban-Infantes spoke to the Officers and troops to be awarded. In a few seconds would start the pounding Russian artillery attack. July 18, 1943.

first plate, the entire palace shook as if coming down. The Russians, knowing of the gathering, decided to participate in the celebration. Hundreds of artillery projectiles hit the Spanish Headquarters to the surprise of guests and hosts, all of whom looked for refuge in the bunker recently constructed (as related in his work *The Blue Division in line* by then Lieutenant Colonel Diaz de Villegas).

This refuge, next to a complicated system of trenches, saved many lives that day, although the death of the German Commander could not be avoided—hurt by a piece of shrapnel—along with three soldiers, and several who were wounded.

The Division praying book, 1941.

ministers who accompanied the Division and the Blue Legion throughout their histories, of which two (Padres Justino Sierra González and Victoriano Freixa Marcall) found death in Russia, and five others were injured. It is essential to emphasize the performance of Father Indalecio Hernandez Collantes, who was proposed for the Individual Military Medal and received the Iron Cross.

The "Spanish military priests" had to also adapt to the German model, beginning with their uniforms. The 3rd Article of the Division Order of August 16, 1941, regulated the uniforms for Military Chaplains. Established in the German Army, the only ones wearing shoulder reinforcement with symbols were the corresponding category of combatant personnel, and they could not be considered as such. So, in agreement with the Geneva Convention the Military Chaplains, in the performance of the Sacred Mission, did not take direct part in the fight. As of that date, Spanish Military Chaplains did not show shoulder reinforcements of any class on their uniforms.

Despite this norm of uniformity, all the Military Chaplains had all the considerations by right of their assimilation and use in the Spanish Army, analogous to those of the German Army. They wore the same equipment as the Chiefs of the Corps, with the same clothes and equipment as other Chiefs and Officers. Also, they were granted and respected as any Chief and Officer of the Spanish and German Army by all the subordinates.

This was aside from the deference and attentions given to them as ministers of religion. In spite of this norm, the use on their part of the purple color bottom was generalized, as it is always characteristic of the ones serving in the Spanish Army and their units.

Because of its originality we include the 24th typical carol song, which was very popular between the divisionaries:

Esta noche es Nochebuena
Y aunque en Rusia me cogió
Voy a pescarme una "curda"
"prima, gut y jaraso"

¡Dale a la zambomba ¡
¡Dale tú al rabel!
Y no despistaros el cabo furriel...

La Nochebuena se viene
La Nochebuena se va,
Si no llega la cantina
¡ni chicha ni limoná!...

La mula dormía
El buey alentaba
Y el imaginaria
roncaba, roncaba...

Los Reyes tienen camellos
Una "tea" tengo yo
y el sargento de semana
tiene mala malako"...

¡La bota esta llena!
Dale a la guitarra
Hoy es Nochebuena
que es noche de farra...

¡Darle a las guitarras!
¡ darle a las zambombas!
Que este año yo pongo
Yo pongo dos botas...

Esta noche es Nochebuena
Y no es noche de roncar
¡deja la cama guripa
que nos vamos a rondar!
Melchor y Gaspar tuvieron
Una seria discusión
Y Baltasar asustado
Gritaba ¡A mí la Legión!

Y es en Nochebuena
Después de dos tragos
Del follón no libran
Ni los Reyes Magos

A los Reyes mis dos botas
les puse el año pasado
y a la mañana siguiente
me las habían "guindado"

Y ver si consigues
Con la cantinela
"pisar" la cantina
de algún "mortadela"

Los Reyes tienen camellos,
y los camellos jorobas,
y los guripas pañenkas,
y las pañenkas károbas..

Ya no tengo nada
pero no lo siento...
¡tengo una tajada!
¡tengo mucho cuento!

Ya no le temo al rebote
Por que en vez de rebotar
Me han mandado de asistente
del Rey Mago Baltasar...

De reales manjares
Llenare la tripa
Pues menudo enchufe
Es para un guripa...

The Division is finally moving to the Front.

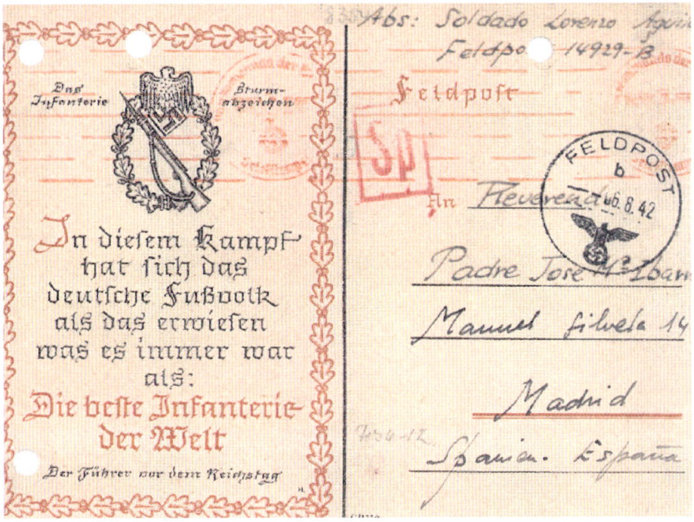

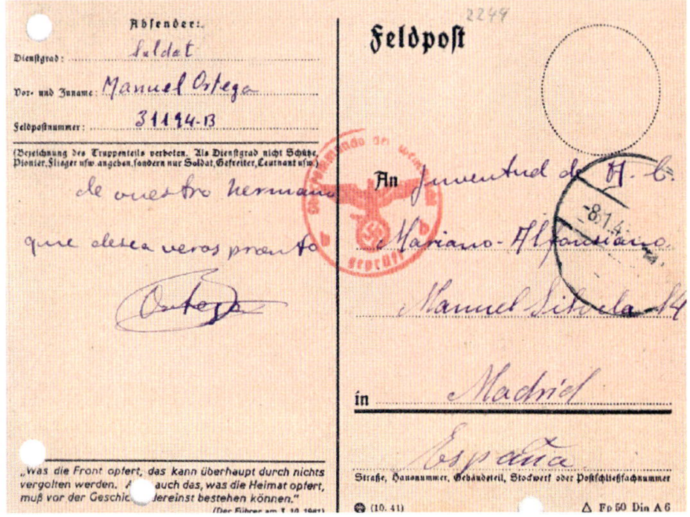

Feldpost mail in and out of the Division.

During these Christmas dates nostalgic and family memories were more present. In order to maintain contact with their families, the Post office Service that existed in the Division quickly acquired an important function. In order to give an idea of the volume of the correspondence, and following General Diaz de Villegas in his mentioned work, the number of letters sent from Russia to Spain went up to around 300,000 being received of approixmately 500,000 monthly letters.

As is traditional in the Spanish Army, there existed in each company a mailman in charge of the collection and delivery of mail. He sent the correspondence to the Service after making one first classification: surface mail (that was shipped by railroad) and aerial (through Junkers airplanes that served as the connection for the Division).

Once received, the mail became reclassified as: mail between the different Units from the Division, surface mail and aerial, and also by destination to Spain, Germany, and other places. Once that work was done the mail bags were sent to Germany, where they started off the trip to their definitive destinations. In addition to letters, the reception of small packages was habitual, of weight no superior to a kilo, with which the relatives palliated the most basic necessities of the soldiers.

The service was organized by a *Feldpost* station, taken care of by a captain, a lieutenant, a sergeant, five corporals, and ten soldiers. Each Unit had a denominated *Feldpost* number.

As it is easy to understand, the day to day life of the troops was bound by the buying capacity of the volunteers. Although it is necessary to consider that, due to the product limitation, the attainment of the objects or foods wished by means of exchange or their acquisition in the black market was habitual.

As we have already seen, the members of the Division received two pays: one on the part of the Spanish government,

Left: Division Officers next to the pilot of the JU 52 covering the line to Berlin. This plane was owned by the Spanish Airline IBERIA, which would place it in the services of the Blue Squadron and the Division. Right: German ship.

Above: Spanish flags parading in Europe card. The note mentioned that they will go up in Gibraltar. Below: Lieutenant Ripoll was an enthusiastic photographer with the camera that went with him during the campaign.

and another from the Germans, and this varied according to the rank, civil state, origin, etc. The base of the Spanish list varied from the 5,000 *pesetas* of a soldier to the 12,500 of a General. On the German part, it oscillated from 260 marks for an unmarried soldier and 382 if he was married, to the 7,000 of a General. These amounts were increased by the bonus front and the allowances for Campaign and Clothes.

The pay was deposited in Spain. For their daily life, the soldiers used different extras and the per diem mainly to obtain, thanks to the service of bar (a form of PX offered by the division quartermaster service, and that worked at least once a month), the objects of first necessity: cleaning equipment; paper, especially for letters; and photographic material.

Some products, such as tobacco, had daily distribution, although they were rationed. Many of the necessities, like eggs, milk, and similar items were purchased from the Russians in the flea markets of the little towns. Between the volunteers, the characteristic icons of the Orthodox Church were very much appraised, and due to the necessities of the war were relatively easy to buy or exchange.

The acquisition of these types of products constituted the main expenditures of the soldiers at the front. If in something the 250

Volunteer Jaime Dolado while in the Hospital of Konigsberg.

Division were distinguished from the remaining units that acted on their side, it was the treatment offered by its components to the Russian population.

The oppression of the Russians for centuries, and the dominated towns of those moments by a ferocious tyranny, created a prototype of man who was characterized by his submission and a great capacity to endure suffering. General Esteban Infantes explained the character of these people the best:

"The Russians that are older than 40 years of age are the prototype of subjects of the czars, with all their defects and virtues. Their spirit is over the material things, their obligations over its wishes. For the Russians that are less than 30 years old, the material totally dominates the sentimental values, and as to the work, it takes more than the fulfillment of an honorable project necessary to complete a mission for their existence, it is the fear of the sanction of the agents of the Party..."

As an example of the treatment of the Russian towns, particularly the prisoners, we relate this recollection by the then Lieutenant Interventor Amaro Lasheras: During one of the night raids done by his unit in December 1942, its section took several prisoners, among them a young scared kid about 16 years old that surrendered to the Lieutenant carrying his gun in stop and shouting: Spain! Franco!

Taken into the Spanish positions and following their custom, the official fed the prisoners and sent them to the rear so that they

Farming markets where they got food and supplies. Grigorovo, 1942.

Alférez Herrera, Nadia, Lela, and Lieutenant Macrino. (Archives Ripoll)

were interrogated by the 2nd Section. All except for the trembling boy, who did not want to move away from his capturer. Since then "MALENI" (small one in Russian) was their faithful assistant to the point of being on duty at night, with a gun, in the *dacha* occupied by Maximiliano Amaro.

In the catastrophe of 10 February "Maleni" disappeared, never to be heard from again.

Any moment was good for "*pelar la pava*" with any close *pañenka*. There were numerous relationships between Russians and Spaniards. In many cases, these "romances" finalized in attempts of marriage, or to take them in their return to Spain, finishing more than an adventure in the camp of Hof, the heart of Germany, or the same Spanish border.

Lela, Lieutenant Ripoll, and Nadia, the two famous Russian women that were working in the Headquarters.

Clockwise from top left: A *panienka* (Russian girl). Russian prisoner that served in the Division Headquarters. The Headquarters Russian assistants with a volunteer. Two Russian boys. Three *panienkas* (Russian girls).

In order to understand the character of the Russian woman we resorted to the "*Russia work is not guilty, Historia de La Division Azul*," which was authored by the member of the Division, Enrique de la Vega Viguera:

"… During our stance in Russia, it was easy to observe the difference of attitude and behavior between the youth and the mature. First, stimulated by the material, they did not have any religious feeling, and nothing of familiar relations worried them.

Two volunteers with a *panienka.*

The older people, however, were loving of their family and of traditions; they even conserved their icons to which they offered orations and respect. In spite of this difference, a peculiar common denominator of feminine discretion existed, the same in the young woman and the most mature, with the particularity that the best way to obtain their friendship and to reach their heart was to court them. In the immense majority of the times, knowing the liberal methods, and not existing moral foundation in the young people, easily resulted in a total union. And it is not necessary to attribute

Hotel Balta liquor receipt. Riga, March 1943.

the common phrase of 'free love.' The feminine respect and the lack of promiscuity was always present in the attitude and privacy of the Russian woman…"

Not with the frequenc commonly desired, but the volunteers had days of rest far from their habitual duties. Personnel coming from the front, and if we added the pertaining ones in Services, the ones in transit (Battalions in march or of repatriation), and personnel and convalescents in hospitals, we will see that an important number of Spaniards were distributed in all the rear positions. The most common destinations to be able to enjoy a permission varied according to their duration, habitually being granted to places near the zone where they operated their unit and, in special cases, in Riga, Vilma, Königsberg, Hof, Dresden, Salzburg, Berlin, Paris, and sometimes Spain.

Muñoz Grandes organized a system of permissions via which, as of May 1942, groups were rotated consisting of twenty Chiefs and Officers, twenty-five selected Sergeant majors, and two hundred soldiers of those that had more service at the front.

The beginning of any permission was always the same: getting out of the state of mind of any soldier coming from the front.

Riga was the place closest to the front that had the infrastructure of a great city, which is why it was the more usual place to rest for

Hotel Balta, Riga, March 1943.

Lieutenant Ripoll during a Services Commission in Innsbruck, September 1943.

Captain Ripoll after his return to Spain, December 1943.

members of the Blue Division. There existed a Spanish Hospital, a Home of Rest and Recovery of the Division, and a Soldiers' club. The hotels Balta, Rome, and Excelsior enjoyed great popularity with the officers, as did the rest of the city.

Going to the cinema or to the Opera to enjoy the performance of some company of varieties or some night club was the usual thing during the duration of the permission. Perhaps the best narration on the importance of the capital of Latvia to the Division came from the U.S. professors Gerald Kleinfeld and Lewis Tambs. On page 258 of their work *The Spanish Division of Hitler* they comment:

"... Also like in the British metropolis, the fog of the wharves raised.

To Spaniards, it enchanted them to see as it was surrounded the tile roofs of ceramics of its European style buildings. It was the West, no Russia. Beautiful women showed their extraordinary pelts or ice skated in the channel of the Duna river, under the envious

Konigsberg, 1943.

Riga, 1942.

Rosón in Dantzig, Oriental Prussia, May 1944. (Archives Rosón)

eyes of Swedish, Dutch, Belgian, French, flamenco, Finnish, Norwegian, Estonians, Spanish and Germans, and, aside from the native Lithuanians. Cosmopolitan city, in which the elephants in the scenes of 'Aida' marched past. Happy city, forgotten the set on fire synagogues, and the haggard Jews who swept the streets. The station of Riga of the *Wehrmacht* emitted programs in Spanish, reinforced with fresh recordings from Madrid, and in main the streets, Spanish newspapers from only three days ago were offered. The bartenders soon learned a few words in Castilian, and *guripas* took to assault the coffee Moon, where they practiced Andalusian chanting, they danced flamenco, and they read eagerly the Campaign page newspaper, that every week left the rotating machines of Riga. All that became the small Spain, the one that knew which soldiers enjoyed a permission…"

In Berlin an excellent Home for the wounded and convalescent existed (that also served for lodging of volunteers, or *guripas* passing by or with permission in the German capital) to the service of the Division, and taken care of by five Spanish nurses, along with a team made up by a Lieutenant Colonel, medical Head of the Service, and three Captains. The patients who had recovered or were awaiting passing the Court hearing to determine their capacity to return to the front were united with the Division members that enjoyed permission in their visits to the city, although the single hospitable regime authorized exit only on Tuesdays and Sundays.

For the lucky ones, the German capital offered extraordinary hotels, or the famous possibility of visiting a night club, of which the *Alexanderplatz* and the *Grosskabarett Berolina* must be emphasized.

Four different views of the Nüremberg stadium, where the spectacular demonstrations of the NSDAP were done. (Archives Dolado)

Konigsberg, 1943. (Archives Dolado)

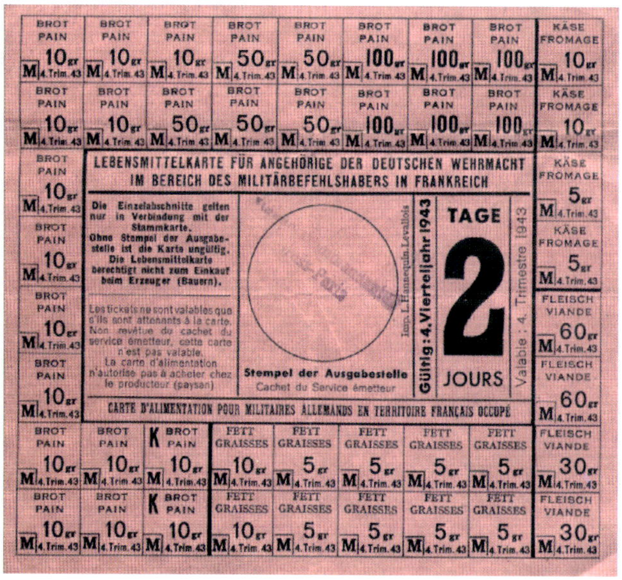

LEBENSMITTELKARTE FÜR ANGEHÖRIGE DER DEUTSCHEN WEHRMACHT IM BEREICH DES MILITÄRBEFEHLSHABERS IN FRANKREICH

Die Einzelabschnitte gelten nur in Verbindung mit der Stammkarte. Ohne Stempel der Ausgabestelle ist die Karte ungültig. Die Lebensmittelkarte berechtigt nicht zum Einkauf beim Erzeuger (Bauern).

Les tickets ne sont valables que s'ils sont attenants à la carte. Non revêtue du cachet du service émetteur, cette carte n'est pas valable. La carte d'alimentation n'autorise pas à acheter chez le producteur (paysan).

Stempel der Ausgabestelle
Cachet du Service émetteur

Gültig: 4. Vierteljahr 1943

Valable: 4. Trimestre 1943

TAGE 2 JOURS

CARTE D'ALIMENTATION POUR MILITAIRES ALLEMANDS EN TERRITOIRE FRANÇAIS OCCUPÉ

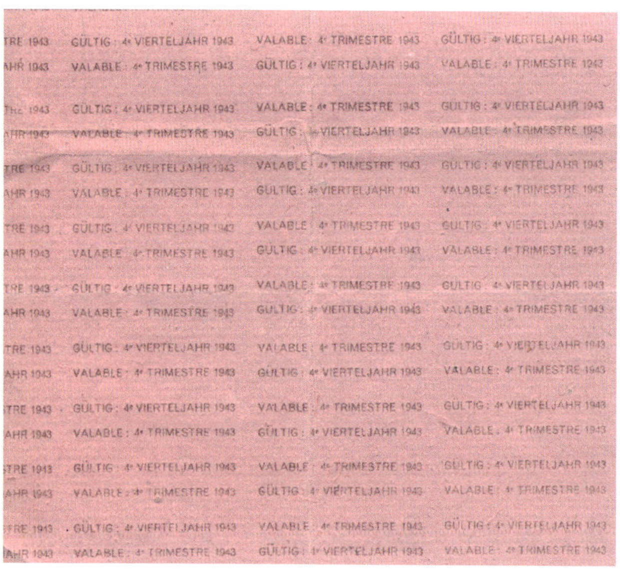

Some lucky members got vacations in Paris. However, you needed, as in any other part of the occupied territories, your ration card to obtain food, liquor, or clothing. (Archives Dolado)

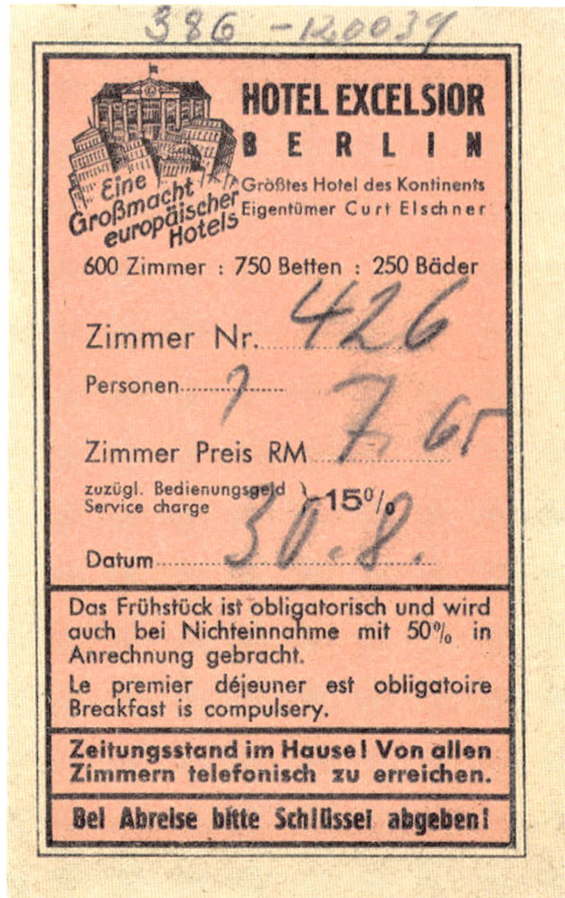

386 -120039

HOTEL EXCELSIOR
BERLIN

Eine Großmacht europäischer Hotels

Größtes Hotel des Kontinents
Eigentümer Curt Elschner

600 Zimmer : 750 Betten : 250 Bäder

Zimmer Nr. 426

Personen 1

Zimmer Preis RM 7.65

zuzügl. Bedienungsgeld
Service charge 15%

Datum 30.8.

Das Frühstück ist obligatorisch und wird auch bei Nichteinnahme mit 50% in Anrechnung gebracht.
Le premier déjeuner est obligatoire
Breakfast is compulsery.

Zeitungsstand im Hause! Von allen Zimmern telefonisch zu erreichen.

Bei Abreise bitte Schlüssel abgeben!

Hotel room receipt at Berlin, 1943. (Archives Dolado)

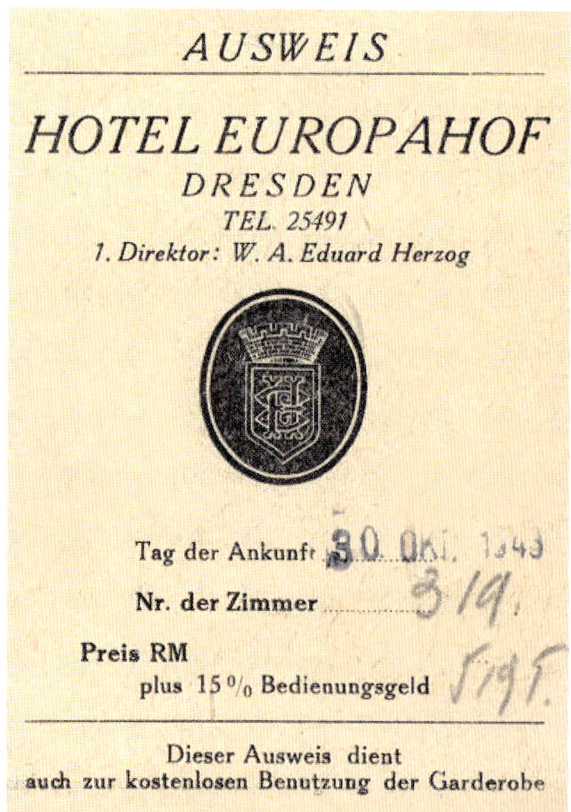

AUSWEIS

HOTEL EUROPAHOF
DRESDEN
TEL. 25491
1. Direktor: W. A. Eduard Herzog

Tag der Ankunft 30 OKT. 1943

Nr. der Zimmer 319

Preis RM
plus 15% Bedienungsgeld 5.95

Dieser Ausweis dient auch zur kostenlosen Benutzung der Garderobe

HOTEL DER FÜRSTENHOF
Berlin W 9 Potsdamer Platz
Sammelnummer:
für Stadtgespräche: 120039
für Ferngespräche 126781
Telegrammadresse: Fürstenhotel

Zimmer Nr. 129

Personen: 1

Preis RM 10

Bedienungsgeld 15 Prozent

Datum: 22.I.43

Hotel room receipt.s (Archives Dolado)

Hotelgemeinschaft
Haus Kossenhaschen
Erfurter Hof
Erfurt
Am Bahnhofsplatz Fernruf 25151

AUSWEIS

ANKUNFT

Zimmer Nr. Preis RM

Zuzüglich 15% Bedienungsgeld.
Bei Nichteinnahme
des Frühstücks erhöht sich der
Zimmerpreis um 50 Pfg.

Bitte Zimmerschlüssel abgeben!

Zimmer, die bis 18 Uhr nicht geräumt sind,
werden für die folgende Nacht berechnet.

Little known was the work made by the women nurses of the Phalange Feminine Section and those from the Army. During the Division there were 109 nurses servicing the Unit.

Like at the front, they could not freely have the goods that they wanted, since the rigors of the war had imposed rationing in all the German territory. The paradox occurred, in spite of having saved more or less important amounts of money, that did not serve for too much if you were not in possession of a rationing record, whose coupons constituted a requirement essential to be served in any establishment.

An important part of the expenses of the volunteers was the purchase of objects of memorabilia or difficult acquisition in Spain, so cameras (the mythical Leika) and clocks were also of great demand, along with the Spaniards' purchase of all types of memories, between which they emphasized a great variety of uniformity articles, emblems, and flags of the German Army and the Nazi party.

Like the rest of the soldiers of any time or place, one of the obsessions of the Division volunteers was to know the women. In this point apparently, there was great success for the Spanish soldiers with the Slavic women.

Nurse and soldier. (Archives Dolado)

Those of them that did not have any luck could resort to the *Wehrmachtbordell*, a service of organized brothels by the Germans (since they had been prohibited to go to the destined civilians), and after passing by the infirmary and receiving the corresponding condom, were granted half an hour in an indicated room.

The examination and liquidation of the accounts of Hospitals and establishments of Health, as well as the elaboration of the corresponding files on these Services were one of the obligations established in the Interventor function. For their fulfillment, different interventors made more continuous visits to this type of establishment, as we saw in the case of Lieutenant Colonel Gomez Garcia, who was ordered to organize its administrative services.

But this was not the only relation with the Medical directorate. The violence of the combats, together with the hardness of the climate caused the Division to suffer a high number of casualties. Jose Antonio Vidal and Gadea in his work *Brief notes on the Blue Division* affirms that 12,726 Division members were battle casualties; of the 47,000 men who formed in their rows, 3,934 men found death serving the Unit, 8,466 were wounded, 326 disappeared, and 345 became prisoners, of whom 97 would never return. To this amount we have to add the 1,600 amputations by freezing and the 7,800 by disease.

More than 22,000 volunteers—almost 50% of the components of the Unit—were casualties. For this reason, it was considered "normal routine" the passage by anyone of the sanitary establishments the Division had. The nine members of the Military intervention service can serve as examples. Manuel Guijarro had to be evacuated due to freezing wounds, and got hurt on two different occasions. Jaime Dolado was entered with paludism, and Maximiliano Amaro was severely wounded after the combats of February 10, 1943. Lieutenant Ripoll had a light entrance for respiratory reasons.

December 24, 1943. Hospital of Konigsberg, Oriental Prussia. (Archives Dolado)

Auditing and account liquidation of Hospitals and sanitary facilities was one of the missions of the Interventor Corps. Captain Ripoll visiting one of these centers while doing one of those services. (Archives Dolado)

Volunteer Jaime Dolado Gonzalo with nurse Maria Socorro Ordesis, both of Navarre origin. (Archives Dolado)

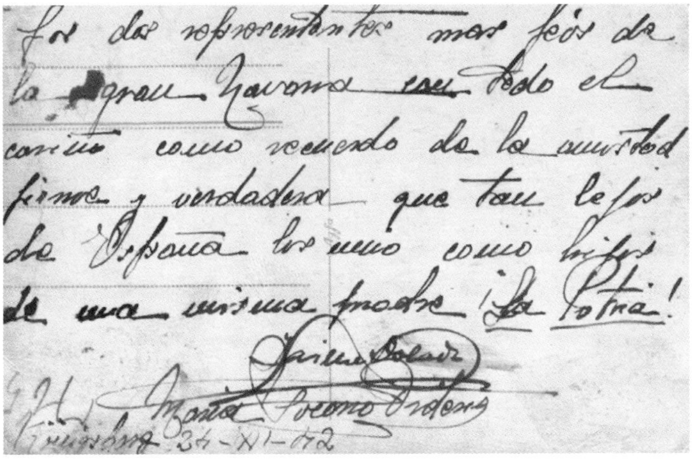

Los dos representantes más feos de
la gran [illegible] en todo el
camino como recuerdo de la amistad
firme y verdadera que tan lejos
de España los unió como hijos
de una misma madre ¡La Patria!
Jaime Dolado
[illegible] 24-XI-42

Letter to his nurse from volunteer Dolado. (Archives Dolado)

Ambulance, Hospital of Konigsberg. (Archives Dolado)

The Division Medical staff was composed of two Medical Units, two sections of ambulances, and one field hospital. The field hospital had as its objective the admission of the injuries coming from the field aid stations, as well as the preparation for the transfer to other hospitals of those who required it. The routes of evacuation for the more seriously wounded patients varied depending on the front where the unit was located. Famous were the trains transporting them. They were called "Lily Marlen" and "Violeta," and were in charge of the transfer of the wounded towards the hospital centers of the rear.

For example, volunteer Jaime Dolado was entered in the field hospital with symptoms of palúdic fevers on 26 August, then evacuated to Luga and Plescao (Russia). He was later sent to Riga, and to Allesteine and Konigsberg (Germany). The Lieutenant Interventor Amaro went from the front to the clearing hospital of Gatchina, and from there to Mestelevo, Vilna, Konigsberg, Hof, and Berlin. In each one of these positions they had Spanish doctors, nurses, and sanitary personnel.

Little is well known of the work of the nurses coming from the Feminine Section of Phalange. With the first expedition they left 40 nurses under the control of Aurelia Segovia. Throughout the stay of the Division another one hundred ninety nurses would follow.

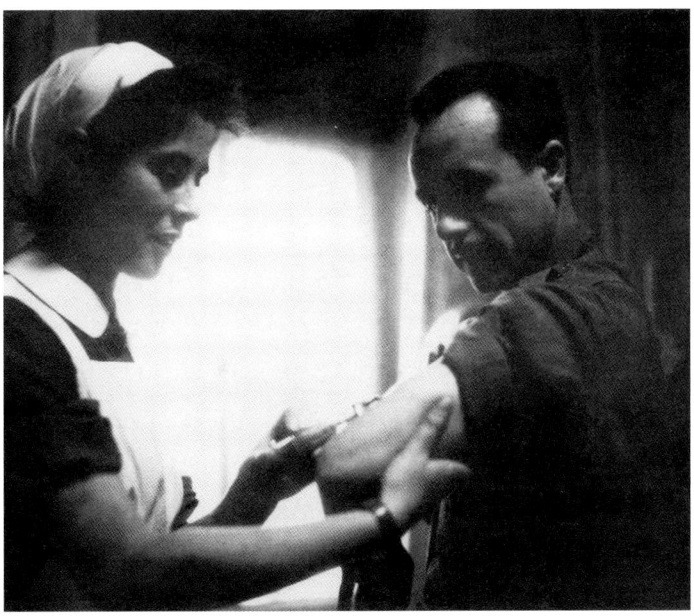

From the nine Interventors participating in the campaign four were hospitalized: Manuel Guijarro evacuated with frozen wounds; Jaime Dolado in the hospital because of the fevers; Amaro mortally wounded on February 10, 1943; and Lieutenant Ripoll because of troubled breathing.

Right to left: Lieutenant Colonel Blas Hidalgo Sanchez, Head of the Sanitary Service of the Division; Lieutenant Colonel Pellicer Taboada, High Command, divisionary; and the soldier José Mª Pellicer. (Archives Ripoll)

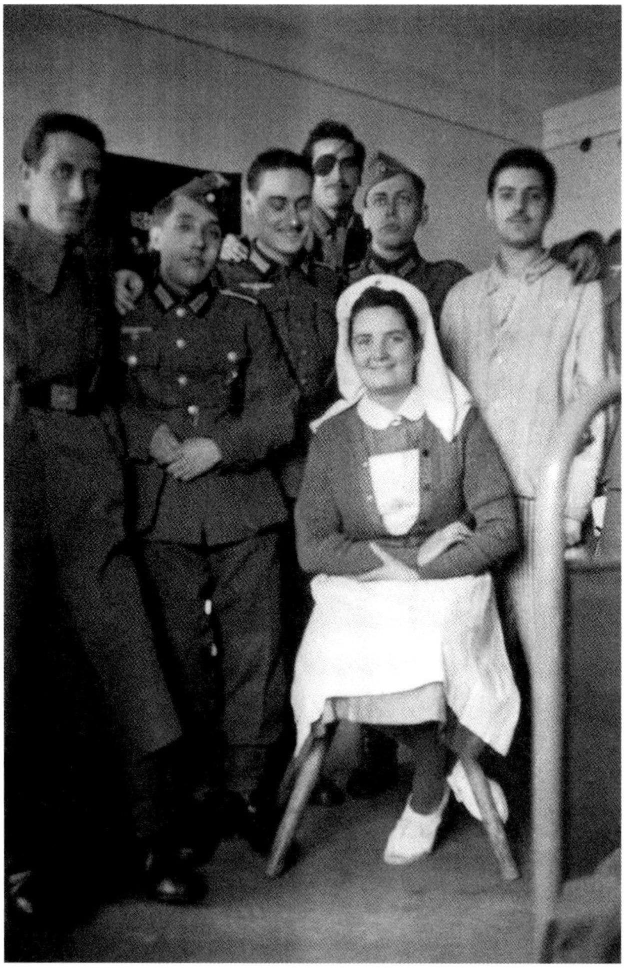

Above: The nurse and the volunteers. (Archives Cuyas) Below: Lieutenant Colonel Pellicer and Lieutenant Colonel Hidalgo, Head of the Sanitary Service of the Division. (Archives Cuyas)

Above: The nurse and the volunteers. (Archives Cuyas) Below: Recovering volunteers (Archives Dolado)

Recovering volunteers (Archives Dolado)

As an anecdote of the operation of the services in the German hospitals, we relate the one of Colonel Interventor Maximiliano Amaro in one interview acquired in the spring of 2003:

"After a wound produced by a tank battle in Krasny-Vor he was admitted to the field hospital. For his evacuation, his companions prepared a small briefcase for him with his more beloved personal objects. Later he began to peregrinate through diverse hospitals of Russia and Germany. At his arrival to any new hospital, he was meticulously washed (a task in charge of prisoners) and replaced his personal items. Finally, once his wounds had improved, he was sent to recover at the Soldier House of Berlin. Transferred in a train hospital, he was taken on a stretcher to the Center, where he received a room. Upon waking up the following day, to his surprise there hung a uniform of captain exactly of his measurements. But this was not the only surprise; when asking for the briefcase that contained his personal objects it did not appear. With the absolute security which it took when it was transported in the train in Hof, personnel of the hospital moved to the station, and there, just in the same place where the stretcher had gathered him, on the platform, and more than 24 hours later, was the suitcase."

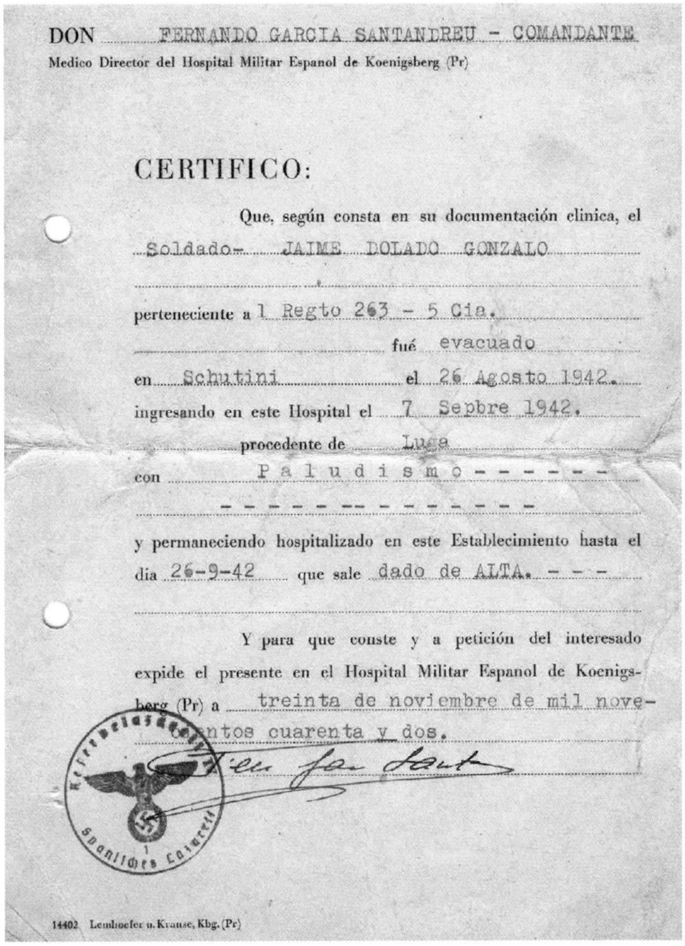

DON FERNANDO GARCIA SANTANDREU - COMANDANTE
Medico Director del Hospital Militar Espanol de Koenigsberg (Pr)

CERTIFICO:

Que, según consta en su documentación clinica, el Soldado- JAIME DOLADO GONZALO

perteneciente a 1 Regto 263 - 5 Cia.

fué evacuado

en Schutini el 26 Agosto 1942.

ingresando en este Hospital el 7 Sepbre 1942.

procedente de Luga

con Paludismo - - - - - - -

y permaneciendo hospitalizado en este Establecimiento hasta el dia 26-9-42 que sale dado de ALTA. - - -

Y para que conste y a petición del interesado expide el presente en el Hospital Militar Espanol de Koenigsberg (Pr) a treinta de noviembre de mil novecientos cuarenta y dos.

14402 Lemhoefer u. Krause, Kbg. (Pr)

Volunteer Jaime Dolado Gonzalo's signed release from the hospital to return to duty. (Archives Dolado)

Group of volunteers from Headquarters. Fist one (seated) is Artillery Lieutenant Juan Ackermann Hanisch. His mission was, in his own words, to be the ears and voices of his superiors. (Archives Ripoll)

In the foreground, and by his extreme height well known, is Artillery Lieutenant Ackermann, brother of the translator, also an Artillery Lieutenant, Juan Ackermann Hanisch. To his right is Colonel Francisco Bandin Delgado, Head of the 250 Artillery Regiment, and Captain Gonzalez Conde. (Archives Ripoll)

The Division was inserted in a very complex frame of Units, and to the difficulty of the operation was added the difference in languages. The necessity that orders, regulations, and dispositions be understood for good normal operation of daily life made the function of the translators essential. To solve this problem a High Command Connection was created, formed by German personnel with a knowledge of Spanish, who ordered distribution of translators by all the Spanish units. Spanish translators also existed, their function being mainly taking care of the essential relations with their German allies.

This was mentioned by Lieutenant of Artillery Juan Ackermann Hanisch in his book *To the Orders of Vuecencia*:

"... my mission consisted of being, practically, the ear and voice of my Colonel in his relations with the Germans and his

To facilitate the idiom problems, a Connection Section was created by the Germans with members knowing Spanish to translate all the documents. *Oberleutnant* Natus and Lieutenant Lamers worked in that Unit, but they lived jointly with the Division offices. (Archives Ripoll)

Oberleutnant Natus. (Archives Ripoll)

Lieutenant Ripoll and Alferez Bashwitz. (Archives Ripoll)

Oberleutnant Havel and Lieutenant Ripoll. (Archives Ripoll)

Group of officers of the Blue Legion. With the arm patch of destroyed an enemy tank, and the Spanish arm emblem, is Lieutenant Constantin Goguidjonachvli, an old czarist officer that joined the Spanish Army during the Civil War and went to combat in Russia. (Archives Rosón)

In the Veterinary Quarters, December 8, 1942. (Archives Ripoll)

In relation to these functions, the relations of the interventors were constant with the Headquarters of the Veterinary medicine division.

Division 250 was a horse-drawn Unit, to which 2,500 horses were assigned, a great majority of which were assigned to personnel without any type of preparation in the handling of this type of animal. In this Headquarters, the Veterinary company was formed with 240 men and structured in six sections: hospitalization, evacuation, motorized, supplying, materiel, and breed.

This Unit served as Veterinary medicine, and at any moment worked next to the Company of Meat supply of Intendance. A good part of its professionals were destined to the support of this Unit.

Since we have been referring in the chapter to the organization of the German Administration, the components of the different administrative specialties did not have the consideration of regular officers. The inclusion of these two Corps, in which the

exits outside the sector of the Division, which did not happen every day. My other assignment, as already indicated, was in the Second Section of the General Staff High Command, denominated to Information. I had to make myself available at all times for my colonel, because telephone calls could come from the adjacent Divisions at any time…"

The Division also had Russian translators. More than a few of the natives, after belonging to the armies of the Czar, looked for refuge in Spain by serving in the Spanish Foreign Legion and, when the Division formed, they asked to form part of it.

D.O. No. 74 of December 30, 1939, declares as functions of the Interventor "to inform on subjects of economic nature, about the personnel, materiel, and cattle," establishing that during campaigns, they report on all movement of personnel and cattle.

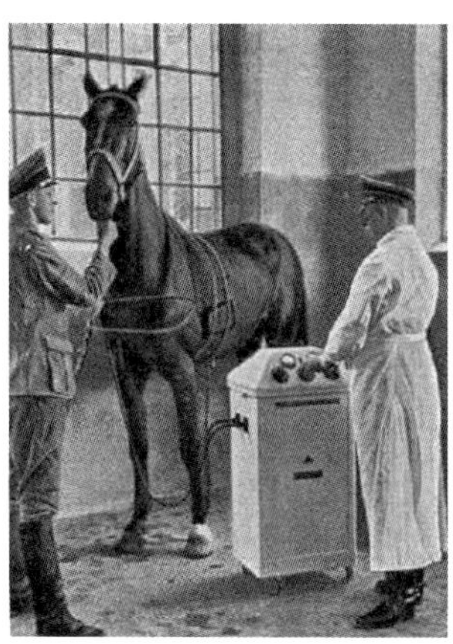

Above: Selection of meat and mount horses. (Archives Dolado) Right: Commandant José Parra Mateos, Head of the Intendance Group.

Procuring to the 263. Chutyni, June 1942. (Archives Dolado)

Moving towards the front in the summer, 1942. (Archives Dolado)

Division members were better known as "the technicians," was the first stumbling block found by the heads of both Services once they arrived in Germany. Such consideration as civil employees was like a cold shower over the officers of the affected Corps, especially in the case of the military Commissioner Gomez Garcia. The Military Intervention of the Army had finished recovering from this denomination recently, as they lost the military condition in 1933, with the creation by the Spanish Republic of the Corps of

Left to right: Captain Joaquin Jimenez de Anta, head of the procurement Company; Commandant Jaime Lopez Varo, head of the Intendance Services; Commandant José Parra Mateos, Head of the Intendance Group; Commandant Pascual; and Captain José Gutierrez, in charge of Dressing and bar services.

Left to right: Lieutenant Edell, Commandant Parra Mateos, Captain Bermejo, and Lieutenant Pascual. (Archives Ripoll)

Civil military Intervention. Although it is sure that the Spaniards accepted this charting from their German counterparts in a very peculiar mode.

The next serious problem was adaptation and operation. The overlapping of functions between the German administrative system (in which both Corps were integrated in one single one) and the Spanish caused more that a few problems between the Lieutenant Colonel of Intendance Perez Iñigo Delgado and the Lieutenant Colonel Interventor Gomez Garcia. Fighting with each other, and each with the German Services, resulted on more than one occasion in the need for the mediation of Muñoz Grandes.

With the first problems solved, intendance and interventors worked in an atmosphere of great camaraderie, sharing on many occasions lodging, means of work, and hours of leisure.

The Division quartermaster service was rated according to the German model, although it did not lose at any moment the military character given to it by the Spanish Army.

A Group (with Headquarters of Supplying, Company of Meat, and another Bread baking company) and an Intendance Quartermaster service organized themselves integratedly like a Service of Headquarters, and that was commanded by Lieutenant Colonel Lopez de Varo Valdes, Para Mateo, and Campos Turn.

From this Headquarters depended the Payroll Financial Office.

As we have already seen, the Headquarters of Intervention was the one in charge of making the numerical state (in which they would be pointed out, on a nominal form, the incorporations and the losses, as well as the promotions and degradation) that was sent to the Intendance Headquarters. This base was used for the requested monetary funding of the Division.

On this subject, our attention is captured by the peculiar way in which omissions and conclusions were arrived at by the General Fernando Lambarri and Yanguas, in his meticulous work *Military Gallery of Intendance*.

The author confirmed that the Payroll Division office was in charge of a Paymaster Officer (Captain, which will do the Chief function) and an Intendance Officer (Lieutenant), voiding the totality of the disposition that, by postal telegram, was sent by the Chief General of the Spanish Division of Volunteers on July 7, 1941, and by which it was settled that it would be an organ dependent on the Intendance Headquarters with a paymaster officer, Intendance officer, and an Interventor.

In Headquarters, at the right, the Head of the Intendance Group, Commandant Parra Mateo. (Archives Ripoll)

The bread. (Archives Dolado)

Right: The food and bread column, sketch. (Archives Dolado)

We do not understand what appears to be a clear example of outlandish corporativism in the affirmation: "... There were no interventions and ties to our organization, that translates in an unnecessary complication of the Service..."

The previous affirmation has little to do, if any, with the real operation of the Division.

The Paymasters of each Battalion were the ones in charge of withdrawing the corresponding amounts of the Payers Financial office, amounts that were audited twice: first by the numerical state of the force, in base to which the requisition of salaries was made to the German Intendance; and another one when it was delivered, since the Interventor also participated in the composition of this service.

It is curious to see how Lambary, who literally translated complete paragraphs from the book *La Division Azul en Linea*, whose Chief of the High Command was Jose the Diaz de Villegas, forgets completely the functions of a Service so near the one of Intendance, and does not mention it. One of the most important rolls and functions corresponding to the Service of Intervention was the management of the payroll of the German Army.

Captain Interventor Ripoll (second from the right) with members of the Intendance Headquarters.

Si Te Dicen Que Caí

I died in a foreign land
and never will return

Sweet eyes in the sky,
Sweet eyes in the sea,
Sweet eyes in the mountains,
Look, look, look

Overseer of my charms,
and of my fortune no par,
tell her in secret one afternoon,
that she should not expect me back

Prayer to the Virgin
candles on her altar
hopes that vanished
embroider, embroider, embroider

And sweet eyes in the sky,
and sweet eyes in the sea,
and, sweet eyes in the mountains,
look, look, look

Overseer of my charms,
and of my fortune no par,
tell her in secret one afternoon,
that she should not expect me back

I will not come back from the mountain,
I will not come back by the sea,
I will not come back from the sky,
Nor will I comeback from the green pines

Sweet eyes of my life,
How much you will cry,
I died in a foreign land,
and never will return.

Pedro Antonio Cuyás
Vieja Guardia, Divisionario, Embajador de España
Old Guard, Blue Division Member, and Spanish Ambassador

In October 1942, Lieutenant Amaro Laheras received orders to welcome and lead to the Division Headquarters a new expedition of young soldiers (*guripas*) just arrived to the front. Once disembarked, the Lieutenant marched towards the old palace where they were to be officially welcomed. Suddenly the officer ordered the troops to halt, and turn to the right. The troops observed an old iron fence and a forest of crosses crowned by helmets.

Soldiers! Harangued Laheras, in this cemetery rest the souls of so many who preceded us. May God grant them a deserved rest, and to us provide the strength to follow their lead and example. Who knows if, when the next expedition passes in front of these gates, some of us will have already won our position next to them in the stars (*luceros*). Out of respect and as an act of gratitude, I request you please join me in prayer for their Eternal Rest.

Hardly had the command been issued for them to remove their hatsthen they begun to intone an Our Father, when the noise of an approaching vehicle stopping was heard behind the formation. From the car three officers, one whose trousers clearly demonstrated the distinguishing red strips, via gestures to the Lieutenant warned him of the arrival of a General.

Muñoz Grandes, the General, indicated to the officer of his General Staff to allow the continuation of the prayer, and he himself joins the prayer. Having finished the prayer, the Lieutenant commands the troops to attention and reports to the General.

The General congratulates him and says:

My Congratulations Lieutenant, remembering the fallen ones is always first. It is also more important to pray than to report, and finally a hero is more important than a General. - Congratulations again Lieutenant, and Thank You....

There was no deeper and costlier pain to all the Generals, Chiefs, Officers, Non Commissioned Officers, and every single volunteer of the Division than the decision to leave behind those tombs of fallen comrades buried in a foreign land.

Sixty years have passed, and there are still some looking in the vast Russian countryside to pay off their debt...

Above left: The future Spanish Ambassador, and Old Guard of Falange, Pedro Antonio Cuyas Ortiz. Above right: The Medal for the widow of the Campaign. (both Archives Cuyas) Right: Volunteer Dolado in a funeral. (Archives Dolado)

This page and following: The funeral of the fallen ones. (Archives Dolado)

RIP

CAIDOS
DE LA DIVISION ESPAÑOLA DE VOLUNTARIOS
¡PRESENTES!
R.I.P.

D. JOSE MAILLO BAENA
22642

RIP
SOLDADO
FAUSTINO-GONZALEZ-CADERON
1c-269
9-1-43

Hoja de Campaña
LEGION ESPAÑOLA DE VOLUNTARIOS
Numero 108 — Por una España mayor y una Europa mas justa — 18 de Marzo de 1944

The Division Campaign Newspaper. (Archives Dolado)

Appendix I: German and Spanish Rank Comparison

GERMANY	SPAIN	COMMISARY	TRANSLATION
GENERALS			
GENERALLEUTNANT	INTERVENTOR DE DIVISION		DIVISION INTERVENTOR
GENERALMAYOR	INTERVENTOR DE EJERCITO		INTERVENTOR OF THE ARMY
W/O EQUIVALENT RANK		Generalstabintendant	Commandant of the High Command War Commissary
		Generalintendant	Commandant of the General War Commissary
		Heeresintendant	Army War Commissary
		Gruppenintendant	Commandant of an Army Group Commissary
		Korpsintendant	Commandant of an Army Corps Commissary
STABOFFIZIERE	JEFES		
OBERST	CORONEL INTERVENTOR	Oberstintendanturrat	War Commissary
O BERSTLEUTNANT	TTE. CORONEL INTERVENTOR	Oberintendanturrat	War Commissary
MAYOR	COMANDANTE		
KOMPANIEOFFIZIERE	OFICIALES		
HAUPTMANN	CAPITÁN INTERVENTOR	Intendanturassessor	Officer of the Commissary Department
W/O EQUIVALENT RANK		Intendant	War Commissary
		Intendanturamtmann	Member of an Army Commissary Department
OBERLEUTNANT	TENIENTE INTERVENTOR		
LEUTNANT	ALFEREZ ALUMNO		

Bibliography

Archives

Archives of The Blue Division.
Institute of History and Military Culture.
General Military Archives of Avila.
Archives of the Historical Room of the Military Intervention Corps.
Personal archives of the Colonel Interventor D. Jaime Ripoll Lecuona.
Personal archives of the General Interventor D. Luis Roson Perez.
Personal archives of the Colonel Interventor D. Maximiliano Amaro Lasheras.
Personal archives of the Commandant Interventor D. Jaime Dolado Gonzalo.
Personal archives of the Colonel Interventor D. Manuel NietoRioboo.
Personal archives of D. Gregorio del Pozo Crespo.
Personal archives of D. Pedro Antonio Cuyas Ortiz.

Militaria

Association Retogenes, Friends of the Military History.

Bibliography

La Division Azul en Linea. – Jose Diaz de Villegas.
La Division Española de Hitler. – R. Kleinfeld and Lewis A. Tambs.
Agonia de un Neutral. – Raymond Proctor.
Lucharon en Krasny Bor I y II. – Fernando Vadillo.
Historia Postal de La Division Azul. – Manuel Vazquez Enciso.
Memoria de la Jefatura de la intervencion de La Division Azul
El Servicio de intendencia en La Division Azul. – Ricardo Recio Cardona.
Das Her. – Ricardo Recio and Antonio Gonzalez.
La Division Azul. – Emilio Esteban Infantes.
A las Ordenes de Vuecencia. – Juan Ackermann Hanisch.
La Division y La Escuadrilla Azul. – Jose Mª Bueno Carrera.
Breves Notas sobre La Division Azul. – Jose Antonio Vidal y Gadea.
Galeria Militar de Intendencia. – Fernando Lambarry y Yanguas.
Handbook in German Military Forces. – US War Department, 1945.
Yo, Muerto en Rusia. – Moises Puente.
La Division Azul, 50 Años despues.. – Francisco Torres.
Rusia no es Culpable. Historia de La Division Azul. – Enrique de la Vega Viguera.
www.deustchesoldaten.com

Acknowledgments

Special Thanks to:

D. Maximiliano Amaro Lasheras.
Dª Mª Antonia Rossete, Widow of Ripoll.
Dª Elena Esteban, Widow of Dolado.
Dª Susana Garcia, Widow of Nieto.
Dª Clementina Bossman, Widow of Roson.
Guijarro Brothers.
De La Vega Fernandez Family.
D. Gregorio del Pozo Crespo.
D. Cesar Ibañez Cagna.
D. Carlos Caballero Jurado.
D. Sergio Brandao Cardoso.
D. Daniel Ribe Benages.
D. Jose Antonio Fernandez Gonzalez.
D. Jose Palau Cuñat.
D. Carlos Lozano.
D. Andres Moreno Ramirez.
D. Ricardo de los Rios Pica.
D. Jose Martin Fernanz.
D. Rafael Aguilar Olivan.
D. Amalio Salguero Ugarte.
D. Antonio Ortiz de Uriarte Urrutia.
D. Arturo Domingo Encinas.
Dª Fatima Incera Peña
D. Carlos Fernandez Martinez.

Endnotes

1 "Si mi memoria no me falla," Edit. Planeta, Espejo de España collection.October 1944.

2 Published after his death by editorial Planeta with the title "Los cuadernos de Rusia," October 1978.

3 As of today, the book *La División Española de Hitler: La División Azul en Rusia* (Madrid, Ed. San Martín, 1983) by U.S. professors Gerald R. Kleinfeld and Lewis A. Tambs is considered the most impartial, complete, and balanced history of the Blue Division, and it is readily available. From the Spanish authors, the most historically important book would be the one by Francisco Torres, *La División Azul, 50 años después*, Fuerza Nueva Editorial, Madrid 1991.

4 Close friend and classmate of José Antonio Primo de Rivera, Serrano Suñer was also brother-in-law of *Generalísimo* Franco. Before the Spanish Civil War he was a member of the right wing party CEDA. He was one of the most important minds behind the Unification of the political parties by Franco and of the creation of the Unique Party named *Falange Española Tradicionalista*. During this time he was president of the Political Caucus of FET and was a cabinet member as the Government Minister, and later as the Foreign Relations Minister. He was known to be a hard line sympathizer of the Germans, but the Germans always looked at him with suspicion.

5 The U.S. Army used a similar approach with their allies during the recent Iraq Gulf War.

6 The Germans denied the offers by the anticommunists exiled from Russia, and other countries, since the German idea was more of a colonizing nature, although not publicly expressed by the German High Command.

7 From a purely opposite ideal, the same relief sensation was felt by the "anti-fascist" camps, to the point that all European communist parties, following Moscow's orders, found that the anti-fascist propaganda used during the "Popular Fronts" just before the start of WWII could not be used now against Germany, placing Stalin and the USSR in a very uncomfortable position. Their only alternative was to condemn the "Imperialist war." But they released, soon enough, that the German attack was a "Holy War," deciding to join against the German occupational forces. In the Spanish case, the Spanish Communist Party proclaimed their campaign with the theme "Not even a man, a gun, nor a wheat grain for Hitler," ideas that they never expressed before from September 1939 to 1941. The Campaign in Spain called for the sabotage in the factories of manufactured products destined to help the German War Machine. These actions were not popular then, and resulted in a positive encouragement in the recruitment for the Blue Division.

8 These three countries deployed units of their regular armies; Finland and Rumania, Russian neighbors, did not send units, but their entire army to the Russian Campaign.

9 As part of the military effort during the Spanish Civil War the Army recruited "temporary officers," thousands of them as "Alfereces provisionales," to group and join new units to the National Army. Most of them were members of Falange, and already promoted to Lieutenants.

10 Contrary to other Spanish Generals, he was not of a traditional military family, but from a modest low income family. He rapidly acquired a name between the ranks for his actions on the Morocco battlefield, gained the "Africanist" nickname, and did not oppose the 2nd Spanish Republic proclamation. He was founder of the Assault Guard Corps, the official political and police corp used during the Republic. Due to the extreme left turn by the Republic he decided to join the anti-republican *Unión Militar Española* (UME) underground. He also assumed position of communicator with Falange, which was declared an illegal party by the Popular Front. He left Madrid at the first presented opportunity and joined the National Army, where he did a competent job. In August 1939 he was named to the position of the *Secretaría General de FET*, from which he would resign in March 1940. At this time he was named Commander of the Armed Forces at the Campo de Gibraltar. At this point the High Military Command decided to take back the British position militarily. If the attack would have started, General Munoz Grandes then would haven taken the military command.

11 On June 25, 1941, the "ABC"newspaper informed of "Overwhelming demonstrations" in Barcelona, and the 24th on Seville, Valencia, Valladolid, Albacete, Badajoz, Almeria y Alicante. Of demonstrations in other towns, like Sabadell, Mérida,.etc. were articles on the following days. In reality, the demonstrations were in all Spanish towns. On the 25th, even in Lerida, they demonstrated (See: Agustí Roca, Carme, "Russia es culpable! Memoria y record de la División Azul", Pagès Editors, Lleida 2003). The 26th, at a union meeting on Mallorca, the workers decided to terminate the meeting to attend a demonstration in favor of the volunteers to Russia (Ver: Negreira Parets, Juan, "Voluntarios Baleares en la División Azul y Legión Azul, 1941-1944"; Ediciones Miramar, Palma de Mallorca, 1991). The 28th in Gerona (Ver, Gay, J. Víctor, "Els gironins de la División Azul", en "Revista de Girona", nº 215, Noviembre-Diciembre 2002. Esta publicación es editada por la Diputación de Gerona.)

12 Jesús Martínez Tessier, "Anticomunistas sin dolares", "Arriba" newspaper, April 1, 1954.

13 Rafael Cañellas, "Centuria de Balillas de la Vieja Guardia (Recuerdo Nostálgico)"."La Nación" (periódico quincenal), nº 410 (January 28, 2004).

14 "ABC" Newspaper, October 29,1941

15 To date, the best overall work of the structure and functioning of the Blue Division is the work of one of the Unit High Commanders, José Díaz de Villegas, La División Azul en línea". Although it was impossible to locate during years, it was recently re-printed (Editorial Acervo, Barcelona 2003, 2ª Edición).

16 Edited by Foundation Don Rodrigo, Madrid 1998

17 Garcia Hispán, José, *La Guardia Civil en la División Azul*, García Hispán Editor, Alicante 1992.

18 The German Public opinion was correct, assuming that the Spanish pride would not allow the German Troops to attack and move the British out of Spanish soil. It appears in the Security Briefing of the SD of July 14, 1941 ("Sicherheitdienst," SD), *Citado en la tesis doctoral de* Victor Kenneth Bennet, "Public Opinion and Propaganda in National Socialist Germany during the Ward against the Soviet Union" (Universidad de Washington, 1990).

20 Inform of the German Army High Command Operations Center (Operationsabteilung, OKH) 15 July 1941 over the necessary forces to occupy the USSR teritories *Kriegstagebuch des Oberkommandos der Wehrmacht*, Vol. II (pág. 1.022), Bernard & Graefe Verlag, Munich, 1982.

21 During 1942 nineteen Marching Battalions arrived in Germany, and eight during 1943. In 1942 eight battalions returned to Spain, and in the next year (1943) until October seven more. Between November and December 1943, after the order was given to repatriate the Division, fourteen Battalions brought back men, except those that were going to give up their lives in the Blue Legion. These were repatriated in three Battalions between March and April 1944.

22 Professor Sigfredo Hillers de Luque calls attention to the Stalin idea in his book *Franco, Hitler, Churchill. España en la II Guerra Mundial*, Editions Arcos, Madrid 2002.

23 The Air Force also contributed, but with minimal presence, with the Blue Squadron and a very symbolic presence of the Navy. See: Caballero Jurado, Carlos y Guillén, Santiago, *Escuadrillas Azules en Rusia. Historia y Uniformes* (Ediciones Almena, Madrid, 1999); and Escuadra, Alfonso, *Bajo las banderas de la Kriegsmarine. Marinos españoles en la Armada alemana (1942-1943)* (Fundación Don Rodrigo, Madrid, 1998).

24 The author has a copy of the archive.

25 A great overview of all the publications can be found at: (1989), Caballero Jurado, Carlos e Ibáñez Hernández, Rafael; *Escritores en las trincheras. La División Azul en sus libros, publicaciones periódicas y filmografía (1941-1988)*, Ediciones Barbarroja, Madrid 1989. However, after that date there are not too many publications made..

26 There are already some notes referenced to that (Negreira, Recio, García Hispán). In the last ones, it should be mentioned Ibáñez Cagna, César, *Banderas españolas contra el comunismo. Las enseñas de los voluntarios en el Frente del Este (1941-1944)*, Fundación División Azul, Madrid 2000, an intense and deep study vexilológic regarding La División Azul; Carrera Buil, Fernando J and Ferrer-Dalmau Nieto, Augusto, *Battalion Román. Historic fotográfica del 2º Battalion del Regimiento 269 de la División Azul*, Foundation División Azul, Madrid 2003, which is more than a bunch of pictures, being a very serious analysis of the famous battle of Krasner Boor by Caballero Jordon. There does exist another documentation with a collective stamps approach made by Vázquez Enciso, Manuel, *Postal History de la División Azul*, Lindner Filatelia Ibérica, Madrid 1995. And another regarding movies: Alegre, Sergio, *El Cine cambia la historia. Las imágenes de la División Azul*, Promotions and Publications Universitarias, Barcelona 1994.

27 As appear in the magazine "Hermandad," nº 14 (IIª Época), Barcelona, May-June 1960, with additional data by Vázquez Enciso, op. cit., although it may be incomplete due to the lack of information regarding new units and posts, or their possible modificatications with time.

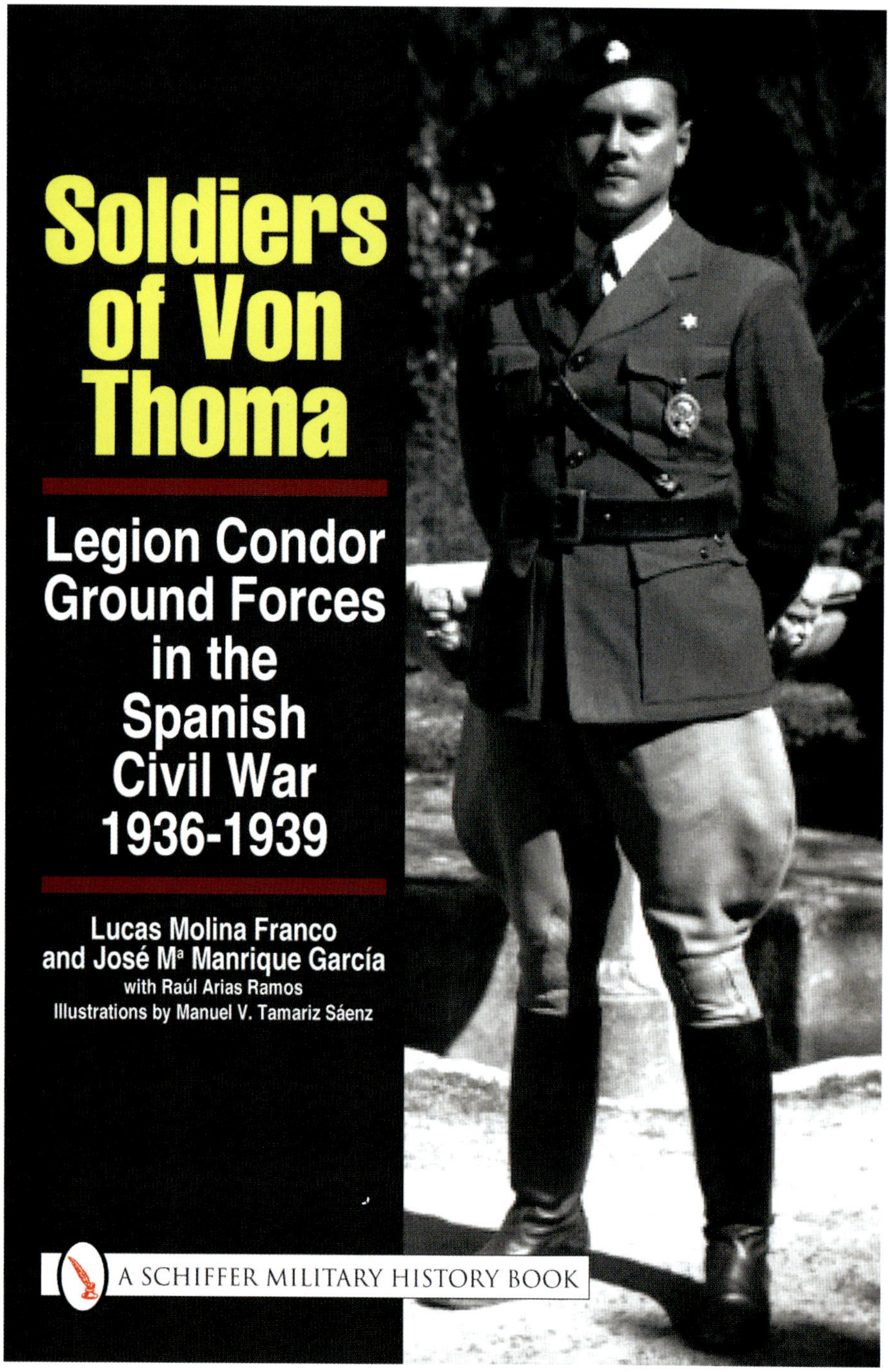

Soldiers of von Thoma
Legion Condor Ground Forces in the Spanish Civil War
Lucas Molina Franco & José Ma Arias Ramos

In October 1936 two German ships arrived in Spain loaded with a Panzer I company and all the services and personnel to establish Franco's army's first armored unit, the so-called Panzer-Gruppe Drohne. The Third Reich chose a pioneer in the development of German ground forces to command this contingent - Oberstleutnant Wilhelm Ritter von Thoma. This book presents the history of von Thoma's units in the Spanish Civil War, from the tank crews to the infantry, and specialties.
ISBN: 9780764329265 6"x9" over 200 bw/color images 240 pp hard cover $39.95